C000220229

A HISTORY OF
THE SOUTHERN
RAILWAY

A HISTORY OF
THE SOUTHERN
RAILWAY

COLIN MAGGS

AMBERLEY

First published 2017

Amberley Publishing
The Hill, Stroud
Gloucestershire, GL5 4EP

www.amberley-books.com

Copyright © Colin Maggs, 2017

All illustrations unless otherwise stated are the
property of the author.

The right of Colin Maggs to be identified as
the Author of this work has been asserted in
accordance with the Copyrights, Designs and
Patents Act 1988.

ISBN 978 1 4456 5271 9 (hardback)
ISBN 978 1 4456 5272 6 (ebook)

All rights reserved. No part of this book may
be reprinted or reproduced or utilised in any
form or by any electronic, mechanical or other
means, now known or hereafter invented,
including photocopying and recording, or in any
information storage or retrieval system, without
the permission in writing from the Publishers.

British Library Cataloguing in Publication Data.
A catalogue record for this book is available
from the British Library.

Typesetting and Origination by Amberley
Publishing.
Printed in the UK.

CONTENTS

INTRODUCTION

The Southern Railway was the only one of the Big Four which truly lived up to its title.

The London & North Eastern Railway entered Wales, which could not be described as London, or the north-east; the London Midland & Scottish Railway served Wales and Bournemouth, neither of which was in London, the Midlands or Scotland; and while the Great Western Railway certainly served the West Country, it also served part of the Midlands as well as London and its environs. The Southern Railway (SR) did indeed only serve southern England and except for a very few miles, all of its lines were south of the Thames.

The SR was formed in 1923 mainly from an amalgam of three companies: the London & South Western Railway (LSWR), mainly serving the south-west of England; the London, Brighton & South Coast Railway (LBSCR), serving central southern England; and the South Eastern & Chatham Railway (SECR), serving the south-east of the country. The SECR itself had been formed from the South Eastern Railway and the London, Chatham & Dover Railway (LCDR).

In due course, these major companies took over smaller companies such as the Surrey Iron Railway – the first railway company in the world – and the Canterbury & Whitstable Railway – the first to use a locomotive to haul a passenger train.

Many settlements not served by a railway felt the need for one, so a small company was formed to build a branch line. Often they proved uneconomic due to the fact that they were insufficiently flexible: if one locomotive was normally used, another had to be available when the other was undergoing repair or maintenance. Although perhaps two carriages were sufficient for normal traffic, on market days four may have been required. A large company had resources to cope with these fluctuations, but it was uneconomic for a small company; the usual result was that a large company bought the small company for a sum considerably less than it had cost to construct, leaving the shareholders of the small company out of pocket.

This history will tell the story of the SR beginning with the LSWR and will then work eastwards.

I

THE HISTORY OF THE LONDON & SOUTH WESTERN RAILWAY: ITS INCEPTION

The story started with a plan for making a ship canal from Spithead to London, but when the scheme proved impracticable due to problems of getting water to its summit, it was realised that a railway would offer a far better means of communication.

On 6 October 1830 a meeting was held at the home of Abel Rous Dottin, MP for Southampton. Dottin was later to become chairman of the London & Greenwich Railway. The idea was adopted, £400 raised to cover expenses and a provisional committee appointed. On 23 October 1830 the *Hampshire Advertiser* published the prospectus of the Southampton, London & Branch Railway & Dock Company, the branch being a line from Basingstoke to Bristol, the Great Western Railway not yet having come into being. This Southampton venture required a capital of £1 million. The London terminus was to be at Nine Elms, Vauxhall, quite a distance from the City. It would then pass through Woking, Basingstoke and over the foothills of the Hampshire Downs to Winchester and Southampton. At a meeting on 5 April 1831 Colonel George Henderson of the Royal Engineers was appointed chairman of the provisional committee, with Francis Giles as engineer.

The proposed line was thought to benefit all classes of society: it was calculated that the railway would save a poor family burning a bushel (a capacity of 2218.192 cubic inches) of coal per week *6d* while middle class families consuming 10 bushels weekly would be *5s* better off. Henderson claimed that a similar saving would be made on other commodities brought into the district such as groceries, sugar and tea, while the railway could ship local produce out on reasonable terms.

A Captain Stephens had issued a report stating that 100,000 passengers used vessels at Southampton annually. Henderson estimated an annual net profit for the carriage of passengers and freight on the railway would amount to £120,000. A railway 60 ft wide would need 566 acres at a cost of £65,000 while construction expenses would be an additional £1,200,000. He said, 'I consider that two locomotive engines, making two trips a day each, will be sufficient for passengers at the opening of the railway.'

A meeting at Southampton Town Hall on 26 February 1831 unanimously voted to promote the company to raise £1,500,000 in shares. That year Francis Giles made a survey of the route.

In view of the fact that it was a longer railway than had hitherto been built, before proceeding further it was agreed to wait to see how Parliament reacted to another long-distance railway, the London & Birmingham Railway, whose bill was to be presented in the following session. An Act of Parliament was essential in order to obtain powers for the compulsory purchase of land. On 23 January 1832 it was decided that the idea of new docks at Southampton would be developed by a separate company, thus reducing the capital required for the railway to just £1 million.

The London & Birmingham Railway received its Act in 1833, and by the time the Southampton proposals came before the House its cumbersome title had become the rather snappier London & Southampton Railway.

A questionnaire was sent to road carriers and stagecoach proprietors who would be affected by this competition. One of these coach owners was William James Chaplin of Chaplin & Horne. Chaplin, an astute businessman, realising that the future of transport was with railways, ceased to support the Anti-Rail-Road League, sold his coach business and invested in the London & Southampton.

In Parliament the bill for the first main line railway south of the Thames received support from both the Admiralty and shipowners, so the Act 5 William IV c.88 received Royal Assent on 25 July 1834.

The London & Southampton Railway was to commence 'at the River Thames, at or near Nine Elms in the parish of Battersea in the county of Surrey, to the shore or beach at or near a place called the Marsh in the parish of Saint Mary in the town and county town of Southampton'.

On 12 September Giles was informed that from 1 September 1834 his annual salary would be £1,500 with an additional £500 for expenses. He asked for three assistants: one, based at Kingston, to be responsible for the line as far as the River Wey; the second, at Frimley, for the section from the Wey to Hook Common; the third, based at Basingstoke, would be responsible for Hook Common to the western end of the proposed tunnel at Popham. It was not until 12 June 1835 that Thomas Dodd, William Lindley and Samuel Giles were appointed to fill these posts.

In 1835 the bill for the branch to Basingstoke, Newbury, Devizes, Trowbridge, Bradford-on-Avon, Bath and Bristol came before Parliament, but was rejected in favour of the Great Western Railway. Right from the start these two companies were in competition, and it was rather ironic that an omission in the London & Southampton bill stating the gauge to be used formed a precedent, allowing the GWR also to omit such a reference; it was then able to lay the broad gauge.

The Southampton line was not built by one major contractor, the route being divided into segments constructed by relatively small contractors, but unfortunately small contractors tended to have poor financial backing and thus were more likely to fail financially. These builders often completed the easy part of their length and then stopped work, asking for more money. These demands of the small contractors meant that the company had to choose whether to yield to their demands, or delay the works.

Work on the line commenced at Shapley Heath, near Winchfield, on 6 October 1834, the contractor being Messrs Treadwell. The initial turf was turned by Mr Bainbridge, a local landowner who had actually given, not sold, part of his estate to the railway.

The same week Robert Stannard was about to start work at Battersea, but Giles sent him to Wimbledon, Kingston and Merton, 'the labourers being there obtainable at cheaper prices than in Battersea'.

At Shapley Heath the men worked two shifts: 3.00 a.m. till noon and noon till 9.00 p.m., with a forty-minute break during each shift for meals. They were paid between 3s and 4s daily, and the boys in charge of horses 10d a day, this at a time when an agricultural worker received about 10s a week, or 15s at harvest time. Horse-drawn 3¼ cu. yd capacity wagons conveyed the spoil, twenty being filled every hour. When track was laid, two locomotives were used.

Giles provided the London & Southampton with good permanent way. At a time when many railways were using stone blocks, Giles laid his 15 ft long 50 lb/yd wrought-iron rails on wood sleepers, timber being chosen due to the cost of carrying stone to the area.

The 9 in. diameter sleepers, cut from circular pieces, were laid with their round surface uppermost. Rails were secured to the sleepers with ⅝ in. bolts with 15 lb chairs used at the joints. The timber was kyanised, that is, preserved by being saturated in a solution of dichloride of mercury, a process discovered by Dr J. H. Kyan. It was not used for many years as creosote was soon adopted. As work progressed, 63 lb rails were used and then 75 lb.

Shares in the company were not bought outright, shareholders receiving calls at intervals. The first call was made on 24 October 1834 for £3 to finance the initial work. Immediately the company's critics opened a campaign, one wit claiming that the line would be used only to convey 'parsons and prawns' – the one from Winchester, the other from Southampton. Criticism became so serious that at the beginning of 1835 it was said that to admit to being connected with the London & Southampton was to choose to be thought either a fool or a rogue.

In October 1835 Giles and Henderson inspected the site of Popham Tunnel and their visit resulted in a report to the directors recommending a deviation 1½ miles west of the authorised line to avoid tunnelling and yet preserve the ruling gradient of 1 in 250. This deviation required a further Act of Parliament.

At the shareholders' meeting on 19 February 1836 it was reported that almost 10 miles of railway had been completed. A few months later David Mackintosh started work on the section between Southampton and Winchester. In December bad weather seriously damaged embankments and cuttings along the line and it was suggested that it would be more economic to proceed slowly through the winter rather than incur heavy costs in restoring slips.

Francis Giles, who had worked as a waterway surveyor under the Rennies and then in 1829 been appointed engineer to the Newcastle & Carlisle Railway, proved a poor choice for engineer. Progress was slow and by 31 August 1835 only 4 miles of the 78 had been completed, earthworks started at twelve major locations, work on some minor stations begun and several bridges built. Half of the company's shareholders lived in Manchester and these northerners, dissatisfied with the poor progress, appointed a committee of investigation which started inspection at Southampton on 12 December 1836 and proceeded along the line. Giles was severely criticised for employing small contractors, 'and it was evident to all but Mr Giles that works executed in that manner, exclusive of uncertainty as to their completion, would in reality cost more than those for which an adequate price should be paid to responsible contractors'.

Francis Giles was also appointed engineer to the Southampton Dock Company, incorporated in 1836, and although not completed, the dock, which could be entered at any state of the tide, was used for the first time in August 1842. Through the years the docks were extended as the volume of shipping increased, exceeding 2 million tons in 1877.

To complete the London & Southampton Railway a further £500,000 needed to be raised, and the northern deputation stated that if Giles remained in office they would not pay the remaining calls. As their money was essential for the line's completion, the directors made two decisions: firstly to engage Joseph Locke to inspect the line and present an estimate for its completion, and secondly to dismiss Giles. To spare Giles' feelings this was not entered in the minutes, but on 13 January 1837 it was recorded that 'Mr Giles having intimated that it would be inexpedient for him to devote the whole of his time to the business of this railway, resigned his appointment as engineer, which resignation the directors accepted'.

Giles was replaced in 1837 by Joseph Locke who in 1823 had been articled to George Stephenson whom he assisted on the Liverpool & Manchester Railway. In 1835 he was engineer to the Grand Junction Railway which ran between Birmingham and Warrington, thus linking the

London & Birmingham and the Liverpool & Manchester. Locke's lines were noted for their economy of construction and his avoidance of tunnels. A skilful organiser, he ensured that the contractors kept within their time and cost limits.

An Act authorising the additional capital and powers for making the deviations was obtained on 30 June 1837. Three minor deviations were authorised and two major: one between Walton Common and Byfleet to avoid St George's Hill cutting, and the other at Popham, the latter over 8 miles in length. Tunnels were not entirely unavoidable: that at Litchfield was 198 yd in length; Popham No. 1 265 yd; Popham No. 2 199 yd; and Wallers Ash 501 yd.

On 26 April 1837, the ex-coach owner William James Chaplin attended his first board meeting as chairman of the London & Southampton. Locke's first action was to dismiss the small contractors working on the remaining 15 miles between Wandsworth and the Wey, replacing them by Thomas Brassey, on the verge of becoming a great contractor, building railways in Europe, America, India and Australia.

Between the Wey and Basingstoke, and Winchester and Southampton, the existing contractors continued work, but now were required to provide their own material. The Basingstoke–Winchester contract, including the Popham diversion, was let to Brassey.

Sir Thomas Baring, one of the landowners through whose land the line passed, showed great concern for the navvies' welfare, instigating a benefit society for them with a substantial donation, this being augmented by Brassey and others.

Sir Thomas suggested that the L&S board donate to the Winchester County Hospital where many navvies received treatment. The directors voted £100 and a further £10 for the cost of the frame used to convey injured men to the hospital.

In anticipation of the opening of the line as far as Woking Common in June 1838, Samuel Davis was appointed locomotive superintendent at Nine Elms in March 1838. On 12 May 1838 the directors and others made an experimental trip over the line, the Down journey taking 45 minutes and 'so smooth and easy was the transit, so utterly undisturbed by even the slightest shock or jar, that if the eyes were closed it was difficult to imagine oneself in motion at all'. The party returned in 43 minutes making an average speed of about 32 mph.

The journey was repeated on 19 May when two trains of nine and ten carriages respectively carried nearly 400 passengers. The Down journey was rather slow due to a headwind and also because some of the gentlemen opted to sit in the luggage space on the flat roofs of the coaches. On the return journey one train reached 30 mph.

The line opened to the public on 21 May 1838 with a service on weekdays of five trains each way and four on Sundays. Only first- and second-class passengers were carried. The 23 miles was covered in 45 minutes. Omnibuses conveyed passengers between Nine Elms and central London while the London & Westminster Steam Boat Company carried passengers along the Thames between Nine Elms and Dyers' Hall Wharf, Upper Thames Street and Hungerford Market. Fares for the distance of 23 miles were 5s first and 3s 6d second class, which compared very favourably with stagecoach fares of about 8s 6d inside and 5s 0d outside.

The opening was successful, the *Railway Times* reporting:

> The servants are numerous and expert at their duty, so that no unnecessary delay is occasioned in taking up or setting down, while the confusion complained of on the first opening of other lines, in regard to the booking of passengers, is altogether obviated.

In the first four weeks the L&S carried a daily average of just over 1,000 passengers and receipts totalled £11,059 17s 3d. No goods or livestock were carried initially.

Nine Elms station was austere with just two platforms. These proved totally inadequate during the second week when race traffic proved overwhelming, Sam Fay in *A Royal Road* recording:

> For the first few days passengers flocked from all over the countryside, and patronized the line for the mere novelty of the thing. Epsom races occurring in the following week, the company advertised their intention of running eight trains to Kingston on Derby Day, for the accommodation of the racing public. To the utter astonishment and alarm of the officials arriving at Nine Elms station early on the morning of that eventful day, a crowd of about 5,000 persons was found at the station gates. Several

trains were despatched, but still the throng increased, till at length the doors were carried off their hinges, and amid the shrieks of the female portion of their number, the mob broke over the booking-counter, leaped through the windows, invaded the platform and rushed pell mell into a train chartered by a private party. Finding resistance useless, the officials sent for the Metropolitan police, and at twelve o'clock a notice was posted on the booking-office window announcing that no more trains would run that day.

A few weeks later the L&S advertised special trains to Woking for Ascot Races and it is believed that temporary seats were placed in carriage trucks and goods vehicles to provide sufficient passenger accommodation.

The directors made a trial trip from Woking to Winchfield, 38 miles from Nine Elms, on 17 September 1838 and this extension was opened to the public on 24 September 1838. The extension from Winchfield to Basingstoke and Southampton to Winchester took place on 10 June 1839, leaving only the intervening 18 miles to be completed. The 2-2-2 *Pegasus* operated trains on the Southampton section. As the splendid terminus at Southampton designed by William Tite was incomplete, until the whole line was finished the following year, trains temporarily terminated at Northam Road. In the first two months, traffic on this section exceeded all expectations.

The winter of 1839/40 proved exceptional, the average rainfall from September to January being exceeded by 50 per cent. The London & Southampton with its high embankments and deep cuttings was particularly severely affected, Locke estimating that repairing the slips between Nine Elms and Basingstoke would cost £50,000.

On 11 May 1840 at 4.30 a.m. twenty-one empty carriages hauled by 2-2-2 *Mars* and 2-2-2 *Chaplin* arrived at Southampton and at 6.30 a.m. the first Up passenger train departed.

At 8.00 a.m. the directors and friends left Nine Elms behind *Venus* in a train of thirteen first-class carriages and at 11.30 was welcomed at Southampton. After 2 hours they returned to Andover Road (renamed Micheldever in 1856), where the contractor Thomas Brassey had erected for them 'marquees amply set forth with delicate viands and rare wines' while the navvies feasted on a roasted ox and unlimited supply of strong beer.

That very day the Northam Bridge Company was at the vice-chancellor's court seeking an injunction to halt the railway within a mile of the Southampton terminus. The action started on 13 March 1839, was not settled until 1840 and cost the L&S £4,000 in legal expenses.

The cost of the line from London to Southampton exceeded estimates, the following being a breakdown:

	£	s	d
Expenditure obtaining parliamentary powers	41,965	14	0
Obtaining land, compensation	295,042	4	1
Premises at Nine Elms	7,461	14	6
Construction of line	1,176,556	12	9
Surveying and engineering	32,887	6	3
Total	**1,551,913**	**11**	**7**

Initially passengers booked their tickets at a counter and received paper tickets bearing date and destination, the company not adopting Edmondson's card tickets until 25 April 1845. The passenger was given a leaflet listing regulations such as not opening a carriage door, or alighting without assistance from the staff. If he lost the ticket he would be required to pay the fare from the station from which the train started. He could only board a train if there was room and passengers travelling the longest distance took priority. If he dared to smoke he would be removed from the railway and forfeit his fare.

In 1837 carriages were ordered from Messrs Wright & Horne: twelve first class, six excursion, twelve second class and twelve third class.

Travelling conditions were spartan: the eighteen first-class passengers, in a vehicle like three stagecoaches on a single underframe, had to endure unlit compartments until December 1841; second-class coaches had twenty-four unupholstered seats, were roofed, but had no windows so thus offered plenty of fresh air. Third-class passengers were not carried until 11 May 1840 when the line reached Southampton and then they could enjoy rain and sunshine in twenty-four seat open trucks attached to goods trains. Second- and third-class passengers had nowhere to store their luggage except on their laps or under the benches. First-class passengers could have porters stow their luggage on the roof. There it was securely strapped down and the youths who carried out this task and cleaned and maintained the leather straps were known as 'strappers' – a term which was in time given to any trainee.

The Board of Trade was unhappy about the safety of passengers being carried in low-sided open wagons when a jerk or bump could throw them out. On 26 February 1842 R. Garnett, the company chairman announced:

> I would also take this opportunity of noticing the alterations which we have made in favour of the third-class passengers. We felt and thought that it was a prevalent opinion that the goods trains were not so secure from danger as the passenger trains, and therefore we adopted a third-class conveyance by an early train in the morning which gave the industrious poor not only a greater chance of security, but also encouraged them for rising early in the morning and travelling to London cheap which could not fail to be productive of considerable benefit. In adopting this plan, our paramount feeling was that of ensuring their security and comfort.

Third-class passengers were those who hitherto and been accustomed to travelling on the outside of a mail coach, so no covering was thought necessary. Sam Fay in *A Royal Road* wrote:

> A frame work with seats, fitted on the bed of a carriage truck, constituted the vehicle in which third class passengers travelled; the frame work was removed upon the truck being required for its ordinary purpose. On a wet day the condition of the poor wretches condemned by poverty to travel in such conveyances may be more easily imagined than described; if they turned their backs to the storm the rain ran down their necks, if they faced it their eyes became blinded and their pockets filled with water; an umbrella was a useless impediment, and their truck really resolved itself into a species of horizontal shower bath from whose searching power there was no escape.

These open coaches were attached to goods trains which, at first, were in the charge of three boys aged about fifteen and took upwards of 6 hours to travel the 77 miles from London to Southampton.

It was soon found that the boys devoted more time to playing games than to the company's goods traffic and so were superseded by guards. Initially there was no guard's van, the guard riding in 'Noah's Ark', which conveyed small packages for stations.

The open wagons had dumb buffers and springless drawgear. When a train was ready to start, the guard scotched the last wagon and the engine backed to slacken the couplings to enable it on starting to take the weight of just one wagon at a time.

The coaches were light – even a fully enclosed first-class carriage only weighed 3 tons 16 cwts. On the night of 30 July 1839 a second-class coach was blown by the wind along a siding at Woking and wrecked when it was struck by a train. The passenger coaches had no brakes, the retardation of speed controlled merely by the driver on the engine, the fireman using the tender handbrake and the guard using the brake in the luggage van if it was one so fitted. In an emergency, guards who sat on the roof of some first and composite carriages could only catch the attention of the enginemen by shouting or whistling.

Joseph Beattie, who had been brought to the L&S by Joseph Locke, designed carriage fitments, patent No. 8741, 16 December 1840, which included wooden-centred wheels, sprung buffers and couplings and brakes, the actual brake shoes being plaited rope. Until about 1860 carriages were only fitted with central coupling hooks and side safety chains, the main couplings being stored at stations.

Early buffers were set at different heights and not until November 1842 did John Viret Gooch, locomotive superintendent and brother of Daniel Gooch, who held a similar post on the GWR, and Joseph Beattie, carriage and wagon superintendent, settle a standard height for engine and carriage buffers.

A guard wrote in the *South Western Gazette* of July 1890:

In September 1858 I was made a Guard and my first trip was with a Necropolis train to Brookwood. I had to take my seat on the roof of a Composite carriage used as a brake, and you may depend I held on tight whilst being a novice in mid-air. In those days we had another brake commonly called a 'booby-hutch' only having an opening on one side and on one journey we had to cross the coupling to reach the platform. Luggage for main line trains had to be loaded on the roof and tied down with tarpaulins, parcels were put in lockers underneath the seats of the carriages. A parcel or two often went beyond its destination!

It not infrequently happened in bitter weather that guards became frozen to their outside seats and needed to be helped down, but at least they were provided with coffee at Woking and Basingstoke stations.

The carriages carried a chocolate livery below waist level and the centre door of each first-class coach was decorated with the company's crest, a dragon's wing painted on the side doors. White lead paint was applied above waist level.

Express trains normally consisted of between three and five carriages plus any carriage trucks and horse boxes as were deemed necessary.

In 1846 the L&S company probably had the fastest trains in the world: the 110-minute schedule to Southampton requiring an average speed of 42.9 mph while on one occasion a the Gooch 2-2-2 *Elk* covered the Up journey in 93 minutes – 50.3 mph.

In September 1848 trials were made with heavier trains, the 2-2-2 *Snake*, new in December 1847, successfully hauled ten carriages on Down trains and eleven on Up, each coach loaded to 7 tons. The result was that normal express trains were lengthened to seven carriages. Some trains were longer; for instance, the *Railway Times* for 17 August 1840 revealed that the 11.00 a.m. Up Mail was formed of thirty first-class carriages hauled by two engines.

Herapath's Journal for 21 May 1842 described an excursion which started from Nine Elms, reached Southampton in 2 hours 20 minutes, passengers then transferring to the PS *Royal Victoria* for a trip round the Isle of Wight.

> Some grumbling was made about the Second class carriages, which being open, and, thanks to the enterprise of the Company, were pulled along at a speed of 35 mph, were rather too windy for a morning and evening jaunt. Had the carriages been enclosed at the sides everyone would have been contented and there would be sufficient disparity between their bare boards and the comfortable cushions of the First class carriages.

Porters were dressed in fustian jackets with arm badges and chocolate-coloured caps, but in 1841 dark corduroy was substituted, two jackets supplied annually with number plates on their collars.

Railway policemen wore swallow-tailed, chocolate-coloured coats, dark trousers and tall hats with leather crowns. Apart from their duties as watchmen, they acted as signalmen and ticket collectors.

Guards wore chocolate-coloured frock coats with dark trousers until 1841 when their uniform changed to scarlet coats, lace collars and silver buttons, first-class guards being distinguished by belts.

5 minutes before the departure of a train from Nine Elms a large bell in the roof was rung, hand bells being used at other stations. The rules stipulated:

> With respect to the starting the trains at stations after the bell has been rung, the trains shall not start until the guard shows a white flag or lamp to the engine man, and he shall see that the passengers are seated and the doors of the carriages closed before he shows the flag.

Nine Elms was the scene of great excitement on 16 March 1841 when the locomotive storekeeper's light ignited turpentine which had seeped from a leaking carboy. The railway authorities insisted that the eight fire-engines be driven to the station. The chief fire officer was assaulted, the railway officials behaving disgracefully and creating confusion while the sightseers were entertained by 'conduct and language used by men professing to be gentlemen, that would be a disgrace to persons in any rank of society'. The chief fire officer said that he had 'never before experienced such ruffian treatment, even in the worst neighbourhoods of the metropolis'. In addition to the store and workshops, three locomotives and tenders were destroyed.

One example of the LSWR's empire-building tactics in trying to keep the GWR at bay (the L&S had been renamed in 1839) was the acquisition in 1847 of the Bodmin & Wadebridge Railway despite the fact that it was some 200 miles distant! This short line had opened on 4 July 1834. The LSWR had no parliamentary authority for its purchase and did not legally absorb the line until 1886 and it was only in 1895 with the opening of the Delabole–Wadebridge section of the North Cornwall Railway that it was joined to the parent system.

Similarly the Exeter & Crediton was regarded as a branch of the broad-gauge Bristol & Exeter Railway, but the LSWR, craftily purchasing shares, gained control and eventually seized most of North Devon, the GWR only reaching Barnstaple.

The station at Nine Elms was inconvenient for London as passengers had to travel onward either by road or river. As early as 1844, 10 acres of delightful 'vacant ground, to a great extent occupied as hay stalls and cow yards, and by dung heaps, and similar nuisances' had been purchased near Waterloo Bridge, while on 2 July 1847 further powers allowed for quadruple track.

Although the electric telegraph was invented in 1817, it was only the development of railways which made practical use of it. In the spring of 1844 it was laid experimentally along the 6 miles between Nine Elms and Wimbledon and by 24 January 1845 the telegraph ran from Nine Elms to Gosport.

In 1847 a wagon turntable offered access to the Southampton Dock Company's estate, so haulage was limited to horses. In 1871 a line was extended across Canute Road and extended from Town Quay to the Royal Pier but horse-powered boat trains continued until 1876 when the Board of Trade agreed to the use of steam locomotives.

The branch from Woking to Guildford opened 5 May 1848, a branch from Weybridge to Chertsey on 14 February 1848, tradesmen not welcoming the railway as it meant that customers could easily travel to London and purchase goods at a cheaper rate than by ordering through the local shops.

The Richmond to Datchet line opened on 22 August 1848. Her Majesty's Commissioners of Woods & Forests required the LSWR to pay £60,000 for the privilege of crossing Home Park, which, with the GWR's £25,000, was used to improve the approaches to Windsor and the castle, and also included the construction of the Victoria and Albert bridges across the Thames. The GWR reached Windsor on 8 October 1849, but due to the settling of two cast-iron piers of the bridge over the Thames at Black Potts, the LSWR could not be opened to Windsor until 1 December 1849.

The line was criticised for failings, one being that a special letter sent by rail informing of a sudden serious illness was despatched from Staines station at noon on 23 December 1848 to London for immediate delivery, yet did not reach its destination until twenty-3 hours later, thus covering the distance at an average speed of less than 1 mph and costing the sender over ½d a mile – this at a time when the Royal Mail would have delivered it the same day for only a penny.

Railways soon became an attraction for the local youths and on 24 November 1849 two boys aged twelve and fourteen were brought before the magistrates charged with throwing stones at a train on the South Western & Windsor Railway injuring the fireman of Rothwell 2-2-2 No. 92 *Charon*. They were given a month's hard labour. Stone throwing was a prevalent practice as earlier one railway employee was in Charing Cross Ophthalmic Hospital having been struck in the eye by a stone.

The Hounslow loop was completed on 1 February 1850.

2

THE LONDON &
SOUTHAMPTON SEEKS
EXPANSION

Almost as soon as the L&S Act was passed, the company turned its eyes towards Portsmouth, intending to build a branch from Southampton, but the proud folk of Portsmouth were unhappy with this, wanting their own direct railway, not one via Southampton. Eventually in 1839 the extension was authorised from Southampton to Gosport, but in deference to the fortifications, the railway was required to build Gosport station no higher than the local officer commanding the Royal Engineers permitted. The Southampton company astutely avoided the citizens of Portsmouth having to use the offensive word 'Southampton' by renaming the company the London & South Western Railway.

The trusted Thomas Brassey was contracted to lay the line and all appeared ready for opening to Gosport on 26 July 1841 when, on 15 July, part of Fareham Tunnel slipped despite having walls 3 feet thick. It was deemed more economic to open out the affected part rather than make a repair. The line opened on 29 November 1841, but on 3 December fresh slips appeared and passenger services were withdrawn until 7 February 1842. Gosport station was used by Queen Victoria when visiting Portsmouth or Osborne House, her residence on the Isle of Wight.

In 1844 the LSWR built a royal saloon for Queen Victoria. Designed by the locomotive superintendent Joseph Beattie, its body was dark maroon with the royal arms in its central panel. The compartment for the Queen and Prince Albert occupied two-thirds of the 17 ft, the smaller compartment being a suite for the children. To prevent vibration, the floor was covered with Axminster carpets over a layer of cork and India-rubber composition. The interior of the saloon was sumptuous.

Its first use was probably on 8 October 1844 when King Louis Phillipe of France arrived at Gosport and left for Farnborough with Prince Albert proceeding by road to Windsor. When he returned on 14 October, Locke drove the royal train and Queen Victoria accompanied her guest to Gosport in the new royal carriage.

As a gale was blowing at Gosport and the waves were high, the king deemed it expedient to travel via Dover and Calais. At 7.45 p.m. King Louis bade farewell to Queen Victoria and Prince Albert and reached Nine Elms at 10.35 p.m. He crossed London to the South Eastern Railway's station at New Cross where he found the building in flames.

A special messenger of the South Eastern Railway met King Louis and informed him that the directors regretted their inability to meet him owing to the late hour at which notice of the altered plans had been received and offered their profound apologies for the fire. *The Times* recorded:

> The King in reply expressed himself perfectly satisfied with the arrangements which had been made. He expressed in strong terms his regret at the unfortunate fire then raging on the premises and concluded by hoping the Company was well insured.
>
> At 11.15 pm the special train, driven by Mr Cubitt, left the station, Dover being reached at 2.30 am. His Majesty spent the rest of the night at the Ship Hotel, and crossed to France next day.

The Richmond Railway Act received Royal Assent on 21 July 1845, three of its directors were also directors of the LSWR. The line passed through Mortlake, Barnes, Putney and Wandsworth, Henry Knill being appointed the contractor for this section and Locke the engineer. It involved a 1,000 ft long viaduct. Construction took only nine months and the line opened 27 July 1846 with a service of seventeen trains daily. The fares of 1s 4d first and 1s 0d second-class were found to be too high and soon reduced to 1s 0d first and 10d second. The company was purchased by the LSWR, Richmond shareholders receiving one LSWR paid-up share for three Richmond £15 paid-up shares, or £25 cash for each Richmond share.

In the Havant district, the lines from Chichester to Havant opened 15 March 1847, Havant to Portsmouth 14 June 1847 and Fareham to Cosham 1 September 1848. The Hampton Court branch was opened on 1 February 1849, horse traction being used initially from the junction. Farnham was reached 8 October 1849 and Godalming 15 October 1849.

Although the proposed L&S branch from Basingstoke to Bath and Bristol was defeated by the GWR, it still had eyes on the west and planned a line from Eastleigh, then called Bishopstoke, to Milford on the outskirts of Salisbury. It was authorised on 4 July 1844.

Initially things appeared inauspicious: landowners proved obstructive and prices offered for their property had to go to arbitration. Then, instead of employing the reliable Thomas Brassey, the contract of the delightfully named Hoof & Hill was accepted since it was £18,000 below that of its competitors. However, it proved an excellent example of cheap proving dear.

The delay in obtaining land meant delaying the start so Joseph Locke, the LSWR engineer, offered Hoof & Hill an extra £1,000 if the line was opened on 10 August 1846. This they were unable to do as farmers gathering the harvest were able to offer higher wages than the contractors. Opening was postponed until October, and then unfavourable weather in November and December caused further delays.

One of the chief benefits the railway brought was cheaper coal, advantageous both to households and industry and thus helping to raise living standards. Because flooding had made Salisbury desperately short of food, the incomplete line was opened to goods traffic on 27 January 1847 when 90 tons of coal arrived for distressed households. The first train was hauled by 0-6-0 No. 52 *Rhinoceros*. The following day three trains delivered beef, mutton, pork, flour, butter, cheese and animal fodder.

The branch opened to passenger traffic on 1 March 1847 and enabled Salisbury citizens to reach London by one of the four daily trains after making a change at Bishopstoke.

In 1844 Charles Castleman, a Wimborne solicitor, proposed a railway between Southampton and Dorchester. His route being circuitous, it was named 'Castleman's Corkscrew' or 'The Water Snake'.

Southampton inhabitants discovered that with the arrival of the railway, travellers, instead of staying in the town for a while as they had in coaching days, were immediately whisked off from train to ship or vice versa. The lack of customers had an unpleasant economic effect on both hotels and shops. In an attempt to counteract this trend, Southampton managed to place a clause in the Southampton to Weymouth Act of 21 July 1845 requiring a station to be built at Blechynden Terrace near the town centre and make most trains call there. (This station became the present Southampton Central.)

Unfortunately the station's site led to a legal dispute. Mr Fotheringham claimed that the location infringed on his agreement with the company that a station would not be built within sight of his home. Then, cunningly, on 30 May 1847 just two days before the line was to be opened, the railway managed to rent a nearby house for two years and use it as a temporary station.

The 'Corkscrew' opened on 1 June 1847, the first train leaving from Blechynden rather than Southampton Terminus as the tunnel between the two stations had collapsed. This was because Peto, the contractor, had appeased the owners of the property above by filling the disused Andover & Southampton Canal tunnel which crossed below the railway tunnel. Damming had prevented drainage from the canal tunnel, thus causing the water to so saturate the clay that it collapsed.

The LSWR, not content at reaching Salisbury, wished to press on deeper into the West Country. At a meeting on 26 January 1846, the chairman, Chaplin, proposed four schemes:

LSWR: Basingstoke to Salisbury, £700,000
Salisbury & Yeovil Railway: Salisbury to Yeovil, £900,000
Exeter, Yeovil & Dorchester Railway: Yeovil to Exeter, £1,300,000
Cornwall & Devon Central Railway: Exeter to Falmouth and Penzance, £3,000,000

The LSWR would subscribe a quarter of each company's capital, and if all were successful in achieving an Act, the LSWR, the Salisbury & Yeovil and the Cornwall & Devon Central would amalgamate and jointly lease the Exeter, Yeovil & Dorchester. The latter three schemes failed in Parliament, but the Basingstoke to Salisbury bill received Royal Assent on 13 August 1846.

West of Salisbury the LSWR was entering broad gauge territory and feelings were strong both for and against the standard gauge.

Louis H. Ruegg in *The History of a Railway*, published in 1878, relates of a meeting held at Sherborne on 26 March 1846.

> The town hall was densely crammed, and, after considerable delay, it began to be known in the room that there was a split in the local railway committee, and that the meeting might go off. This gave fresh excitement to the feeling in the hall and when, after an hour's delay, the members of the committee struggled through the mass which had overflown the floor and covered the platform, the cheering was tremendous.
>
> On behalf of the Exeter Great Western ... it was averred that it [the broad-gauge route] could not be more than 5 miles further from the locality in which the meeting was being held than the line via Salisbury. A part of it, it was said, was actually made (a part of the Wilts & Somerset). It would open up some of the best corn markets in the world and tap the great coal measures of Somerset. It would give communication with the North, and carry them down to Land's End. With cheap coal and communication, North, East, West and South, what more, it was asked, could they want? The meeting enquired the sort of line they were to have, and when it was described as a branch from Sparkford, they indignantly declared 'It won't do!' and the continued mention of 'the drop line from Sparkford' was received with shouts of laughter. Would that line, it was asked, carry their wheat to Salisbury, or their cattle to London? It was said that the two great companies, the Great Western and the South-Western, were tied by some sort of agreement with the Board of Trade which prevented them entering upon this territory; and amidst loud cheering, Mr Crombie [secretary of the London, Salisbury & Yeovil] asserted that but for the London, Salisbury & Yeovil Company the Great Western would never have seen the district at all.

Nine Elms was situated on the edge of the built-up area and although convenient for steamers, was set too far from the City and many passengers had to travel onward by road or river. The answer was an extension to the south end of Waterloo Bridge. The line required the destruction of about 700 homes, the construction of a 235-arch viaduct and it and the new station at Waterloo demanded over 80 million bricks.

In order that the arches could be let and the company receive a return for its outlay, they were waterproofed with asphalt. The six-road terminus with four platforms, designed by Sir Francis Tite, opened on 11 July 1848, Nine Elms then being given to goods traffic.

Waterloo had four platform roads 300 ft in length, with two centre lines. Being 22 ft above road level, the station was reached either by inclines of 1 in 25 or by staircases. As platforms were added over the years, Waterloo became a complete mishmash and was one of the London termini without an adjoining hotel. Developing was piecemeal: four platforms, the North Station, were added in 1860 and the two-platform South Station in 1878, and a further six platforms in 1885 known as 'Abyssinia' or 'Khartoum'. Even on opening Waterloo was too inadequate for the number of trains using it, so working was eased by making as few engine movements as possible. Consequently a procedure, fraught with danger, was enacted.

Waterloo being an open station, tickets were checked at special platforms at Westminster Bridge Road, and while this was being carried out, the locomotive was uncoupled and a rope placed between it and the leading carriage. When the train was in motion the rope was unhooked, the train then freewheeling into a platform controlled by the guards' brakes. A lever at Westminster Bridge Road sounded a gong near the end of the platform to sound a corresponding number of beats to indicate to the points man the number of the platform to which the train was to run. Meanwhile the engine accelerated rapidly into a siding. The locomotive, accelerating away from its train, was diverted into the turntable road.

As the coaches entered the station, they were greeted by a man with a long-handled hammer in one hand and a grease can in the other. As the carriages passed him into the station he tapped each wheel with his hammer to see if by the ring it was sound.

Initially no buffers existed at Waterloo, the tracks running right to the end wall, but in June 1849 stops were erected when a train narrowly escaped overshooting the parapet and plunging into Waterloo Road. Although the practice of slipping a whole train ended before 1878 for loaded trains, it continued until 1895 for empty main-line trains brought in from Clapham Common.

An unusual feature of Waterloo was the six sets of carriage turntables provided to enable trains to be re-marshalled and for horseboxes and carriage trucks to be loaded or unloaded.

The opening day to Waterloo was advertised as 30 June 1848, but when the Board of Trade inspector Captain Laffan examined the works he found the tracks badly laid and poorly ballasted, and suspected that the strength of the 90 ft skew span over Westminster Bridge Road was insufficient. On 7 July 1848 Captain Simmons, the senior inspector, checked the deflection and found it not to exceed ³⁄₁₆ in. He therefore passed the line which opened on 11 July 1848, the day Nine Elms closed to passengers. Temporary timber buildings were used at Waterloo until the opening of permanent structures in 1853.

Waterloo was not intended to be a terminus, the company hoping to extend the line to Southwark or the City. Due to an agreement with the London & Brighton Railway, no goods facilities were provided at Waterloo. At least until 1853 one of the Down roads as far as Vauxhall was used as a carriage siding, and it was not until 1860 when a fourth track was opened between Nine Elms and Clapham Junction that they became Up and Down Windsor lines and Up and Down main lines. The offices at Waterloo, built parallel with the departure platform, were of timber until 1853.

Growing suburban traffic caused congestion and in 1859 the Waterloo Station Enlargement Committee reported that the station was 'insufficient for conducting the traffic either with satisfaction to the public or credit to the Company.' It submitted plans for an extension 'in such form as not to interfere with, but on the contrary be available for, any extension to Charing Cross, or for a new station in the York Road'. In 1860 four additional platform roads were opened on the Windsor side of the station.

Road 5 was an interesting through connection to the South Eastern Railway. Opened on 11 January 1864, from 6 July 1865 to 31 December 1867 it ran across the station concourse and was only used regularly by London & North Western passenger trains. Subsequent trains were just for occasional transfer and special traffic, such as Queen Victoria travelling from Windsor to Woolwich on 22 March 1900. When the line was out of use, an opening bridge allowed passengers to cross the concourse on the level. The connecting line and movable platform were abolished in the 1922 Waterloo rebuilding.

As the intermediate station at Vauxhall served the fashionable Vauxhall Gardens, the third-class waiting room and stairs were suitably separated from those of the other classes.

The Exeter, Yeovil & Dorchester Act was passed on 22 July 1848 and the LSWR was permitted to subscribe £900,00 of its total capital of £1,400,000.

Due to the economic depression following the Railway Mania of 1846 and the shortage of capital, work on the Basingstoke to Salisbury line was slowed and eventually ceased but work restarted in 1851. Chaplin resigned as LSWR chairman on 3 December 1852 and was replaced by Francis Scott. Unfortunately on 14 May 1853 a special train carrying him and his fellow directors killed an LSWR servant at Farnham. The coroner's jury gave a verdict of manslaughter and Scott and his traffic superintendent were charged, but the hearing was stopped, the jury being told that the defendants were no more responsible than any other passenger and that the death had been due solely to the deceased's inattention.

Scott had a short and unhappy chairmanship, being accused of insulting the proprietors and aggravating in conduct, and resigned in November 1853.

When the contractor Brassey was invited to invest in the Salisbury & Yeovil Company he made three conditions:

1 That the LSWR should work the line for 45 percent of gross receipts.
2 That the LSWR should pay 25 per cent of receipts from traffic the Salisbury & Yeovil (S&Y) brought to it.
3 That the LSWR should run four through trains daily each way.

The S&Y Act received Royal Assent on 7 August 1854 with powers to raise a capital of £400,000.

Powers for constructing the Basingstoke to Salisbury line having lapsed, an Act of 4 August 1853 was passed for its completion. Good weather favoured Brassey, and the single line with its high embankments and deep cuttings opened as far as Andover on 3 July 1854 and reached Milford station, Salisbury on 1 May 1857. The Act for an extension from Yeovil to Exeter was passed on 21 July 1856.

The first turf of the S&Y was cut at Gillingham on 3 April 1856. As Brassey had refused to construct the line, Leslie & Davidson won the tender to construct the single line for £300,000, the work to allow future doubling. On 1 October 1857 Leslie & Davidson transferred the contract to Brassey. The navvies near Wilton and Buckhorn Weston were particularly rowdy and the S&Y had to pay the local authorities for additional constables.

The broad-gauge GWR branch from Westbury opened to Salisbury on 30 June 1856, the S&Y laying a parallel line between that city and Wilton.

The S&Y opened to Gillingham on 2 May 1859 and that same day Milford station was closed, passengers using the rather more central station at Fisherton Street, Salisbury. At the time, its glass-roofed platform, almost 800 ft in length, was the longest in England.

Beyond Gillingham, water in the greensand delayed work on the 742 yd long Buckhorn Weston Tunnel and additional shafts had to be sunk to improve drainage. Sherborne was reached on 7 May 1860 and Yeovil on 1 June 1860. Here a joint station was made with the broad-gauge Bristol & Exeter Railway, each company having separate booking offices and stationmasters' houses. The mixed gauge was continued to Hendford.

Taylor won the contract for the line on to Exeter and employed 3,000 men, 600 horses and two locomotives on the project. The 206 yd long Crewkerne and 263 yd long Black Boy tunnels gave little trouble, but water proved a problem in the 1,345 yd tunnel at Honiton.

On 18 July 1860 the LSWR directors left Waterloo at 8.00 a.m. in a train of twenty carriages hauled by Etna class 2-2-2 No. 122 *Britannia*, Canute class 2-2-2 No. 151 *Montrose* and Volcano class 2-4-0 No. 115 *Vulcan*. West of Yeovil they stopped at each of the new stations, reaching Exeter at 3.00 p.m., the event also being marked by an eclipse of the sun. The line opened to the public on 19 July 1860 with three trains each way daily, one from Yeovil and two from Waterloo. Goods services are believed to have begun on 1 September 1860.

The LSWR covered the 171¾ miles between London and Exeter in 310 minutes compared with the GWR's 305 minutes for its 194 miles. In February 1862 the LSWR introduced a new express that covered the distance in 285 minutes, causing the GWR to introduce the Flying Dutchman to reach Exeter in 270 minutes.

Although initially the line had no branches, the Salisbury Railway & Market House Company constructed a branch from Fisherton Street station to the market house and this opened on 24 May 1859.

Meanwhile in Cornwall, looking very much into future expansion, as mentioned earlier the LSWR had purchased the Bodmin & Wadebridge Railway, principally to carry sea sand, used as a fertilizer and ore, from Wenford to Wadebridge. The line still being detached from other

LSWR lines, 0-4-2 No. 42 *Atlas* was transferred by ship from Rotherhithe Docks in September 1852 as the existing engines could not handle the developing granite traffic, while sister engine No. 44 *Pluto* joined her in December 1854. The line had one passenger vehicle, the *Omnibus*, with fares 1s inside and 8d outside paid to a conductor. The service was infrequent – the passenger train ran on alternate days.

Another LSWR detached line was the broad-gauge Taw Vale Railway to serve Fremington harbour. A separate undertaking, the Taw Vale Extension & Dock Company, extended the line from Barnstaple to the Exeter & Crediton Railway. In December 1846 the LSWR leased the Taw Vale Railway, while on 4 December 1846 the LSWR directors authorised Locke to lease or purchase the Exeter & Crediton, hitherto leased to the broad gauge Bristol & Exeter. The LSWR through nominees, illegally purchased sufficient shares in the Taw Vale to control the Exeter & Crediton. These new shareholders rejected the Bristol & Exeter lease and for four years refused to open the completed line on the broad gauge.

Regarding the Exeter & Crediton, eventually sense prevailed and the line opened on 12 May 1851 and worked on the broad gauge by the Bristol & Exeter. The Taw Vale, renamed the North Devon Railway, opened on 1 August 1854 and the Bideford Extension on 2 November 1855, both lines being leased by the contractor Brassey, who obtained much of the rolling stock second hand from the Bristol & Gloucester Railway, which had been taken over by the Midland Railway and converted to standard gauge rendering the broad-gauge stock redundant. Through trains ran from Bideford to Exeter St David's, Brassey's locomotive coming off at Crediton and being exchanged for one owned by the Bristol & Exeter.

The growth of London, coupled with the cholera epidemic of 1848–9, meant burial space was proving a problem, so from October 1849, nightly the LSWR carried coffins to Woking in goods trains. The charge was 5s per coffin, mourners travelling second class at single fare for the return journey.

The London Necropolis and National Mausoleum Company obtained a private Act on 30 June 1852 and in 1854 purchased almost 2,200 acres of land at Woking and arranged with the LSWR to have a dedicated platform at Waterloo. Designed by Sir William Tite and three storeys high, it had a grand entrance hall and staircase for mourners attending the better classes of funerals, and another hall and staircase for the lowest classes. Steam powered coffin lifts linked all floors. Brookwood was the largest cemetery in Western Europe and was served by its own ¾-mile-long branch line opened on 13 November 1864.

Not far inside the cemetery gate was the North station serving the Nonconformist chapel and that part of the cemetery, while at the far end was the South station and the Church of England section. A siding midway served the statuary and monumental masonry works.

The London Necropolis Company required to be notified of the number of funerals and attending mourners by noon the preceding day so that the LSWR could assemble stock. The coaches (owned by the LSWR) were divided into three classes, while the hearse vans (the property of the Necropolis Company and which had been purchased in 1854 for a very reasonable £20 each) were also divided into three sections, the main distinctions being the quantity of ornamentation on the doors. Each of the six vans could carry twelve coffins. In 1899 two new replacement vans, one Anglican and the other Nonconformist, cost £224 6s 11d each.

A train had Anglican and Nonconformist portions, the hearse vans placed in the rear of the relevant portion of the train. In the early years, trains left Waterloo at 11.35 a.m. on weekdays and 11.20 a.m. on Sundays, arriving at 12.25 p.m. and 12.20 p.m. respectively. The Sunday train was withdrawn on 1 October 1900. From 1928 funeral trains normally only ran on Tuesdays and Fridays.

Initially black horses drew the train along the cemetery branch, but locomotive working began in 1864, the train being propelled through the cemetery under the guard's supervision.

The funeral of Charles Bradlaugh (1833–91) a radical free-thinker, proved memorable. When his funeral took place on 3 February 1891 a special train was provided to accommodate the mourners, but as over 5,000 turned up and jammed the approaches to Waterloo, two further trains were provided to carry them to Brookwood.

The LSWR's mechanical engineer, Dugald Drummond, is buried at Brookwood in plot 38 near Church Avenue and South station.

The only accident on the branch occurred 13 May 1938, when a propelled train struck a Necropolis lorry emerging from the masonry works. The coffin van severely damaged the vehicle.

Visitors to the Necropolis and the village of Brookwood were served by a station on the main line, Brookwood (Necropolis) opened 1 June 1864. Maximum charges between Waterloo and Brookwood were:

	£	s	d
For each corpse of the pauper class	0	2	6
For each corpse of the artisan class	0	5	0
For each other corpse	1	0	0

(Note that only single fares were available!)

Fares to and from the cemetery, not exceeding six mourners per funeral:

	s	d
First class each person	6	0
Second class each person	3	6
Third class each person	2	0

As these fares were fixed under the Necropolis Company's Act, they could not rise. By 1902 the normal return fares for Waterloo–Brookwood were 8s 0d first, 5s 2d second and 4s 0d third, thus some economically minded golfers dressed as mourners and used the Necropolis train to reach the links at Brookwood. Although second class was abolished on the LSWR on 22 July 1918, coffin tickets continued to be issued in three classes.

The funeral trains, known colloquially as 'The Dead Meat Trains' or 'The Stiffs' Express', generally consisted of two brake-firsts, a saloon and some hearse vans.

In 1877 the two-road Necropolis train shed at Waterloo was demolished, a line sold to the LSWR, and an awning constructed to shelter the remaining single road. As increasing LSWR traffic demanded further track widening, the station site at York Road was transferred to the LSWR which in return built a new Necropolis station in Westminster Bridge Road, offered a 999-year lease at nominal rent, £12,000 compensation and new rolling stock. The new terminus opened in February 1902.

Funeral trains declined to once weekly and the service was terminated when a parachute mine fell on the Waterloo terminus and funeral train during the Blitz on 16 April 1941. As the motor hearse had taken over, the Necropolis station was not rebuilt after the war.

On 12 January 1867 the driver of the Up Necropolis train was so drunk that the fireman had to carry out both driving and firing duties. The driver was dismissed and the LSWR wrote to the Necropolis Company asking that it ceased offering drink to railwaymen. The reply was that no drink was offered, but railwaymen adjourned to a nearby public house while the funeral services were taking place. Learning this, the LSWR suggested it would be better if the Necropolis Company provided bread, cheese and a single pint of beer.

On 28 July 1852 the Guildford to Farnham line was extended to Alton. A very useful line was the North & South Western Junction Railway which joined the LSWR at Kew and offered a link with the London & North Western Railway and thus brought mineral traffic to the LSWR. It opened for goods 15 February 1852 and to passengers on 1 August 1853. In January 1854 4,096 tons of coal travelled over the line to the LSWR averaging seventy wagons daily.

In May 1855 the LSWR abolished the use of open carriages in excursion trains and ensured that all passenger-carrying vehicles were covered.

The Lymington Railway from Brockenhurst opened on 12 July 1858 terminating at the temporary Town station; a permanent station replaced it on 19 September 1860. In due course the line was extended to the Pier station on 1 May 1884.

The exciting Battle of Havant occurred on 28 December 1858. The contractor Thomas Brassey had planned and built the Portsmouth Railway, now known as the 'Portsmouth Direct', from Godalming to Havant with the intention of leasing or selling it to any interested party. Initially the LSWR and the LBSCR were not interested as they earned more money from passengers using the longer existing routes, but when the South Eastern Railway threatened to lease the direct line, the LSWR took the lease which included running powers over the London, Brighton & South Coast Railway (LBSCR) from Havant to Portcreek Junction. The LBSCR was not happy with this new competition for Portsmouth traffic so delayed the opening. The LSWR announced that it would begin traffic on 1 January 1859 but would send a goods train through to Portsmouth on 28 December 1858.

Expecting trouble, the LSWR traffic manager, Archibald Scott, arranged for over a hundred platelayers and others to be at Havant. Sir Sam Fay, general manager recorded:

> The South Western train was not expected until about 10 o'clock, but Mr Scott took time by the forelock and reached the junction at 7.00 am. He found the Brighton people had prepared a surprise by removing the points, and placing an engine [0-4-0T No. 99] on the crossing during the night. No time was lost in relaying the points and … the Brighton engine was forcibly seized … By this time the rival army had mustered in force and before Mr Scott could get clear, they had lifted a rail on their main line. The South Western goods was then on the crossing, blocking both lines, and in that position Mr Scott and his force remained for two hours … At one time a serious fight appeared imminent, but at length Mr Scott retreated.

Passenger traffic began on 1 January 1859 but with bus connections from Havant. The LSWR obtained an injunction and through running commenced on 24 January 1859. This was followed by a fare war between the two companies before sense prevailed and receipts were shared. In 1860 the Havant to Portcreek section became joint property.

The Epsom & Leatherhead Railway opened on 1 February 1859 and was taken over by the LSWR in 1860 to make a connection with the LBSCR's Dorking to Epsom line. This extension came into use on 23 December 1866.

The Exeter & Exmouth Railway had an inauspicious beginning. The ceremony of turning the first sod took place on 27 November 1856 and coincided with the twenty-first birthday of the Hon. Mark Rolle who was to turn the first turf. He arrived 2 hours late and then, presumably famished, alighted as the directors' carriage passed the Market House where the feast was to be held after the ceremony, Mark leaving the honours to be performed by the chairman John Walker. In lifting the turf, Walker broke the spade handle and completed the task with his hands. In due course the line was completed and the first train ran on 1 May 1861.

Christchurch was reached from Ringwood on 13 November 1863, but Bournemouth had to wait for a rail connection until 14 March 1870. The line taken over by the LSWR on 16 December 1874.

Stokes Bay Railway opened from Gosport on 6 April 1863 and was acquired by the LSWR 17 June 1875. Chard Junction to Chard opened 8 May 1863 and was taken over the following year.

The Botley to Bishop's Waltham branch was a line built rapidly. Its Act was passed on 17 July 1862 and in April 1863 the secretary announced that the Board of Trade inspector had received a month's notice of opening – yet on this date no tenders for a station at the terminus had been sought! A temporary station was erected in a fortnight at a cost of £103 and the 3¾-mile long line opened on 1 June 1863. Minerva class 2-4-0WT *Salisbury* was shedded at Bishop's Waltham and in March 1867 and October 1868 its driver was fined 'for failing to ensure that the fire was correctly banked at night to ensure that the first train of the day departed punctually'.

A branch from Twickenham to Kingston-on-Thames opened on 1 July 1863.

A useful link line was the West London Extension Railway (WLER). 4 miles long and opened on 2 March 1863, it ran from the West London Railway at Chelsea to Battersea. It linked four companies who held shares in proportion: the London & North Western Railway one-third; the Great Western Railway one-third; the LSWR and the London, Brighton & South Coast Railway one-sixth each. In order to accommodate GWR traffic, the line was mixed gauge. The WLER enabled the LNWR to operate a service between Euston and the South Eastern Railway station at London Bridge via Willesden, West London Junction, Waterloo, then across the concourse to Waterloo Junction and thus to London Bridge.

The Petersfield Railway to Midhurst opened on 1 September 1864, while the Thames Valley Railway promoted a line from Strawberry Hill to Shepperton. Opened 1 November 1864, it was taken over by the LSWR in 1865.

The line from Andover to Redbridge was beset with troubles. Lord Palmerstone, who lived nearby, turned the first sod on 20 September 1859. As the railway would take its trade, the Andover Canal was purchased for £25,000, half this sum being in railway shares. Richard

Hattersley, who won the contract, proved a rogue and instead of immediately draining the canal so that the mud would harden, waited until he was almost ready to build the railway on its site and then charged the cost of removing the sticky mud. Eventually he was dismissed in May 1861 for poor work. He had been aided by John Burke, the company's engineer, who resigned two months later.

Henry Jackson & Co. replaced Hattersley, but eventually all work on the line ceased. Rowland Brotherhood enthusiastically started work on the line nine months later, but suddenly stopped in July. In December the financial situation was eased when the LSWR took over the company. The line opened on 6 March 1865 and was known as the 'sprat and winkle' line. Its inauguration was hardly a roaring success as the first train from Southampton only carried five passengers and twice slipped to a standstill climbing the 1 in 62 gradient near Andover Junction because the locomotive was not fitted with a sandbox.

Road users were distressed at the opening due to the fact that the level-crossing gates remained closed due to zealous observance of the traffic manager's order to keep the line always clear. Branch finances were given a boost by the opening of the Swindon, Marlborough & Andover Railway on 1 May 1882, that company running through trains from Swindon to Southampton, while with the opening of the Midland & South Western Junction Railway to Cheltenham, it was used by expresses running between the Midlands and Southampton.

Following the opening of the line to Alton, residents of the area to the west pressed for a line to Winchester. This was constructed and opened on 2 October 1865, Medstead station set at the line's summit, 650 ft above sea level. The Mid-Hants Railway was displeased with the manner in which the LSWR worked the line because it failed to offer more than one reasonable train between Waterloo and Southampton and neglected to develop through traffic because the LSWR wished to protect its own line via Basingstoke. The MHR's share of income for the first three years averaged about £3,600 – an inadequate return on an expenditure of some £200,000. On 30 June 1884 the LSWR purchased the line for £237,500.

On 5 March 1866 a branch was opened between St Denys and Netley with an extension to Fareham in mind, though this did not take place for another twenty years.

On 1 October 1866 the Chertsey branch was extended to Virginia Water, while on 20 December 1866 a line opened which proved useful for Saturday specials to the south coast was that from Salisbury to West Moors where it joined the Southampton & Dorchester.

Following the opening of the LSWR to Exeter in 1860, a line was laid from Exeter Queen Street to St David's and mixed gauge to Bideford, the LSWR took the lease of the Exeter & Crediton of which it owned 60 per cent of the shares; the North Devon Railway of which it owned 40 per cent and the Bideford Extension. On 3 February 1862 LSWR standard gauge trains ran through from Waterloo to Crediton and on 1 March 1863 to Bideford, though one daily Bristol & Exeter broad-gauge mixed train to Bideford ran until 1877. The Exeter to Crediton broad-gauge trains lasted until the end of that gauge in 1892.

The Seaton branch opened on 16 March 1868 and its plans were unusual insofar as they included a road bridge over the River Axe. The bridge, which still stands, is unusual for the period in that the whole of the bridge and the tollhouse are of concrete, the house being reputed to be the oldest concrete house in England. The bridge was not opened until 24 April 1877 when a toll of 4*d* was charged for each horse and cart crossing the bridge, a penny a leg for animals in harness and a halfpenny a leg for those not in harness. The story runs that one miserly farmer unharnessed his horse at one end of the bridge and made his son pull the cart across! The staff of Seaton station were allowed to cross toll-free.

1 October 1868 the Tooting–Wimbledon line opened connecting with the LBSCR's Peckam–Sutton line.

On 1 January 1869 the line from Kensington through Gunnersbury and Kew Gardens to Richmond opened and in 1877 the District Railway was given running powers. Also on 1 January 1869 the line from Wimbledon to the Twickenham–Kingston branch at Kingston opened.

The line was extended from Christchurch to Bournemouth on 14 March 1870, and on 2 May 1870 the branch from Brookwood to Farnham.

A branch from the North Devon Railway at Coleford reached Okehampton 3 October 1871, Lydford on 12 October 1874 from where the South Devon Railway's Launceston branch was mixed into Plymouth where on 17 May 1876 LSWR trains used a terminus at Devonport. Traffic developed to such an extent that the LSWR laid its own double track line on 2 June 1890, Devonport being converted to a through station and a terminus opened at Plymouth Friary on 1 July 1891. The LSWR used a joint station with the South Devon, Plymouth, North Road, from 28 March 1877.

The extension from Bideford to Torrington opened 18 July 1872 and on 2 December 1872 a branch from Broadstone Junction to Poole, enabling LSWR and Somerset & Dorset trains to run through Poole to Bournemouth West when the line was extended there on 15 June 1874. The original Poole station became Hamworthy Goods Station.

On 20 July 1874 the Somerset & Dorset Railway opened its extension from Evercreech Junction to Bath, thus completing a standard gauge link between the LSWR at Bournemouth and the Midland Railway at Bath. A junction at Templecombe facilitated exchange traffic to and from Plymouth and Salisbury.

A further incursion into GWR territory occurred in 1876. The opening of the Somerset & Dorset Railway's extension over the Mendips from Evercreech Junction to Bath on 20 July 1874 had bankrupted the company. Forced to find a purchaser, it approached the GWR and the Bristol & Exeter Railway who, in view of the Quadruple Treaty, whereby the B&E, GWR, LSWR and the South Devon Railways shared traffic in common areas, courteously informed the LSWR secretary, Scott of the position.

Scott's directors told him to contact the Midland Railway, the S&D books were inspected on 15/16 August 1875 and on 18 August the LSWR and the MR had made a better offer than the GWR and B&E. The LSWR and MR took the joint lease from 1 November 1875. The Somerset & Dorset Joint Railway was managed by three members from the board of the LSWR and the MR, as well as a committee of two general managers, plus the MR's locomotive superintendent and the LSWR's chief engineer. For the public it was the best outcome as the two standard gauge companies developed traffic, whereas had it come into the possession of the broad gauge party, it is likely that it would have been left to stagnate.

On 6 July 1874 the branch to Sidmouth opened; unusually the celebrations were spread over no less than four days. The station was 200 ft above sea level and a quarter of a mile from the beach. *Lethaby's Sidmouth Journal & Directory* reported: 'There was a seeming incongruity in linking the railway opening with a waterside rollicking; and in providing an amusement which is proverbial for bringing together all the rowdyism of a district ... giving knaves a welcome and thereby attracting the fools on whom such knaves flourish.' Select Sidmouth was experiencing just the sort of behaviour it feared would occur when the branch was opened. The line proved a financial success and unlike most other branches was not taken over by the LSWR but lasted as an independent company until the SR was formed.

On 2 October 1876 the LSWR and the LBSCR extended their joint line to Portsmouth Harbour with the new station adjacent to the Isle of Wight ferry quay, the companies purchasing the ferry boats in 1880. The new line required the station at Portsmouth Town to be on a higher level.

On 1 June 1877 the Metropolitan District Railway inaugurated a passenger train service from Mansion House to Richmond joining the LSWR at Studland Road Junction near Hammersmith.

The Meldon Junction to Holsworthy line opened on 20 January 1879. Meldon Junction at 950 ft above sea level was the highest point attained by the LSWR, while the viaduct itself has a height of 150 ft.

On 2 June 1879 the line between Ascot and North Camp, Aldershot was completely opened, the section between Ascot and Sturt Lane Junction have been used since 18 March 1878.

Waterloo station proving to have an inadequate number of platforms it was enlarged between 1877 and 1879, this requiring the demolition of homes and the provision of new dwellings. Another problem was that the wall of the London Necropolis Company's train shed stood where the approach roads required widening. A satisfactory agreement was concluded and as mentioned earlier, one of the Necropolis platform lines converted into an approach road to the Waterloo extension. The two new platforms at what was termed the South Station were brought into use in December 1878 to serve 'suburban trains going down the main line' as opposed to those taking the Windsor lines at Clapham Junction. Concurrently platforms in the main station were raised and widened. In 1878 the 'A' signal box was cunningly enlarged by building a new one around it and adding thirty-five levers making a total of 144.

In 1878 the LSWR purchased the Salisbury & Yeovil Railway paying £260 stock for every £100 of Salisbury shares.

The development of railways meant that it became more economic to send milk from rural areas to large cities rather than produce it in urban dairies. The cooling of milk before its despatch was carried out in rail-served depots, the first opening at Semley, Dorset in 1871. At first milk was carried in the guard's van, or in a ventilated milk van attached to a passenger train, but soon the quantity was sufficient to warrant running special milk trains.

The Great Storm of 1881 caused chaos on the LSWR. The Exeter to Lydford line was blocked from the morning of the 18th, the Ilfracombe line was blocked for days, and on the 19th a train from Okehampton arrived at Exeter having taken 8 hours for the journey of 26 miles. On the morning of the 21st a train left Devonport, struck a drift at Lydford and remained there for the rest of the day. Blockages began to be cleared on the 24th.

In the 1880s, when William Jacomb was the LSWR's resident engineer, the company first started using concrete to a significant extent.

The LSWR was a believer in burrowing or flying junctions to obviate hold-ups caused by flat junctions. The Kingston line flyover at Twickenham dated back to 1882 while Raynes Park, on the Epsom line, and Malden, on the Kingston line, came with quadrupling in 1884. The Aldershot Up line flyover at Pirbright Junction came into use in 1901 while at Byfleet the Down connection from Feltham made a burrowing junction in 1903. The Battledown flyover at Worting Junction is another example, as was the Lyme Regis branch at Axminster, while a burrowing junction could be found at Newton Tony.

A creosoting works was established at Redbridge in 1884, a switch, crossing shop and foundry being added in 1924–5.

The LSWR obtained most of its ballast from its Meldon Quarry and in the Southern Railway era the crushing and screening plant was modernised so that 40-ton hopper wagons could transport it to the whole system. In the busy season eight or nine trains of ten wagons left the quarry weekly.

The continued growth of suburban traffic demanded six new platforms at Waterloo of which three were opened on 12 March 1885 and the remainder later that year. Called the North Station, or more colloquially 'Abyssinia' or 'Khartoum', it was actually almost due west of the Windsor line station. Between 1888 and 1892 the viaduct from Nine Elms was widened to accommodate six roads. From 1881 the South Station was lit by electric lights installed by the Brush Company, while in 1883 the Edison company installed electric lighting on the Windsor platforms. In 1890 staff at Waterloo comprised 218 porters and carriage cleaners,

71 signalmen, 52 ticket examiners and ticket examiners, 46 policemen, 25 booking clerks, 24 telegraphists, 11 waiting room attendants, 4 bill posters, 2 messengers, 62 carmen and stablemen, 20 lamp cleaners, 2 hydraulic enginemen and 5 scavengers. On an average day, 720 trains and light engines entered and departed.

The South Station had an indicator for the platform staff, and to inform them when a train arriving was, say, for departure to Leatherhead or Kingston, a letter from a line of capital letters was turned: L for Leatherhead or K for Kingston. When a letter was not applicable, it was turned edge-on. These letters were worked from 'A' signal box.

The station covered about 22 acres and had twelve platforms and eighteen roads, all used for both arrivals and departures. Due to the intensive use of the station, a train which started from, say, platform No. 6 one day might start from No. 7 the following day and perhaps No. 8 the day after. This led to passengers being confused, and the description of Waterloo in Jerome K. Jerome's *Three Men in a Boat* has little exaggeration.

The Bodmin & Wadebridge was absorbed in 1886 and the work of improving the line was completed 3 September 1888, but it remained isolated from the rest of the LSWR until 1 June 1895.

After thirty-two years of holding the office of general manager, Archibald Scott resigned on 10 November 1884 and was succeeded on 1 March 1885 by Charles Scotter, goods manager of the Manchester, Sheffield & Lincolnshire Railway.

On 2 February 1885 the Surbiton–Cobham–Guildford line and its branch from Leatherhead to Effingham Junction were opened. On 20 May 1885 the Swanage branch was inaugurated, while the line from Fratton to Southsea worked jointly with the LBSCR opened on 1 July 1885. The North Cornwall line from Halwill to Launceston opened on 21 July 1886.

Experiencing financial difficulties, the Southampton Dock Company approached the LSWR and in 1886 Parliament sanctioned the LSWR lending the dock company £250,000. This fund was used to construct the Empress Dock, with a water area of 18½ acres compared with the 16 acres of the Outer Dock and 10 acres for the Inner Dock; the Empress Dock was opened by Queen Victoria 26 July 1890. Still more quayside accommodation was required and the only source of finance was the LSWR, so in February 1891 negotiations began and, following parliamentary approval, the docks became LSWR property from 1 November 1892.

This was a highly important date in the history of the LSWR. From 14 August 1848 the LSWR had been authorised to operate steam packets and the following year ran services from the Royal Pier, Southampton to Le Havre, Guernsey and Jersey. Seasonal potato traffic with the Channel Islands was important and over twenty-three days in 1883 the LSWR carried potatoes in 139 special trains from Southampton to London.

Immediately on purchasing the docks in 1892, the LSWR set about their enlargement, the Prince of Wales Graving Dock being at the time the largest in the world. On 4 March 1893 the liner *New York* called at Southampton and this marked the start of the transatlantic traffic which developed at the expense of Liverpool, Southampton having the great advantage of being so much closer to London. In 1898 the largest cold store in Europe was opened on the Test Quay.

The LSWR operated highly efficiently. Imported meat was packed into horse-drawn carts which were placed on flat wagons where, on arrival in London, they could be drawn immediately to their destination. Bullion from South Africa was sent to Waterloo in a specially strengthened bogie parcels van with an asphalt floor. One interesting import was South African crayfish, curiously transported from Southampton to Folkestone and then exported to France.

Many discerning passengers preferred the LSWR's Southampton to Le Havre route when travelling from London to Paris rather than one of the shorter sea crossings, because when travelling via Southampton you left Waterloo in the evening, crossed the Channel by night and French railways took you to Paris next morning. Between 1892 and 1911 goods traffic at Southampton increased by about 90 per cent and passenger traffic by 70 per cent.

0-4-0Ts were used for shunting the sharply curved dock lines. Dock locomotives were subject to marine law, and when one driver had been found carrying contraband his locomotive had been placed in a siding with its motion officially sealed.

A pupil of I. K. Brunel, resident engineer William Jacomb, died on 26 May 1887 after eighteen years in office. He was the uncle of J. W. Jacomb-Hood, who was to become the chief engineer from 1901 to 1914.

5 March 1888 saw the opening of a direct line from Brockenhurst to Christchurch coupled with a line from the former terminus at Bournemouth East to Bournemouth West, thus offering a more direct route to Bournemouth, a fast-growing resort. Engineering works included an embankment at Sway, which, although only 60 ft high, required a base 500 ft wide to prevent slipping. To further attract passengers a Pullman car was added to a train from 21 April 1890.

The line from Putney to Wimbledon opened on 3 June 1889. On 2 September 1889 the Southampton to Netley branch was extended to Fareham, thus offering a direct line between Southampton and Portsmouth and tapping the important market gardening area around Swanwick, which was to place important traffic on the line.

A rather curious line was that from Edington Junction on the Somerset & Dorset Joint Railway to Bridgwater, opened on 21 July 1890. Although owned by the LSWR, it was well detached from the rest of the system and therefore leased to the Somerset & Dorset.

14 July 1890 saw the opening of a tramway from Brookwood station to the National Rifle Ranges, which had been transferred from Wimbledon Common to Bisley.

Around 1893, G. T. White, superintendent of the line, introduced the custom of labelling each coach with a destination board on both sides.

On 20 May 1893 the Holes Bay curve was opened, allowing Weymouth trains to travel via Bournemouth rather than Wimborne, while on 1 June 1893 a curve at Branksome enabled trains to run direct from Bournemouth Central to Weymouth without having to reverse at Bournemouth West.

The 1890s marked the expansion of the LSWR in Cornwall, Launceston–Tresmeer opening 28 July 1892; Tresmeer–Camelford 14 August 1893; Camelford–Delabole 18 October 1893; Delabole–Wadebridge 1 June 1895; and Wadebridge–Padstow 27 March 1899. Bude had been reached from Holsworthy on 10 August 1898. In 1900 Padstow despatched 24 tons of fish, raising receipts of £65, but in 1911 the weight was 3,074 tons and receipts £6,879.

The Lee-on-Solent Railway was unusual in that it was not built under an Act of Parliament, but by an order of the Railway Construction Facilities Act of 1864. The intention was to develop the hamlet of Lee Britten into a resort. When the line was inspected on 15 July 1895 it was found that the platforms were only 4 inches high and devoid of shelters and booking offices, while in places the line had been built outside its legal limits. Following a re-inspection, it opened on 12 May 1894. It was economically worked – at intermediate stations a lad with a red flag signalled to the driver if he was required to pick up passengers, while those wishing to alight were required to inform the guard before leaving the terminus. Between Fort Brockhurst and Fort Gomer the railway ran unfenced like a tramway beside the road.

Rolling stock consisted of a hired LSWR engineer's department 2-4-0T No. 21 *Scott* and 0-6-0ST No. 392 *Lady Portsmouth*. The two coaches were tramway-pattern lightweight bogie vehicles with longitudinal seats and end platforms. Due to the light permanent way, speed was restricted to 10 mph.

In June 1908 the LSWR broke the news that both the hired locomotives were worn out and no other suitable engines with an 8-ton axle loading were available. As the company never paid a dividend and expenses usually exceeded receipts, on 26 July 1909 the LSWR took over the working using an H13 class steam railcar.

In 1895 the case of the Mansion House Association *versus* the LSWR came before the Railway & Canal Commission, the defendants charged with offering undue precedence for imported traffic in contrast to home produce, contrary to the Railway & Canal traffic Act 1854.

The LSWR showed that the traffic imported at Southampton, principally meat, bacon, cheese and butter, was taken direct from ship to railway wagon and conveyed in full train loads and generally consigned to just one firm. Home produce was generally in small consignments for numerous firms and did not usually make a trainload. Home produce demanded greater clerical work and thus a higher rate was reasonable. The court found in favour of the LSWR.

William Adams, locomotive superintendent, retired 31 July 1895 and was succeeded on 1 August 1895 by Dugald Drummond, a rather ferocious character who had worked with William Stroudley both at Inverness and Brighton.

On 14 May 1897 Mrs Hugh Williams-Drummond wife of the chairman of the Budleigh Salterton Railway, 'drove' the inaugural train. Unfortunately she overran Budleigh station and had to set back. The LSWR worked the line and absorbed the company on 1 January 1912. The line had been extended from Budleigh to Exmouth on 1 June 1903.

After being general manager for thirteen years Scotter retired in 1897 and was succeeded by Charles J. Owens. G. T. White, superintendent of the line, died on 17 March 1899 and was succeeded by Sam Fay, who had originally worked in Scotter's office before being appointed general manager of the Midland & South Western Junction Railway. He had led the company out of Chancery, completely turning its traffic receipts round. In four years he had increased them by 73 per cent with only an 18 per cent growth in expenditure. Fay had honed his managerial skills on the MSWJR and it was said that he could make an empty sack stand upright.

A fair proportion of passengers arriving at Waterloo were destined for the City. An overground railway would have been prohibitively expensive and even a line with standard-size tunnels like the Metropolitan Railway would have cost £5 million, but as the first electrically operated underground line, the City & South London Railway, had proved profitable, the LSWR backed the Waterloo & City Electric Railway.

This tube railway only needed a capital of £540,000 and £180,000 loans. Messrs Mowlem started work in June 1894 using a Greathead shield. Shafts were dug beside the Thames and excavated material barged to Dagenham Marshes while construction material was barged in, thus obviating the need to use the streets. As the route was mainly beneath roads, only a very few easements were required. The terminus at Waterloo was 41 ft below the main-line platforms.

The City station was 59 ft below the surface and commuters had to trudge up a gradient of 1 in 9, as the cost of acquiring property to provide lifts was prohibitive. The slope was eased to 1 in 18 by the insertion of short flights of steps in 1918.

The line opened on 8 August 1898 with four-car trains – two motor cars with a pair of intermediate trailers. Westinghouse braked, the one-class timber-built cars with perforated plywood seats were constructed by Jackson & Sharpe of Rochester, New York. Reassembled at Eastleigh, they were hauled to Waterloo by steam locomotives. The cars were powered through a central 500V DC rail from a small generating station at Waterloo. As no dead man's handle was fitted, a crew of two was required in the motorman's compartment. In the event of a signal being passed at danger, a contact arm tripped the main switch on the train.

The motor coaches, in addition to the low-level buffing gear, had standard buffer beams to facilitate movement on the main line. Although the line initially adopted green headlights, they were soon changed to red. In 1899 single cars were introduced for handling off-peak traffic.

Initially tickets were issued at turnstiles, but from 1900 on-board staff used tramway-style bell punch and tickets. It was worked as a part of the LSWR and through tickets were available. Passenger number increased from 3,485,556 in 1899 to 4,545,535 in 1902, with receipts of £26,029 and £34,296 respectively, while in addition were many through season ticket holders. The LSWR absorbed the company on 1 January 1907.

At first Manning Wardle *Pioneer* was sent below to shunt dead stock, but was replaced by a four-wheeled-Siemens electric engine (later No. 74S). A larger Siemens Bo-Bo was provided as a spare but spent most of its life as Durnsford Road shed and works pilot. Coal wagons were lowered down the hoist from the Windsor line sidings and hauled by an electric engine via the Up line and the departure platform to the power station. When Durnsford Road power station was opened in 1915, current for the Waterloo & City was supplied from there and the Waterloo generating station relegated to stand-by before being dismantled in 1917.

By 31 December 1888 points and signals on the LSWR were 99.5 per cent interlocked, while important routes were widened: the Portsmouth Direct 1 March 1878; the Thames Valley 9 December 1878; Crediton-Lydford 22 December 1879; Andover and Redbridge 20 November 1885; Ilfracombe-Barnstaple 1 July 1891; and Ascot to Frimley Junction 11 June 1893.

3

THE LSWR 1900 TO 1922

On 1 March 1901 E. Andrews retired as chief engineer, being succeeded by J. W. Hacomb-Hood, hitherto the Exeter divisional engineer and the son of R. Jacomb-Hood, engineer and later director of the London, Brighton & South Coast Railway.

The Basingstoke & Alton Light Railway opened without ceremony on 1 June 1901. It saw very little traffic that day, only about fifty tickets being sold at the intermediate stations. A great advantage of the line was that passengers could travel from Basingstoke to Alton in an hour at the cost of 1s 2d, whereas the previous route via Winchester took 2 hours and cost 3s 0½d.

The *Hampshire Herald & Alton Chronicle* of 8 June 1901 commented:

The man in the street expects to find the village somewhere near the station. But such little details do not trouble the promoters of railways, who, if the station is somewhere in the parish named - the parish may be a dozen miles in area - are quite content to take the name, which, with common people, is generally associated with the villages. And so it has turned out on the Basingstoke & Alton Railway. The three intermediate stations are named Cliddesden, Herriard, and Bentworth & Lasham respectively. But the villages bearing those names are a long way from the stations and not a glimpse of them can be seen from the train.

The line worked by the LSWR, reached a summit of almost 600 ft above sea level at Herriard. A private siding served Thornycroft's works, while near Alton a siding was laid to a hospital and convalescent camp with accommodation for 500 men built under the auspices of the delightfully named Absent-Minded Beggar Fund. This curious title came from the fact that at fundraising concerts for the construction of the hospital during the South African War, Rudyard Kipling's poem *The Absent-Minded Beggar* was recited. The siding was lifted, but replaced on 5 April 1910 for delivering coal to the Lord Mayor Treloar's Cripples' Home in the former hospital.

As was often the case, the last line to open was the first to shut. Military demand for track during the First World War caused the Basingstoke & Alton Railway to be closed on 1 January 1917, though the sidings to Messrs Thornycroft and Lord Mayor Treloar's Cripples' Home remained open. Two of the intermediate stations remained open for milk and parcels traffic which was carried to and from Basingstoke station on an LSWR Karrier bus converted to a lorry. In 1921 the LSWR directors considered potential traffic insufficient to warrant relaying the line.

On 1 August 1901 three sets of vestibuled trains of corridor coaches with dining or luncheon cars were introduced to the West of England service.

In March 1902 Sam Fay, superintendent of the line, was appointed general manager of the Great Central Railway and H. Holmes took his LSWR office. Fay visited the USA to observe operations and as a result the LSWR was the first English line to introduce automatic signalling on a steam-worked railway. Pneumatically powered automatic points and signals were brought into use between Andover Junction and Grateley from 31 July 1901 to 20 April 1903. Arising from Fay's appointment to the Great Central, a through service was inaugurated on 1 July 1902 between Bournemouth and Newcastle-upon-Tyne.

On 29 April 1902 the branch line from Grateley to Amesbury opened, extended to Bulford on 1 June 1906 and was to prove highly valuable in First World War giving access to Salisbury Plain for both army and air force.

The development of horse tramways had drawn some urban passengers from the railway and tramways became an even greater threat when electrified. One line that was affected by tramway electrification in 1901 was the Southsea Railway jointly owned with the LBSCR, when in 1902 the branch working expenses of £2,149 did not balance well against receipts of only £287.

Something had to be done, and that something was singling the line and abolishing signals, unstaffing the East Southsea terminus and having the guard issue tickets. The most important innovation was a steam railcar. The latter was a novel concept, though not entirely new as one had been used on the Bristol & Exeter Railway in 1849. It was a combined coach and locomotive, and in the LSWR design could be driven from either end, thus obviating the need to run round at the end of each trip, saving time and the cost of a signalman.

Railcar No. 1 commenced its regular working of the branch on 1 June 1903 operating a 20-minute interval service from 8.00 a.m. to 7.30 p.m., working alternate days with No. 2. Unfortunately their steam-raising ability was poor, and for the rush-hour services a steam engine had to be attached, thereby cancelling out any savings.

In September 1903 No. 1's vertical boiler was replaced by a larger version in the horizontal position. This improved steaming and No. 2 was also modified enabling the pair to work all traffic unaided. Occasionally a railcar stopped with the piston towards the top of the stroke – this meant that the driver had to ease his 24½-ton vehicle forward a few inches from dead centre with a long pinch bar. The locomotive section of both cars was painted Drummond green, but the coach section of No. 1 was in the LBSCR livery of chocolate and cream, while No. 2 was in the LSWR's salmon and dark brown. Lettered 'SW & LB&SCR Joint', they were one of the few English examples of a joint line having its own locomotive power.

To increase traffic, two intermediate rail-level halts were opened on 1 July 1904. Halts were devised by the Great Western Railway the previous year, simple low platforms with just a shelter, unmanned and with no toilet or waiting-room fire. These were an economical means of providing a stopping place where a conventional station would have been uneconomical.

On 1 June 1903 the Budleigh Salterton branch was extended to Exmouth permitting a circular service to be run from Exeter. On the same date the Meon Valley line from Alton to Fareham opened. Its construction caused problems. R. T. Relf, the railway's contractor, offered higher wages than local farmers and the latter, threatened with also having to pay higher wages in order to retain staff, stated that if any of their men, or their families, worked on the line, they would be thrown out of their cottages. One lad employed as a fireman on the contractor's engine had to leave his home on the Basing Park Estate, Privett and lodge with an aunt in West Meon in order to avoid his father being thrown out on the street.

The Meon Valley Railway Act also permitted a 2-mile-long deviation line to be made between Knowle Junction and Fareham, where two tunnels caused trouble through slipping. The problem was the clay through which the railway was cut. It had the unpleasant characteristic that when dry it was so hard that explosives were required to assist excavation, yet became slurry after exposure to heavy rain. The problem was never really solved, and the line suffered slipping until closure.

Another modern development was operating a motor omnibus between Exeter and Chagford, a second-hand Milnes-Daimler being purchased which inaugurated the route on 1 June 1904. The service prospered, sometimes having more passengers than the regulation sixteen. The overspill piled itself on the roof with the luggage, a practice forbidden by the Exeter municipal authorities, but passengers were not defeated. Within the city they crowded the narrow aisle and the conductor's platform, then, when beyond the boundary, ten or more would climb up the luggage ladder on to the roof. Even ladies did this, sometimes exhibiting articles of dress not normally on display. The service was withdrawn during the winter and two Clarkson's steam buses used the following year. In July 1905 the LSWR inaugurated a Clarkson steam bus service between Lymington, Milford-on-Sea and New Milton.

On 23 August 1903 the Axminster & Lyme Regis Light Railway opened, half its capital being provided by the LSWR. The principal work was the ten-arch Cannington Viaduct, one of the first viaducts in England to be constructed of concrete. Unfortunately one of the arches started slipping a fortnight before the line was due to be opened. The problem was cured by inserting a jack arch. For the first three years after opening, a watchman was posted to keep an eye on the stability of the viaduct.

Another modern feature was that the branch crossed the main line at Axminster by means of a fly-over. The LSWR took over the line 1 January 1907 and in 1908 the branch was used by 60,000 passengers,

10,000 parcels and 8,000 tons of goods. That year the line experienced particularly heavy traffic as from January till June sightseers came to view the burning cliff caused by natural deposits of bituminous shales and iron pyrites which had ignited spontaneously.

Locomotives working the branch proved interesting to enthusiasts. As the LSWR had no suitable class of engine to work the line, it purchased for £500 each two 0-6-0T Terriers from the LBSCR, No. 668 *Clapham* and No. 646 *Newington*. Repainted and numbered No. 734 and 735 they proved insufficiently powerful for the heavy summer traffic and the tight curves caused extensive flange wear and strained frames. In August 1905 an Adams O2 class 0-4-4T No. 228 assisted but due to the line's severe weight restriction, the tanks and bunker could only be partly filled, which decreased the engine's usefulness. Its side tanks were marked to indicate the maximum permissible volume of water allowed within the weight restriction.

In May 1907 the Terriers left permanently, No. 734 being sold to the Freshwater, Yarmouth & Newport Railway in 1913. It now works on the Isle of Wight Steam Railway. No. 735 was used on the Lee-on-Solent Light Railway and from 1930 until its withdrawal in 1936 acted as Carriage & Wagon Work's pilot at Ashford.

The O2 class engines did not prove satisfactory and, like the Terriers, suffered from excessive flange wear and strained frames, so in 1913 Urie took Adams' 415 class 4-4-2 No. 0125 and modified the bogie to give greater side play and thereby ease the negotiation of severe curves in which the branch abounded. This alteration proved successful and two more were modified and masterfully worked the line for the ensuing forty-five years.

One curious fact is that although the branch was never electrified, some of its rail was run over by electric trains. An LSWR minute of 16 December 1915 records that electric rail for a siding at Dunsford Road power station was old rail from the Lyme Regis branch because expensive, high-conductivity 100 lb/yd rail was not required in this location.

The LSWR cast envious eyes at the prestigious traffic the GWR received at Plymouth from its ocean liner traffic, so when in 1903 the American Line announced that all its ships travelling eastwards across the Atlantic would call at Plymouth before reaching the LSWR's docks at

Southampton, the LSWR felt it essential to provide facilities at Plymouth to equal those of the GWR.

At Stonehouse Pool Quay, just upstream from the GWR's Millbay Docks, it constructed a covered 350 ft long platform with waiting and refreshment rooms, ticket, inquiry and telegraph offices, and customs and luggage hall. The floors were covered with a cork carpet and the refreshment room was lit by gas and electricity. The station bore bold letters on the roof: 'London South Western Railway' – the '&' deliberately omitted to please Americans who appreciated brevity. A steam crane lifted luggage in specially constructed wheeled crates from the tender's deck to the railway platform. In 1907 the platform was extended to permit two boat trains to be dealt with simultaneously.

The first American Line vessel to call was the *St Louis* on 9 April 1904. Only passengers were carried by the LSWR, the Post Office refusing to take the mail contract from the GWR whose route via Bristol gave connections to the Midlands and north of England. On 23 April 1904 the LSWR challenged the GWR boat specials with a luxurious five-coach corridor train which ran from Stonehouse Junction to Waterloo in 4 hours 3 minutes. The vehicles had electric light and were 6 inches wider than the LSWR's normal stock.

The SS *Victoria*, a 709-ton vessel constructed in 1896 for the LSWR's Jersey–St Malo service, was adapted in 1904 for duties as a tender, visiting the same ships as the GWR tenders. The service was not always profitable: on 18 February 1907 only eleven passengers disembarked from the SS *New York* and only three used the boat train to Waterloo. In the summer, to fill in time between tender duty, the SS *Victoria* ran excursions to Dartmouth, Falmouth, Fowey, Looe, Salcombe and Torquay.

When the White Star Line announced that its vessels would call at Plymouth from 1907, the LSWR realised that traffic would be sufficient for a purpose-built tender and so ordered the SS *Atalanta* which was completed by 29 May 1907, allowing the SS *Victoria* to return to the Channel Islands service.

Events proved that competition with the GWR for ocean traffic was uneconomical and an agreement was signed on 13 May 1910 providing for the pooling of all competitive traffic based on the figures for 1908. The LSWR withdrew its Plymouth Ocean Liner specials while the GWR withdrew its Plymouth to Brest ferry.

In 1906 the LSWR had obtained powers to double the remainder of its Exeter to Barnstaple line. The work was begun and earthworks and bridges completed, but in consequence of this agreement, the second track was never laid. Another sequel to the agreement was the inauguration on 1 July 1910 of a GWR through train from Birkenhead to Bournemouth via Basingstoke.

When the War Office asked the LSWR in 1902 to construct a line to serve the new Longmoor military camp in Woolmer forest, the LSWR obtained powers under a Light Railway Order. Unusually, instead of a contractor being engaged, the LSWR's engineer's department carried out the work of building the 4½-mile long line, completing it in only eighteen months.

The line opened on 11 December 1905 and on 7 March 1906 a steam railcar service was introduced, but later 2-2-0T motor tanks and trailer cars appeared. Most of the station buildings at Bordon were of corrugated iron and lit from a small coal-gas producing plant. The station was capable of handling up to four ten-coach trains. As housing was short in the area, the LSWR built ten terraced houses for its staff and a detached station master's residence. The partition walls between houses were of brick, but those within a house were tongue-and-grooved timber.

Comparative statistics of passenger trains working on the Bordon Branch:

	Railcar	Motor Tank	O2 class 0-4-4T
Pounds of coal burnt per mile	13.2	18.6	26.8
Cost of working per mile	3s 4d	5s 9d	10s 6d

The East Cornwall Mineral Railway (ECMR), a 3 ft 6 in. gauge mineral line, opened on 7 May 1872, running from Calstock Quay to Kelly Bray a mile east of Callington. Initially prosperous, eventually some of the mines it served closed, making the line poorer economically. Taken over by the Plymouth, Devonport & South Western Junction Railway (PDSWJR), a standard-gauge line was laid from the main line at Bere Alston to Calstock and the ECMR converted to a standard-gauge line. This extension opened 2 March 1908. Remarkably, this work was undertaken without suspending traffic for more than two days, and the navvies were required to work on only two Sundays. Also on 2 March 1908 a new standard-gauge line was opened from a junction with the main Plymouth line at Bere Alston to Calstock, together with a lift from Calstock Quay. The LSWR took over the PDSWJR in 1922.

In 1891, when the LSWR decided to construct its carriage and wagon works at Bishopstoke, the nearby novelist Charlotte M. Young was asked to propose a name and suggested Eastleigh after the manor, rather than New Bishopstoke.

Initially the works consisted of six buildings 330 ft by 200 ft, while a wagon shop erected later measured 375 ft by 300 ft. Nothing was wasted: all sawdust and chippings were fed into boiler furnaces. The population grew from about 700 in 1888 to 7,500 in 1898.

As territory covered by the LSWR expanded, its locomotive works at Nine Elms became inadequate and required a larger site. Eastleigh was developed and there the country's most advanced locomotive works was opened to enable the LSWR to construct its own locomotives instead of having them erected by tendering firms. Additionally, Eastleigh offered a much more pleasant environment for the works' staff than South London.

A running shed was constructed to replace that at Northam, Southampton, and when opened in January 1903 Eastleigh became the second-largest shed on the LSWR. When the footplate crews and depot staff arrived at Eastleigh, they added 250 more men and families to the crowded area. In view of the grave shortage of homes, in January 1903 the LSWR agreed to build fifty-four cottages at £255 apiece and all were completed by December 1904.

Although the decision to construct the locomotive shops had been taken in December 1902, progress was slow. The works were planned and supervised by Dugald Drummond, who made special visits in his special saloon 'The Bug'.

He designed the works so that as many tasks as possible could be carried out under one roof, while the separate buildings required for the forge, foundry and stores were given space around them for expansion. Stone for the concrete was nearly all obtained on site.

As the boiler shop at Nine Elms had only been built in 1892–3, part was transferred to Eastleigh, as were many of its machine tools. The yard floor was composed of chalk and ash brought from various parts of the LSWR system.

In 1908 the LSWR announced that it would not erect houses for its works staff as their needs would be satisfied by private enterprise.

The reason behind this was that the LSWR was experiencing a temporary cash shortage due to a greater expenditure than usual on capital projects.

By the summer of 1909 some locomotive repair work was carried out at Eastleigh and by the end of the year 350 men were employed. Land prices rose and no speculative building was carried out, so workers transferred from Nine Elms tried fruitlessly to find accommodation. Many had to take lodgings in nearby towns and villages thus facing a daily commute to the works, the LSWR sympathetically supplying cheap tickets. Additionally the LSWR provided a special train to Waterloo at midday on Saturdays, with a return on Sunday evenings, to enable the workers to travel home at weekends to see their families and friends.

This housing shortage was quite intolerable, so in January 1910 a hundred more cottages were erected by the LSWR. Built at a cost of £30,758 they were let at a weekly rent of 5s 6d. The main transfer from Nine Elms involved 1,500 men and at the company's half-yearly meeting in February 1910 Drummond reported: 'The locomotive works at Nine Elms are now closed and the men and machinery are removed to Eastleigh. This transfer has been accomplished without an employee of the department being one hour out of work or the output of the works interfered with.' Eastleigh turned out its first new locomotive on 12 September 1910, 0-4-0 motor tank No. 101.

By 1911 many railwaymen were aggrieved at their pay and conditions of work. The government offered to set up a royal commission to examine the workings of the conciliation boards, which had been organised to enable employers and staff to discuss pay and conditions, but made no promise that any recommendations would be implemented.

The four railwaymen's unions believed this offer unsatisfactory and on 16 August 1911 sent an ultimatum to all the railway companies stating that unless there was an immediate response within 24 hours all labour would be withdrawn from the railway industry.

The Prime Minister, H. H. Asquith replied:

We cannot allow the commerce of the country to be interfered with in the way it would be by a national dispute, and we want you men to realise in the event of it reaching that stage, His Majesty's Government have decided that they will use all the civil and military forces at their disposal to see that the commerce of this country is not interfered with.

The strike began on 18 August 1911 and many lines, stations and goods yards became silent. Labour MPs persuaded the Cabinet that mediation and not bloodshed was the way forward and railway companies told that they must agree to a meeting between their general managers and the unions, which they had so far refused to recognise.

The companies agreed that if the strike was called off and all strikers reinstated that the railwaymen's grievances would be examined by a royal commission on which they would accept equal representation with the unions. The strike ended on 20 August.

In 1913 Jacomb-Hood, the chief engineer, established a concrete yard at Exmouth Junction making such items as fencing, gates, mile and gradient posts, electric light standards, platform coping slabs, sectional buildings and footbridges. The weekly capacity of the works was about 4,500 articles.

The outbreak of war on 4 August 1914 had serious implications for the LSWR on account of the great use made of its Southampton Docks and the fact that the company served Aldershot and Bulford camps, many on Salisbury Plain making a total of 176 camps served by the LSWR.

Practically all of its docks at Southampton were taken over by the government and most of the cross-Channel steamers withdrawn. When war was declared 4/5 August 1914 the War Office gave the Railway Executive Committee 60 hours to assemble locomotives and rolling stock to convey the British Expeditionary Force to Southampton. This was achieved in 48 hours and embarkation began on 9 August and completed by 31 August during which from Southampton had been shipped 5,006 officers, 125,171 men 38,805 horses, 344 guns, 1,575 other vehicles, 277 motor vehicles, 1,802 motor cycles and 6,406 tons of stores carried using 711 trains. The busiest day was 22 August when seventy-three trains were dealt with, eight timed to arrive between 6.12 a.m. and 7.36 a.m., another eight between 12.12 p.m. and 1.36 p.m. and twenty-one between 2.12 p.m. and 6.12 p.m. The rapid arrival of the British Expeditionary Force in France surprised the Germans.

To ease the transport of locomotives and rolling stock to the Continent, a train ferry terminal was made at Southampton. Eastleigh works produced parts for gun carriages and shells. Fifty locomotives were loaned to the government, mainly for use overseas.

Southampton was one of the principal ports for hospital ships and during the war dealt with a total of 1,234,248 wounded, requiring 7,822 trains. After the Battle of the Somme, 1 July 1916, no less than twenty-nine hospital trains were required and during the week ending 9 July some 151 hospital trains ran. During the First World War Southampton was so busy that sometimes between twenty-five and thirty vessels left in a single night. The LSWR carried an average of 13,000 soldiers each day during the war.

On 22 July 1918 the LSWR abolished second class, second-class stock being converted to third class. The abandonment of second class saved coal by avoiding hauling partly filled coaches.

Following the District Railway's electrification of the LSWR's line from Hammersmith to Turnham Green 1 July 1905, to Richmond on 1 August 1905 and to Wimbledon on 27 August 1905, the South Acton Junction–Gunnersbury and Kew East Junction–Kew Bridge were electrified for London & North Western trains from Broad Street to Richmond and Kew Bridge on 1 October 1916.

Seriously concerned by decreasing passenger numbers, the company's electrical engineer, H. Jones, visited the United States, and his findings combined with the advice of consulting engineers Messrs Kennedy & Donkin led the LSWR to adopt 600V DC third-rail system with running rail return. Sir Herbert Walker's aim was not just to rival tram and bus competition, but to extend the outer suburbs to Guildford.

Work started in July 1913, but was delayed by the outbreak of First World War in August 1914, so the electrified line from Waterloo to East Putney was not opened until 25 October 1915. Power came from an installation to the east of Durnsford Road bridge, Wimbledon. Modern in concept it contained sixteen Babcock & Wilcox boilers with chain-grate stokers. Above was a bunker containing 1,400 tons of coal served by a siding laid over a viaduct. The turbine room contained five Dick, Kerr 500kW turbo-alternators generating three-phase AC current at 11,000V, 25Hz. Cooling towers adjoined the River Wandle, and two brick chimneys were 230 ft in height. Transformers, rotary converters and switchgear for the substations were supplied by British Thomson-Houston Co. Ltd.

Conductor rails of special high-conductivity steel weighing 100 lb/yd were laid on porcelain insulators 16 inches from the side of the running rail with the upper surface 3 inches above it. The running rails were bonded for the return current with two copper bands under the fishplates and cross-bonded at intervals. Signalling track circuits were converted to use alternating instead of direct current, and station lighting on the Kingston Roundabout was converted to electricity.

A coasting mark indicating where a motorman should cut off current was a white diamond, while stopping places at platforms were indicated by enamelled plates bearing the figure 3 or 6 on a blue ground. Station name boards on the electrified lines were glass, the name in white letters on a blue ground.

Compartment-type rolling stock was former steam-hauled stock suitably converted and placed in eighty-four close-coupled three-coach sets, each end coach having one motor bogie powered by two 275 hp British Westinghouse motors. They were equipped with Westinghouse brakes. Accommodation was only first and third class. Livery was dark green.

Electric trains over the Kingston Roundabout and Shepperton were to have started on 5 December 1915 but the Post Office claimed that the substation interfered with long-distance telephone lines. Following modifications, services began on 30 January 1916, the Hounslow loop on 12 March 1916; Malden–Hampton Court on 18 June 1916 and Surbiton–Claygate 20 November 1916.

Trains ran at the same regular intervals throughout the day, leaving at the same number of minutes past the hour, thus making it easy for passengers, the only alteration in peak hours being that trains were of six coaches rather than three. Letters were used as head codes to differentiate between the different routes.

A certain flour miller spotted that the letters spelled 'Hovis' and devised a suitably illustrated advertisement.

Electrification proved an excellent choice, for in 1921 Sir Herbert Walker said that in 1915 the LSWR carried just under 500,000 passengers in the electrified area weekly but that in 1921 the figure was over a million. Wartime and post-war costs on electrified lines had risen by 100 per cent, whereas steam working had gone up by over 200 per cent.

In 1922 the goods concentration yard at Feltham was opened. Gravity worked, a locomotive propelled a train up a gradient of 1 in 140, wagons were uncoupled and rolled down 1 in 50 to one of nineteen Up sidings. Points were operated electrically by push-button and up to 3,390 wagons could be dealt with in 24 hours while a train of seventy wagons, involving fifty-six 'cuts', was dealt with in 12 minutes.

By the end of the nineteenth century Waterloo station had become so chaotic that rebuilding was essential. It was extended to thirteen platforms and twenty-one platform lines, eight of the platforms having two platform faces. Every road was given hydraulic buffer stops capable of withstanding the impact of a 400-ton train at 10 mph. Of the twenty-one platform lines, twelve were equipped for electric traction.

One of the main entrances was the Victory Arch, the LSWR's war memorial, with Britannia holding the torch of Liberty while on the left was Bellona, Goddess of War and marked 1914, while on that on the right was dated 1918 and represents Peace. Four bronze tablets inside the archway record the names of the 585 LSWR servants who were killed in the First World War. A vast ridge-and-furrow roof and a spacious concourse transformed it from the worst London terminus to one of the finest. The curved frontage by J. R. Scott housed the company's offices. The enlargement of Waterloo, the largest British railway terminus, was formally opened by Queen Mary on 21 March 1922.

4

ACCIDENTS ON THE LSWR

In its early years the LSWR proved a line remarkably free from accidents, but on 20 June 1858 a third-class coach was derailed at Bishopstoke (Eastleigh) involving the death of a passenger and injury to others.

The first accident of any note occurred on 7 June 1864. The first of two race trains left Ascot at 7.10 p.m. and its first stop was Egham for ticket collecting and the ejection of card sharpers, while the second departed at 7.15 p.m. and its first stop was Staines. Unfortunately the driver of Hercules class 2-4-0 *Milo*, working the second train and travelling tender-first, was not informed that the first was to call at Egham – a serious oversight seeing that services were run on the time interval system. When 200 yd away he saw the adverse distant signal, but as it was only 513 yd from Egham station and he was on a falling gradient with no continuous brakes and a load of fourteen coaches with only two manned brake vans he was unable to stop in time and collided with the 7.10. Seven passengers were killed and twenty-three injured. *Milo*'s fireman was thrown from the footplate and buried under the wreckage, yet only received a cut forehead. The guard saw *Milo* approaching and jumped, leaving his severed coat-tails in the smashed door.

The Board of Trade inspecting officer, Col Yolland, criticised the lack of continuous brakes, the use of the time interval and the lack of a turntable at Ascot resulting in tender-first running on fast trains.

This accident caused the block system to be installed on the LSWR, thus ensuring a space between trains. A further result was that the ends of

LSWR vehicles were painted in a vermillion made from mercuric oxide, which was both extremely toxic and expensive.

On 9 September 1873 the 12.20 p.m. Up Portsmouth express between Peasmarsh and Guildford struck a bullock. Tweed class 2-4-0 No. 148 *Colne*, tender and leading van passed over the carcase, but it derailed all ten coaches killing three passengers and injuring many more. The coupling between the van and coaches snapped allowing the driver to continue on to Guildford to raise the alarm, the stationmaster there sending a special train to assist. Two passengers and their two attendants were from the Convalescent Lunatics' Home, Witley, a branch of Bethlem Hospital. One patient, a medical student before his affliction, kindly extricated his attendant from the wreckage of the second-class carriage and then tended his wounds.

On 11 September 1880 0-6-0 No. 309 arrived light engine at Nine Elms Locomotive Yard box and stood on the main line awaiting clearance to enter the shed. The signalmen were exchanging duties, No. 309 was forgotten and the 10.00 p.m. Waterloo to Hampton Court passenger train accepted. It was headed by Beattie 2-4-0T No. 76 *Firefly*. Five passengers, a driver and fireman were killed in the crash and forty-two passengers injured. The only brakes were on the engine and a van in the train. In 1882 the automatic vacuum brake was adopted and passenger stock gradually fitted at a cost of £100,000.

On 3 June 1884 the 4.33 p.m. passenger train from Salisbury to Wimborne was well filled with folk returning from market. It consisted of two first-class and four third-class coaches sandwiched between two guard's vans headed by two engines. Just beyond Downton the train derailed, couplings parted behind the leading brake van.

The train bumped along the permanent way for 100 yd before plunging over the embankment down 12 ft to a muddy ditch filled with 4 ft of water. The coaches struck a willow tree. Three women were killed; one was the fourteen-year-old daughter of the Fordingbridge stationmaster. Two of the three met their death by drowning. Two men were also killed. A total of forty-one passengers were injured.

Colonel Rich of the Board of Trade censured the LSWR in his report:

... the numerous complaints which have been made, and the violent shaking which passengers experienced when travelling on parts of the London & South Western Railway, leave no room to doubt that a great deal of reform in the management, and improvement in the working of this railway is required. I believe the complaints are caused in a great measure by bad driving, using inferior stock, and by the coaches of the trains not being properly coupled up. I would strongly urge the company to make a thorough examination of their system and stock, to classify their drivers, to classify their stock, to classify their several lines and parts of their system, and to classify their trains. It cannot be expected that the whole of the company's stock and railway shall be of the best description; but the public has a right to expect, that old and inferior stock shall not be run over old, weak, and inferior parts of the railway, at such speed as to make it unpleasant and dangerous to all that use it.

An accident occurred on 18 November 1885 when Adams 395 class 0-6-0 No. 442 was derailed at 30 mph near Yealmpton while working the 4.00 p.m. Exeter to Plymouth passenger train. No. 442 struck a rock face, rebounded across the track and, with the leading brake van, fell down an embankment, fatally injuring the driver. The inquiry blamed the engine's 16 ft 6 in. wheelbase and faulty elevation of the curved track. Subsequently this class of engine was banned from working passenger trains west of Exeter and restricted to 25 mph on goods services.

The LSWR's most serious accident occurred on 1 July 1906 when an Up boat train from Plymouth headed by L12 4-4-0 No. 421 was derailed on a sharp curve at Salisbury, killing twenty-four of the forty-two passengers while four employees died. Although a speed limit of 30 mph was imposed, the engine came through at between 50 and 60 mph. Reasons for the driver's actions remain obscure. One plausible suggestion is that as Driver Robins had come on duty after a rest of only 9.5 hours, he may have had a ten- to thirty-second micro-sleep. This is particularly likely as his booking-on time moved anti-clockwise, the shift pattern most likely to result in disruption to the Circadian rhythms.

A collision at Vauxhall on 29 August 1912 was caused through having eight roads. The signals for the Up Main Through were at 'danger' as a train was calling at the station, but signals for the Up Main Local were 'clear'. Unfortunately the driver of a light engine T9 No. 312 on the Up Main Through believed he was on the Up Main Local and ran into the standing passenger train, killing two passengers.

5

LSWR LOCOMOTIVES & COACHING STOCK

The company's first engine was an E. Bury & Co. standard 2-2-0 built in 1839; it was followed by three similar locomotives constructed by Nasmyth & Co; as was the usual contemporary practice they were named but not numbered. They were not famed for longevity: the Bury was destroyed by fire at Nine Elms on 16 March 1841 when leaking turpentine was ignited by a storekeeper's lamp, while the other three were reported 'worn out in 1843 and 1844.

Experience suggested that six-wheeled engines would be more practicable, but the Rennie 2-2-2s ordered proved to be under-boilered and their construction was insufficiently robust and necessitated rebuilding in 1841. Engines of the same wheel arrangement were ordered from various other manufacturers.

The Locomotive Committee had appreciated that the 2-2-0s and 2-2-2s, with relatively little adhesion, would not be suitable for goods traffic, so 0-4-2 'Sharpies' with 4 ft 6 in. diameter wheels were ordered for such duties.

Engine building at Nine Elms started on 16 January 1843 when two 2-2-2s were ordered with boilers purchased from outside manufacturers. Although the first, *Eagle*, ran on 12 October 1843, precedence was given to repairs and rebuilding and the second was not completed until March 1844. Unfortunately the frames of the Eagle class proved too light and by 1847 required rebuilding. In 1847 Nine Elms produced improved and enlarged Eagles called the Mazeppa class, which cost less to operate than similar engines supplied by outside firms, burning an average of 24.1 lb coke per mile compared with 24.5 lb – coke was used as the law forbade engines to emit smoke.

In the summer of 1844 it was not unknown for goods trains to be as much as 12 hours late and part of the trouble was unsuitable engines. The locomotive superintendent J. V. Gooch designed Bison class 0-6-0s, the first entering service at the end of December 1845.

In 1848 the Etna class 2-2-2s appeared and one member, *Britannia*, was fitted with a coal-burning firebox, having a small auxiliary box and grate placed at the front of the ordinary firebox. Coal was fired to the latter while any partially consumed gases were burnt in the auxiliary box. After modification the idea proved successful.

In 1850 Clemente Masserano interested the LSWR directors in a cheap form of locomotive named *Impulsoria*. Basically it was a 2-2-0 locomotive frame with an endless belt on which two horses trotted. One excellent feature was that its axles had roller bearings. Its advantage was that horses cost 2s 0d a day whereas steam locomotives used 6d of coal per mile. It could draw thirty wagons up the incline at Nine Elms Goods. In the event, none were ordered.

Joseph Beattie, when appointed locomotive superintendent, developed the idea used in *Britannia* and his engines, with their double coal-burning fireboxes, feed water heaters and balanced slide valves, were arguably the most economical passenger engines at that time, though this was partly offset by the cost of the fireboxes.

Although the Bison 0-6-0s were powerful, they were slow and thus unsuited to hauling passenger trains, so in 1851 Beattie designed the Hercules class coke-fired 2-4-0s. In 1855 he produced the Saxon class 2-4-0s with outside cylinders to avoid crank-axle breakage.

The planned opening to Salisbury demanded four-coupled engines and Beattie supplied Tweed class 2-4-0s with 6 ft diameter wheels.

The LSWR appreciated the usefulness of tank engines on short workings as they could run in reverse without causing too much discomfort on the footplate, whereas with tender-first running on a bitter day, the crew had been known to shelter behind the smoke box where signals could not be readily observed. Beattie favoured 2-4-0 well tanks, the water being carried in a tank between the frames rather than having a saddle, or side tanks.

In 1861 Beattie's Standard well-tank appeared, of which 85 were built, most by Beyer Peacock & Co. In due course they were fitted with a conventional coal-burning firebox with brick arch – much cheaper to maintain than the Beattie fireboxes. Feed water injectors replaced donkey pumps. In addition to working suburban services, they appeared on branch lines and were so successful on the Bodmin & Wadebridge branch that three of the class remained there until August 1962, though most of the class was withdrawn by the 1890s.

As Nine Elms works was busy, in 1864 Beyer Peacock was asked to supply six Lion class 0-6-0s, but when the quoted price of £3,485 each was queried, Charles Beyer suggested a reduction of £385 if the design was based on his standard 0-6-0. This offer was accepted. The Beyer Peacock engines proved slightly cheaper to maintain than the comparable Beattie engines.

In 1873 locomotives were required for the Coleford Junction to Plymouth line and Charles Beyer recommended 4-4-0Ts that his firm had designed for the Metropolitan Railway. The track was unsuited to these 48-ton engines, and rails were spread, points damaged and rails broken.

In November 1876 Patrick Stirling of the Great Northern and F. W. Webb of the London & North Western Railway were asked to report and said:

> The class is well constructed, free steaming and economical to operate, but being based on engines designed for the moderate speeds and frequent stops of the Metropolitan Railway, are not really suited to main line service. The engines inspected rolled, nosed and pitched excessively on trains at 35 to 40 mph, while at 50 mph the running was so violent that steam had to be shut off and the brakes applied. The class could usefully and safely employed on the company's outer suburban services if more robust springs were fitted to the coupled wheels, the compensatory beams being modified as per enclosed diagram and greater control given to the leading end by fitting either an Adams' bogie, or a Crewe type Bissell truck.

As by 1875 the 2-4-0s were having difficulty maintaining schedules of expresses in poor weather, William George Beattie, who had succeeded his father Joseph Beattie, designed an outside cylinder

4-4-0. Delivered in 1877, the engines suffered many failures so W. G. Beattie resigned and was replaced by William Adams from the Great Eastern Railway.

Suitable locomotives were required for the steeply graded and lightly laid Ilfracombe branch and in 1872 Charles Beyer suggested 0-6-0s similar to those he had built for the Swedish Government Railway in 1866. Until the end of the Beattie era shunting was carried out by horses, winches, train engines and engines awaiting repair and it was not until 1873 that an order was placed with Beyer Peacock for six of their standard 0-6-0Ts for use as shunters.

William Adams became locomotive superintendent in 1878, his first engines being robust 46 class 4-4-0Ts, but unfortunately their steaming was poor, they rode uncomfortably and their bunker and tank capacities were too limited. He also designed a similar tender engine, the 380 class, which were nicknamed 'steamrollers' due to their solid bogie wheels. The next 4-4-0s, the 135 class, had larger driving wheels and were very elegant.

In 1882 he produced the 415 class 4-4-2Ts, an improved and lengthened version of the 46 class 4-4-0Ts. The exceptionally short side tanks were supplemented by a well-tank below the bunker and footplate. Perhaps influenced by the neighbouring LBSCR, Adams' subsequent tank and mixed traffic engines had coupled wheels at the front, his T1 0-4-4Ts proving efficient and long-lasting, as were his O2 class with smaller driving wheels. In 1881 the 395 class 0-6-0s appeared, the smoke box front angled back from bottom to top, giving a streamlined effect. During the First World War they were loaned to the government and saw service in the Middle East and the Balkans. Only two were scrapped by the SR, and eighteen lasted long enough to be taken over by BR.

In May 1884 Adams borrowed London & North Western Railway compound No. 300 for trials between Waterloo and Exeter. Its advantage was that it was supposed to save fuel, but it proved to consume more than Adams' engines; some burnt in the firebox, some in the smoke box, which developed a red-hot door, while some coal shot out of the chimney and burnt along the embankments. It also lost 5 minutes on the schedule.

Adams rebuilt 4-4-0 445 class No. 446 to a Worsdell-von-Borries compound, the right-hand 18 in. cylinder being replaced by a low-pressure one of 26 in. Although its coal consumption was slightly lower, it was insufficient to compensate for the extra cost and the greater use of oil and tallow so was returned to simple working after four years.

At the end of the nineteenth century the 460 class 4-4-0s were used on Weymouth expresses. There was a surprising timing of 60 mph start to stop for the 15 miles and 5 chains between Dorchester and Wareham. Although the working timetable allowed 17 minutes, drivers liked to do it in the 15 minutes of the public timetable and often succeeded.

The 395 class 0-6-0s proved slow and rough riders when used on passenger trains, so this led to Adams designing the Jubilee class 0-4-2s in 1886, numerically his largest class, eighty being built, some being constructed by the LSWR at Nine Elms. Nine Elms Works also constructed B4 class 0-4-0Ts for shunting sharply curved lines. Larger yards were worked by his G6 class 0-6-0Ts, many parts being common with the O2 class 0-4-4Ts. By 1888 traffic was proving too heavy for Adams' early 4-4-0s, so he produced the larger X2, T3, T6 and X6 classes.

When Dugald Drummond took over in 1895, his first LSWR design was the M7 0-4-4T followed by the 700 class 0-6-0s. His first express passenger locomotives were the E10 class four-cylinder 4-2-2-0s, their most unusual feature being the double single wheels. Not a huge success, they were heavy coal burners and were stored during the winter part of the year when passenger traffic was lighter; thus they were nicknamed 'butterflies'.

The C8 class were conventional 4-4-0s using the same boiler as the M7s and the 700 classes, but unlike those classes, they had steam reversers. They were less powerful and consumed more coal than the Adams' X2 4-4-0s. In 1891 the T9 class 4-4-0s appeared. A most successful series, some lasted until well into the British Railways era, the last being withdrawn as late as 1961 – very late for a pre-grouping engine.

Circa 1900 the introduction of faster services and heavier steam-heated rolling stock demanded a more powerful engine and in 1904 the L12 class appeared with a chassis similar to the T9 married to bogie, cylinders, motion, boiler and tender of the mixed traffic S11. The 4,000-gallon double bogie tender was heated by exhaust steam.

When more mixed traffic engines were required in 1900 to supplement the Jubilees, Drummond modified his C8 class design, giving them smaller wheels and a T9 firebox, thus producing the K10 4-4-0. Working main-line reliefs they lacked sufficient steaming ability, so when more were required Drummond used the larger T9 boiler. The S11s were similar to the K10s but were given larger wheels and boiler.

Ever heavier and faster trains demanded larger locomotives and in 1905 the F13 class 4-6-0s appeared. They appeared massive and more powerful than they actually were. They were not free-steaming and were the only LSWR engines which could not be pushed down banks by the weight of the trains, steam always having to be applied. Useless on expresses, they were found suitable for freight and mineral trains until their withdrawal in 1924.

In 1907 Drummond produced the E14 4-6-0 based on the F13, but with larger cylinders and Walschaerts valve gear. An unusual feature was two glass doors in the splashers giving access to this valve gear. It proved even worse than an E14 and had enormous coal consumption. Not to be defeated, in 1908 the G14 4-6-0 appeared, similar to an E14 but with a slightly smaller boiler. It proved rather better than the earlier 4-6-0s, but its performance was seldom better than a T9 or L12. In 1911 the P14 appeared, a G14 with minor alterations, while the T14s were broadly similar engines but with 6 ft 7 in. diameter wheels designed for working the services from Waterloo to Salisbury and Bournemouth, but their modified front end and higher working pressure offered greater performance.

Most of Drummond's engines proved strong, long-lasting machines, many eventually being taken over by BR.

Although Drummond's steam rail cars (**see page 52**) proved successful to a certain extent, they were not above criticism: being combined, the carriage section became dirty when maintained at a locomotive shed and the failure of a locomotive meant that the carriage section was also out of use. The answer seemed to be a separate small 2-2-0T based on an engine unit of a rail motor, but fitted with a larger boiler. Like the rail motors, there was no need to run round at the end of a journey as wire cables enabled a driver to operate the regulator from a control compartment of a trailer car at what had been the rear of the train. They were not an outstanding success: lack of adhesion caused slipping problems, while the 8 ft wheelbase caused them to buck and corkscrew at speeds over 30 mph. In due course they were converted to 0-4-0Ts and used for shunting while push-pull trains were successfully worked by suitably converted conventional tank engines of the M7, T1, O2 and 0415 classes. In push-pull trains an engine pulled a train to a terminus and then the locomotive remained at what became the back and propelled coaches to the starting point. These coaches had lazy-tong gates and pierced plywood seats.

A curious engine which Drummond designed was No. 733 a 4-2-4, a combined tank locomotive and coach he used when he was out inspecting. A neat-looking vehicle, all its bogie wheels were fitted with small splashers. The compartment had a table, six chairs and a lavatory. Communication with the footplate was by electric bell or a sliding panel in the front bulkhead. Lighting was by gas.

Built at Nine Elms, 'The Bug', as it was nicknamed, entered service in June 1899 and was used daily by Drummond to carry him from his home at Surbiton to Nine Elms, and later Eastleigh, as well as on his inspection tours over the system. It could reach over 80 mph, but riding was exciting at this speed.

C. Hamilton Ellis, in *The South Western Railway* recounts:

On the four-track main line down to Basingstoke, enginemen might be loafing down the line of a peaceful summer morning when suddenly and stealthily 'The Bug' would be alongside, with the droplight down and a fierce, bearded face glaring out. That was the time to become acutely conscious of an untidy footplate, a drift of dirty smoke or a blowing gland; a gust of sultry language would boom across the flying six-foot and a peremptory summons would follow.

William Eaton, sometime fireman of 'The Bug' reminisced: One morning the engine was going down with Drummond and some guests to Exmouth. It was a lovely day as they skimmed past the pleasant meadows, but its peace was broken by a gruff shout through the trap: 'Hey! We're no' going to a funeral!' The driver let the engine go, as she could, until the voice spoke again: 'Hey! I'm no' wanting tae go tae Hell yet!'

Urie, his successor, used 'The Bug' much less, so it was transferred to departmental stock in 1913. In 1916 it was laid aside but in the 1920s was overhauled and used for transporting officials around the new docks at Southampton, often trailing a six-wheeled coach for additional accommodation. With the completion of the dock works, it was returned to store until 1940 when it was broken up but the frame retained and used minus the driving wheels, for transporting heavy items around Eastleigh until 1957.

Drummond died in November 1912 and was succeeded by Robert W. Urie, works manager at Eastleigh. He favoured high footplates offering easy access to Walschaert's valve gear, and in the ten years prior to Grouping, for economy, his five engine types used largely interchangeable parts. Until December 1914 he retained the Drummond royal green livery, replacing it with olive green which after wear became more yellow.

The H15 4-6-0s with 6 ft wheels appeared in 1914 and the similar N15 in 1916 with 6 ft 7 in. wheels and these latter, after improving modifications became part of the SR's King Arthur class. In 1920 the S15 with 5 ft 7 in. wheels were designed for heavy goods trains.

With the development of hump shunting (Feltham Concentration Yard opened 1 May 1921), the standard G6 0-6-0T was not man enough for the job and in 1921 the G16 4-8-0 appeared with 5 ft 1 in. coupled wheels. Drivers appreciated that the reversers were steam operated, as were the brakes.

An LSWR director travelled on an Eastbourne express hauled by a superheated 4-4-2T. Impressed by its performance, he wondered whether the LSWR should build something similar. Little progress had been made before Drummond's death and by 1918 the Running Department did not require a fast passenger tank but one which could transfer wagons between the various London yards. Urie suitably modified his design and the H16 4-6-2T appeared in 1921. In the spring of 1922 No. 518 was tried on Bournemouth–Southampton and Waterloo–Basingstoke passenger trains but was found to ride roughly when going bunker-first and its limited water capacity was a problem. Normally the class was used on freight transfer between various yards, but due to their annual outing on race trains to Ascot they were painted in passenger green and lined out.

In 1919 the LSWR was short of locomotives and the loan of seventeen Royal Engineers' Railway Operating Division 2-8-0s was accepted. Their condition was so poor that it was February 1920 before they had all been made fit to run. Due to their weight and long wheel base, the routes they could run on were restricted and as the S15s were being delivered by the summer of 1920, the 2-8-0s were all either placed in store or transferred away.

Until *circa* 1859 the livery of LSWR locomotives was Indian red with black bands; then until the early seventies chocolate-lined with black and white with the addition of vermillion on the best express locomotives. About 1875 the lining of express engines consisted of dark yellow edging divided from the chocolate by a thin white line. In 1878 Adams changed the chocolate to umber, with black bands and fine orange and pea-green lining. In 1885 Adams changed to pea-green with black edging and white lines while goods and elderly engines were painted dark green with black edging and fine pea-green lines, this scheme lasting for goods engines until the end of the company. In 1900 Drummond introduced a passenger livery of grass-green with chocolate bands and black and white lines.

The early rolling stock of the London & Southampton Railway was similar to that of other railways: unroofed wagons with seats for third class, roofed open wagons for second, and enclosed first class coaches with three compartments looking like three stagecoaches joined together. Luggage was carried on the roofs of the first class and in boots in the second. Guards and brakemen were seated at the end of the roofs.

Until around 1860 coaches were only provided with central coupling hooks and side chains, the actual couplings stored at stations. Those used by the London & Southampton had a tensioner to draw the buffers together and thus offer a smooth ride when a train was accelerating or decelerating. Screw couplings were introduced on the LSWR *circa* 1860.

Following the first murder on a British train, committed by one Franz Muller on the North London Railway in 1864, in order to make closed compartments less isolated, the LSWR cut portholes, known as 'Muller's Lights', in the partitions. These were not given general approbation, particularly by romantic couples.

The LSWR was an early pioneer in communication between passengers and railway servants and in 1865 introduced Preece's electric bell system. It was highly susceptible to dust interrupting the contacts. Indeed this happened when Preece was demonstrating his invention to the Institute of Civil Engineers and someone remarked that if there was sufficient dust to affect it in the Civils' lecture theatre, there would be more than enough on the LSWR!

From 1882, eight-wheel coaches on American-type compensated bogies with spiral outside springs and volute bolster springs appeared and were equipped with Pintsch gaslight. In 1885 a tricomposite coach had two third-class compartments, two of the second class and two first class, while in the centre of the coach and accessed by corridor were two lavatories with Beresford's zinc-hopper, pull-up-handle apparatus and folding hand-wash basins. Tricomposites were very useful for the LSWR which ran many expresses with through coaches to a variety of destinations and therefore added or subtracted coaches.

To aid the development of Southampton for transatlantic passengers, carriage superintendent W. Panter in 1893 built sumptuous coaches for the American Eagle express. Equipped with internal corridors, mostly central, they were provided with lavatories. These coaches ran on Fox's pressed-steel bogies. Initially there were no gangways linking coaches. A block set comprised nine coaches with a six-wheeled van at each end. In 1901 Panter adapted the Eagle carriages, giving them connecting gangways and installing kitchens in full-length luggage brakes at one end.

Early passenger coaches were chocolate and then many of Beattie's carriages were varnished teak or mahogany. In the 1870s new stock was brown with dark cream upper panels, dark brown below the waist with upper panels and mouldings in salmon; ventilated milk and meat vans were salmon all over and wagons dark brown.

When William Adams was appointed Locomotive, Carriage & Wagon Superintendent in January 1878 he was instructed to visit Paddington and inspect the GWR vehicles. One result was that many subsequent coaches were six-wheeled.

Although the Midland Railway and the Great Northern Railway had bogie coaches in 1874, it was not until 1880 that the Pullman car *Victoria* was transferred from the Midland, renamed *Alexandra* and placed on the Exeter service. It was not a success, partly due to the Pullman supplement and partly due to the fact that it was on open saloon and lacked privacy.

In 1880 the LSWR placed in service six composite bogie coaches 42 ft long, with equal-sized compartments, the four centre ones being first and the two end ones second. The first third-class bogie coaches appeared in 1890.

Panter retired in 1906 and was succeeded by Surrey Warner. Panter had already adopted Stone's electric lighting system and this was continued by Warner. In 1908 he produced four sleeping cars for the American boat expresses with movable brass bedsteads.

The LSWR gradually introduced steel outer panels on timber-frames with traditional wooden beading strips, but when the beading was abandoned in 1921 the resultant coaches were nicknamed 'Ironclads'.

Towards the end of the LSWR it had three types of train: a corridor set for a long-distance express; a lavatory set, with access to a lavatory direct from a compartment; and a bogie block, and the latter was not to run more than 30 miles without a stop nor at speeds exceeding 40 mph.

LSWR Steamer Services

As railways were not allowed by Parliament to run steamer services, in 1845 the LSWR set up the South Western Steam Navigation Company to run from Southampton to the Channel Islands, Le Havre and St Malo. In 1847 the French Western Railway reached Le Havre so the shipping service was improved. In 1848 the LSWR obtained powers to operate steamers but initially decided merely to lease them. In 1857 a Channel Islands company established a service from Weymouth, and the South Western Steam Navigation sent a steamer to work to and from Weymouth. In August 1862 the LSWR absorbed the navigation company while in 1888 the Weymouth & Channel Islands' Steam Packet company was purchased by the GWR and the two railway companies competed, though the LSWR had the privilege of carrying the mails. As of December 1899 the Channel Islands' traffic was pooled. In 1865 a service was inaugurated between Southampton and Honfleur.

In 1889 the LSWR's fastest steamer ran at 16½ knots, but by 1894 20 knots had been attained. The vessels had separate cabins, rather than open berths in the saloon.

By 1911 the LSWR owned thirteen vessels plus four small cargo ships. Early ships were paddle steamers, but later vessels were screw-driven by triple expansion engines. The approach to the Channel Islands is dangerous, and several LSWR ships were lost.

The LSWR SS *Ardea* had a particularly unusual history. Built in 1915 as *HMS Peony* as a mine-sweeping sloop, she was purchased by the LSWR for the summer-only Southampton–Cherbourg service. In 1925 the SR transferred her to Southampton–Caen, and following the withdrawal of this service she was sold. Taken over in 1940 by the Greek government, she was sunk by German aircraft. Raised and repaired, she served in the Kriegsmarine only to be sunk by a mine in 1943.

6

THE LYNTON & BARNSTAPLE RAILWAY

The contract for constructing the Lynton & Barnstaple Railway (L&B) was awarded to J. Nuttall but the cost of blasting the 1 ft 11½ in. gauge line through unexpected rock bankrupted him. The railway was formally opened on 11 May 1898 by Sir George and Lady Newnes and opened to the public five days later. Later that year the publisher Newnes said: 'I believe that Lynton has for some time enjoyed the distinction of being the only place in England extensively visited by tourists, despite the fact that it is twenty miles from any railway station. It has been the regular thing in July and August to see twenty or thirty coaches and *chars-a-bancs* from Ilfracombe crowd into Lynton between 11 and 12 o'clock in the morning.'

The company proved just about profitable, generally paying dividends of one half per cent per year. The company was unaffected by the Railways Act of 1921, but the Southern Railway purchased the line for £39,267 in March 1923. Despite improvements made by its new owners, the line was unable to compete with the growth of road transport and ticket sales dropped dramatically from 72,000 in 1925 to 32,000 in 1934. In 1935 a decision had to be made about whether to undertake the expense of permanent way renewals or to close the line. The latter course was adopted. A protest meeting was held at Barnstaple to try and reverse the decision, but the fact that all the railway's supporters had travelled from Lynton by car rather ruined their case. The last train ran on 29 September 1935.

The line purchased three 2-6-2Ts from Manning, Wardle & Co., but then found that it required a further engine. This British builders could not supply owing to a strike coupled with an ordering boom, so the L&B purchased a Baldwin 2-4-2T from the USA. When the SR took over an additional engine was ordered from Manning, Wardle & Co.

Although the line was fenced, the engines were fitted with cowcatchers. They were designed to draw a load of 50 tons up an incline of 1 in 50 at 20 mph. On favourable stretches, the maximum speed was 25 mph. Passenger rolling stock consisted of seventeen bogie carriages on roller bearings; some had a central compartment left open to waist level for passengers to enjoy the view. Freight was carried in twenty-five wagons which, unlike contemporary main line wagons, were all fitted with vacuum brakes. In dry summers a water shortage at Lynton station meant that the public was requested to refrain from using the lavatories.

The L&B ran the first railway motor bus feeder service in Great Britain. From the opening of the line, a horse-drawn coach operated from Ilfracombe to Blackmoor station, but early in 1903 the enterprising Sir George Newnes decided to motorise the service. He purchased two twenty-two-seat 16 hp Milnes-Daimler motor wagonettes and began the service on 30 May 1903. Following difficulties with the police when vehicles were found 'speeding above 8 mph', the two buses were sold to the Great Western Railway.

7

THE ISLE OF WIGHT RAILWAYS

The first railway on the island was the Cowes & Newport which opened on 16 June 1862. 4½ miles in length, it linked the capital with the sea. In 1877 the company opened Medina Wharf just south of Cowes to land coal and heavy goods.

The Isle of Wight Railway (IWR) opened from Ryde (St John's Road) to Shanklin together with a short branch from Brading to a quay on 23 August 1864, an extension from Shanklin to Ventnor being inaugurated 10 September 1866. The contractor experienced serious difficulties with keeping labour during the summer months when men could earn wages more easily at seaside resorts. In March 1863 forty navvies were brought from County Kerry but created so much mayhem in the district that their employment was soon terminated and the men repatriated.

The Isle of Wight (Newport Junction) Railway was to have been opened from Sandown to Horringford in June 1872, but the Board of Trade inspector seriously objected to the use of double-headed rails which had been turned and re-used by the LSWR and then sold to the island railway. A fair number had cracked ends and furthermore the fish bolts were too short. The line opened between Sandown and Shide 1 February 1875, to Pan Lane 6 October 1875, finally reaching Newport 1 June 1879 on which date the temporary terminus at Pan Lane closed. The company fell into receivership in 1879 and on 1 July 1887 it, together with the Cowes & Newport and Ryde & Newport, became the Isle of Wight Central Railway (IWCR).

The Ryde & Newport Railway opened on 20 December 1875 and under an agreement of 4 December 1872 was run jointly with the Cowes & Newport.

The island had great holiday potential, particularly after Queen Victoria purchased Osborne. The LSWR and the LBSCR were keen to develop traffic, but passengers landing at Ryde and needing to use onward rail transport had to use a horse tramway to reach St John's Road station – not easy with the mountain of luggage that Victorians liked to have with them. The LSWR and LBSCR jointly built a new pier carrying a railway half a mile out to sea and linked it to St John's Road, the line opening on 12 July 1880. The joint line was used by both the IWR and the IWCR.

On 27 May 1882 the Brading Harbour Improvement & Railway Company opened a line from Bembridge to the IWR's quay branch at Brading. A wagon ferry operated by the LBSCR from Langston on the Hayling Island branch was inaugurated in 1882, using the vessel *Carrier*; the service proved uneconomic and ceased in 1888. On 2 August 1898 the IWR purchased the line for £17,000.

The Freshwater, Yarmouth & Newport Railway opened to goods 10 September 1888, but not for passengers until 20 July 1889. It was worked by the IWCR until the FYNR took over working in 1913. Several schemes to link this line with the mainland by a tunnel proved abortive.

The Newport, Godshill & St Lawrence Railway from Merstone on the Newport–Sandown line to St Lawrence opened 26 July 1897 and reached Ventnor (Town) 1 June 1900. The line was worked by the IWCR, which absorbed the company in April 1913.

Most of the early tank engines on the island were second-hand, some even having just a single driving wheel. In 1904 steam rail motors were the latest thing and seemed ideal for the lightly used Merstone–Ventnor (Town) branch. In due course R. W. Hawthorn & Co. constructed the engine and Hurst, Nelson & Co the carriage which worked in steam from Motherwell to Southampton where it was shipped to St Helens. Its cost, excluding delivery charge, was £1,450. Trials began on 5 October 1906 and it entered regular service on 2 November 1906. In December comparative tests were made with a Terrier 0-6-0T hauling three four-wheeled coaches and a brake van. Results were:

	Coal burned per mile
Rail-motor No. 1	13.2 lb
No 11 and train	17.8 lb

During the winter months, when traffic was particularly light, the rail-motor worked with a crew of two: a driver and conductor.

The rail-motor proving a success, it was thought that the Newport to Sandown service could be operated by a larger vehicle, but quotes were found too high. In 1907 a composite bogie carriage fitted with Westinghouse brake and electric lighting was purchased for £250 from the Midland Railway and run with 0-4-2T No. 3, which was adapted by encasing its boiler and footplate, fitting mechanical push-pull gear and close-coupling it to the coach which was equipped with a driver's vestibule at one end. Although not a true rail motor, Newport Works considered it one and the total cost, including purchase of the carriage, was only £437 9s 5d. It proved a failure and only worked 6,892 miles before being divided into a separate coach and locomotive.

In 1908 rail motor No. 1 was transferred to the Freshwater line, but the tight curves and lightly ballasted track caused excessive oscillation and during the winter of 1910 it was divided, the carriage portion given a second bogie while the engine was given a small bunker and used at Newport for light shunting and ballasting.

The compactness of the island made its railways vulnerable to competition from sea and road, particularly when the first motor bus service was established in 1905. The seasonal nature of the traffic caused problems when stock required in busy summer periods lay idle for much of the year, or if not enough was available, there was a loss of revenue.

With the 1923 grouping the five island railways became part of the SR. Initially a traffic superintendent was based at Newport and a CME representative to supervise locomotives and rolling stock, but these two posts were combined in 1930, A. B. Macleod being in charge of everything. Ryde Works at St John's station undertook repair of locomotives and wagons while the former locomotive works at Newport dealt with coaches.

Ryde Pier was purchased by the SR in 1924 and three years later its electric tramway replaced by petrol-engined cars while even later, diesel-engined cars were used. Electric cranes were installed at Ryde pier head to speed transfer, particularly on summer Saturdays. Some loops were lengthened, enabling trains to keep to the timetable more easily.

On peak Saturdays 35,000 passengers could be carried on the island's lines. The SR improved the island's railways and by the end of the 1940s some 3 million journeys were made annually, though there was a large disparity between peak summer traffic and the rest of the year, when Southern Vectis buses were overcrowded and trains almost empty. To avoid the O2 class 0-4-4Ts having to break off for coaling when running an intensive service, they were given enlarged bunkers. The arrival of four E1 class 0-6-0Ts on the island enabled coal trains from Medina wharf to be increased from twenty-five to forty wagons and worked between the close-headway passenger trains on the Newport–Cowes single line. To interest visitors and to engender pride in the island's motive power, engines carried local place names on brass plates.

Many coaches to replace elderly stock were ex-LCDR teak bogie coaches. Macleod designed a geared, hand-worked trolley for moving locomotives and rolling stock within Ryde Works, thus avoiding the need to light up a shunting engine.

8

THE LONDON & GREENWICH AND LONDON & CROYDON RAILWAYS

The London & Greenwich Railway was the first line actually in London to come into operation. It received its Act on 17 May 1833 to build a 3¾-mile-long line set on a viaduct of 878 brick arches; in total 60 million bricks were used. It was envisaged that it would eventually be extended to Dover. The first experimental trip, which was free, took place on 8 June 1835 when *Royal William* covered a mile in 4 minutes. In November 1835 *John Bull* recorded: 'One of the carriages in which a party of noodles ventured themselves was thrown off the rail, but although it ran a vast number of yards no serious accident occurred.' The company's engineer, Lt-Col G. T. Landmann, observed that the derailment showed how safe accidents were.

This statement was in fact true, because in addition to the 4 ft 6 in. high parapet walls, the carriages had an unusually low centre of gravity, only 4 in. above the rails. As an additional safety measure, gas lamps illuminated the viaduct at night.

London Bridge was the terminus in the metropolis, its two platforms formally opened by the Lord Mayor on 14 December 1836, though trains had been running from a temporary station at Spa Road to Deptford since 8 February 1836. As there were only two running lines, in order to avoid the need for a second engine to release the incoming engine, or work the train back, fly shunting was adopted.

On approaching Spa Road or Deptford the engine driver would slow his engine to enable the coupling to go slack and allow the front guard to release the coupling by means of a rope. When uncoupled, the driver would accelerate while the train was being braked by the guards so the engine could run over a set of points which could then be changed to allow the coaches to enter a different road.

As the existing crossovers were trailing for left-hand running, to avoid laying new crossovers, right-hand running was adopted so that the existing crossovers were facing.

The final half-mile to Greenwich opened on 24 December 1838. As the company had received complaints of noise from the stone sleepers and leakage through the arches, this final section was laid on wooden sleepers and the arches made watertight with asphalt.

The first slip coach in the country was operated by the London & Greenwich Railway in 1840 using detachable rope couplings.

The London & Greenwich Railway provided perhaps the earliest Park & Ride facilities, gentlemen riding their horses to stables provided beneath the viaduct at Greenwich and then continuing to London Bridge by train.

After the initial excitement traffic declined, in January 1842 the company reduced first-class fares and abolished the second to boost the number of passengers.

The Greenwich company possessed nine locomotives constructed between 1835 and 1840. In March 1845 a William Marshall four-wheeler which had been converted to a 2-2-2 was purchased by the Admiralty and installed aboard HMS *Erebus* to drive a screw propeller. She sailed under Sir John Franklin to search for the North West Passage and was lost with all hands.

Wealthier men were moving from the City to live in pleasanter areas, one of these being Croydon. An Act was obtained on 12 June 1835 to build a line from West Croydon to Corbett's Lane where the company would have running powers over the London & Greenwich for the 1¾ miles to London Bridge, where the Croydon line would have its own station. The original intention was to lay track along the bed of the Croydon Canal, which it had purchased, but this proved impracticable.

The line was formally opened on 1 June 1839 and public traffic began on 5 June 1839 with a service of twelve trains daily, almost on a time-interval basis. The Croydon company developed commuter traffic by encouraging those who worked in London to live in Croydon, charging the same fares from London to Penge and all stations beyond, thus offering Croydon passengers 4 miles of free travel.

On 2 November 1841 the clay cutting north of Dartmouth Arms slipped, halting traffic on the Croydon and Brighton lines for seventeen days.

Trains of the London & Brighton Railway and the South Eastern Railway had running powers which led to congestion as the Croydon company's stopping trains tended to delay the London Brighton & South Coast Railway and the SER's longer-distance trains. An important development came in 1841 or 1842 when Charles Hutton Gregory, the company's resident engineer, erected at New Cross the first semaphore signal used on a railway; previously boards or discs had been used. He did not actually invent the semaphore signal, the idea having been given to him by John Urpeth Rastrick, resident engineer of the London & Brighton and partner in the firm which built Trevithick's locomotive *Catch Me Who Can*. The first signal box was built on the south side of Greenwich viaduct in the fork of the junction at Corbett's Lane. A similar box was erected at London Bridge.

It was believed that timekeeping could be improved if the Croydon company laid its own independent line for its local traffic. Furthermore it was decided to use the Samuda brothers' atmospheric system where instead of using locomotive power, a pipe ran between the running rails. Into this pipe, a piston slung under a special wagon was fitted and when air was withdrawn by means of stationary engines set at intervals along the line from ahead of the piston, atmospheric pressure from the rear would propel the special wagon and likewise the train to which it was attached. A wheel closed the leather valve along the top of the pipe, a seal being effected with a composition of beeswax and tallow by means of a copper heater filled with burning charcoal which re-melted the composition that had been broken when the valve was lifted. Stationary pumping engines at Forest Hill, Norwood and Croydon exhausted the tube ahead of the piston. A greased leather flap sealed the tube ahead and behind the piston.

The first section, that from Dartmouth Arms to Croydon was inspected by General Pasley on 1 November 1845 when the 5 miles was covered in 6¾ minutes at an average speed of 44½ mph. William Cubitt, the London & Croydon's engineer, said that the atmospheric system was well adapted to hilly districts and heavy passenger traffic which required to go short distances quickly at frequent intervals.

This preceded atmospheric traction on the South Devon Railway, which did not start until 13 September 1847. Although passengers were freed from the annoyance of coke dust and the smell from a locomotive chimney, atmospheric propulsion proved impracticable due to the fact that at points the piston had to be lifted, while shunting had to be carried out by horses of locomotives. The atmospheric line from New Cross to Croydon was condemned in May 1847 and converted to locomotive working by 19 August 1847.

One thing the atmospheric railway brought about was the first flying junction, which was installed south of Norwood to enable the atmospheric line with its central pipe to cross the running lines of the two toll-paying companies. Although atmospheric working was initially fairly satisfactory, it was abolished soon after the amalgamation of the London & Croydon in 1847 with the Brighton company.

The Croydon company possessed eight locomotives built in 1838–9. Its No. 3, *Sussex*, built by Sharp, Roberts in 1838, was sold to the Antwerp & Rotterdam Railway in June 1855.

Opening procession of the Canterbury & Whitstable Railway at Whitstable, 3 May 1830.

A Bodmin & Wadebridge carriage exhibited at Waterloo *circa* 1900. Its stagecoach ancestry is obvious.

The opening procession of the Bodmin & Wadebridge Railway at Pendovy Bridge, 30 September 1834. The twenty-two coaches are hauled by *Camel*.

'Help', the Scotch collie trained by Guard John Climpson. He encouraged passengers to donate to the Associated Society of Railway Servants' Orphans' Fund.

Clapham Junction, view Up *circa* 1882. LSWR tracks on the left; the LBSCR centre and those of the mixed gauge West London Railway, right, the broad gauge from beyond terminating at the platforms.

Charing Cross *circa* 1870.

The mobile section of the platform at Waterloo, which could be moved to allow trains to run from the LSWR to the LCDR.

Shanklin station on the Isle of Wight *circa* 1865.

Whitstable harbour in 1890.

Three Bridges, view Up *circa* 1903. The lofty signals can be seen from a distance and it is hoped that the lamp boy did not suffer from vertigo.

Clayton Tunnel *circa* 1860, the scene of a disaster on 25 August 1861. The red flag indicates that the tunnel is not clear. Notice that ballast covers the sleepers.

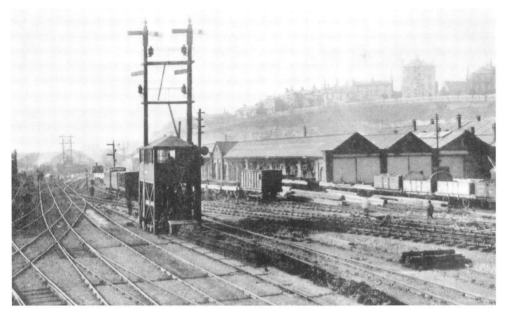

The approach to Brighton *circa* 1860. The old custom is followed of having the signals mounted on the signal box. Signals for both directions are set on each post.

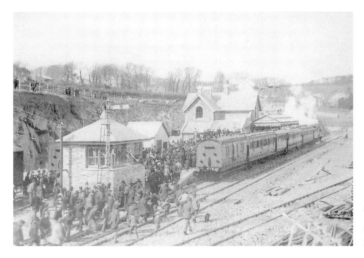

The first passenger train arrives at Padstow on 27 March 1899.

Left: 2-4-0WT No. 3329 at Wadebridge. Built in December 1892, it was not withdrawn until December 1962. (E. L. Scaife)

Below: The stately Adams 445 class 4-4-0 No. 448; the fireman stands a respectful distance from his driver.

H16 class 4-6-2T No. 520 designed for hump shunting at Feltham. This class was also regularly employed working the Ascot race specials.

Snapper Halt on 29 August 1924 when Lynton & Barnstaple Railway coach No. 23 derailed. *Lyn* on the left leaves with the first coach to fetch assistance. (R. L. Knight)

Terrier No. 11 near Ventnor West on the Isle of Wight. She was given a gold medal at the Paris Exhibition.

LBSCR 2-4-0 No. 248 received a gold medal at Paris in 1867. She was built by Messrs Kitson.

D3 class 0-4-4T No. 388 working a Down train approaches Betchworth Tunnel.

J1 class 4-6-2T No. 325 at Streatham Common working a train under electrified wires.

Maunsell's K class 4-6-2T No. 790 at Honor Park with a Newmarket–Epsom train of mainly Great Eastern Railway horse boxes. Post-WW1 she was named *River Avon*. The name was removed when she was converted into U class 2-6-0 No. A790. (Colin Roberts collection)

The royal train at Epsom Downs headed by 4-4-2T No. 600.

J1 class 4-6-2T No. 325 passes mile post 19 with the Down Brighton Belle.

In 1940 Stroudley D1 class 0-4-2T No. 2215 negotiates Grove Street, Deptford en route to the docks. Notice the white bands on the lamp post enabling it to be more easily seen in the blackout, and the van's headlights are masked.

Billinton E5 class 0-6-2T
No. 2572 hauling a
'birdcage' coach.

Marsh C3 class
0-6-0 No. 2308.

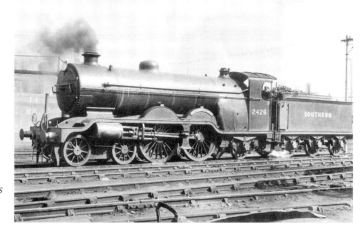

Marsh H2 class
4-4-2 No. 2426 *St Alban's Head* at New Cross Gate,
20 March 1948.

Stroudley E1 class 0-6-0T No. 4 *Wroxall* at Newport, Isle of Wight. Notice the Westinghouse pump on the cab side and the air reservoir below the bunker.

LBSCR petrol railcar No. 3.

Above: Queen Victoria's funeral train passes Carshalton on 2 February 1901 headed by 4-4-0 No. 54 *Empress*. Her coffin is in the third vehicle, a GWR saloon.

Right: The locomotive erecting shop at the LCDR Longhedge Works, Battersea.

Wainwright o1 class 0-6-0 No. 1379 at Ashford, 8 July 1950.

Above: Wainwright E class 4-4-0 No. 516. It was exhibited at the Franco-British Exhibition in 1908.

Left: SECR 4-4-0 No. 132.

An F1 class 4-4-0 passing Purley with an Up horsebox special.

Wainwright J class 0-6-4T No. 207 with a Forest Hill–Sydenham train. In 1927–8 she was re-numbered 595.

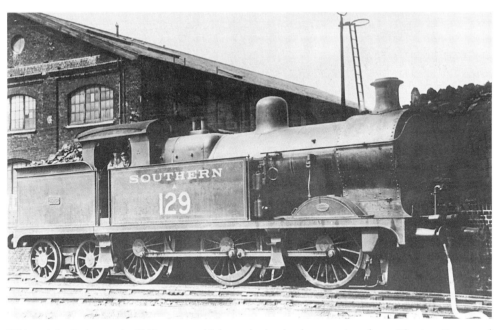

Wainwright J class 0-6-4T No. 129 which worked suburban services from Charing Cross and Cannon Street. In 1927–8 she was re-numbered 596.

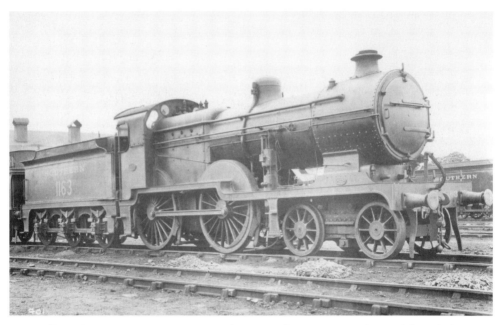

Maunsell E1 class 4-4-0 No. 1163. Notice the Westinghouse pump in front of the splasher.

Wainwright H class 0-4-4T Nos 1329 and 1503 at Stewarts Lane, 17 June 1939. (L. Lapper)

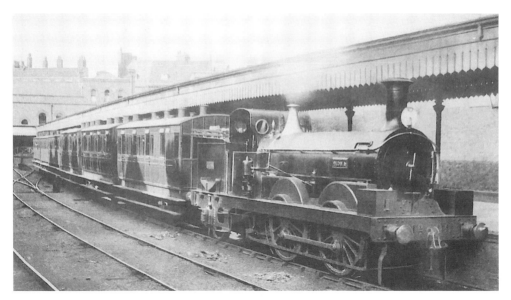

LCDR 0-4-2T No. 99 *Mona*, built by Neilson & Co. in 1873, at Greenwich Park with period coaches *circa* 1896. The branch closed on 1 January 1917 as a WW1 emergency measure.

SER 4-2-0 *Folkestone* at the Great Exhibition in 1851. This could be the first photograph of a locomotive ever taken.

Martley's LCDR 2-4-0 *Mermaid*.

Above: Stirling 240 class 4-4-0 No. 198 near Upper Warlingham, working the 7.36 a.m. Tonbridge-Victoria, via Oxted. (C. Laundy)

Below: Wainwright H 15 class 0-4-4T No. 1554.

Above: LCDR PS *Calais-Douvre* with double hull and fore and aft identical.

Right: Salisbury accident 1 July 1906: the overturned express engine L 12 class 4-4-0 No. 421 being lifted.

L12 class 4-4-0 No. 421, involved in the Salisbury accident, seen here in Nine Elms erecting shop.

Above: A wagon-lit through sleeping car London–Paris, on board a train ferry being jacked and secured to the deck to prevent oscillation. The noise seems to have woken at least one sleeper.

Below: The original Waterloo & City stock.

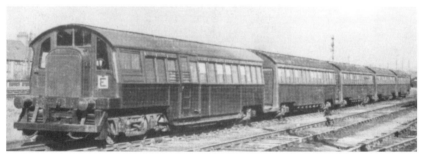

WW2 damage to SR stock and buildings.

Canvas screen being placed over the gap between a locomotive cab roof and tender to prevent the fire glow being seen at night by enemy planes.

D3 class No. 2365, which brought down a German fighter when its boiler exploded. It is seen here at Lydd in 1942.

SR fire-fighting locomotive with a water pump capable of delivering one ton of water per minute.

Ex-US Army 0-6-0Ts No. 1402, left, and No. 1974, right, awaiting overhaul for use on the SR.

O2 class 0-4-4T W28 *Ashey* at Cowes, 6 September 1964.

Right: O2 class 0-4-4T No. 27 *Merstone* on Ryde Pier. 'British Railways' is written on the side tank in SR style.

Below: Schools class 4-4-0 No. 923 *Bradfield*.

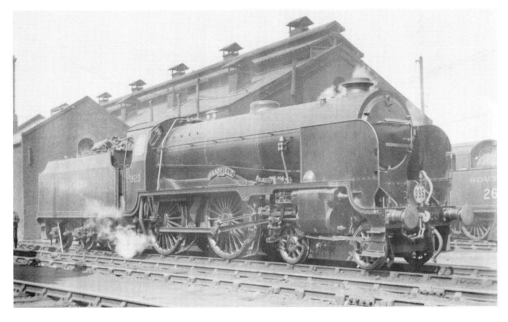

Bulleid's wartime Q1 class 0-6-0 in ex-works condition, 1942.

Left: Bulleid's West Country class 4-6-2 No. 21C128 before being named *Lundy*.

Below: SR mixed traffic electric locomotive No. CC1 with a train of fourteen bogie carriages in 1942.

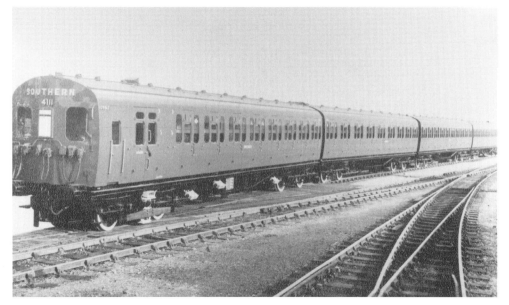

Bulleid electric set No. 4111 in ex-works condition.

0-6-0T No. 700S fitted with fire pump and beyond is a 4-4-0 converted to oil-burning – the oil tank can be seen in its tender.

Leader class No. 36001 at Eastleigh, 14 April 1951. (A. E. West)

Bulleid's double-deck electric train set No. 4002 between Charing Cross and Waterloo.

9

THE LONDON, BRIGHTON & SOUTH COAST RAILWAY

The Surrey Iron Railway was the first public railway in the world, all earlier lines being ancillary to other undertakings such as collieries. The bill received royal assent on 21 May 1801 for constructing a line from a dock near the confluence of the Thames and Wandle at Wandsworth to Croydon, with a branch from Mitcham Common to Carshalton. On payment of tolls the line could be used by anyone.

William Jessop was the engineer and used edged plate rails so that ordinary carts could run over the line. Double track was laid on stone blocks and the gauge 5 ft from centre to centre of the stone sleepers and 4 ft 8 in. between the outer faces of the rails. The line opened on 26 July 1803. Wagons were drawn by horses, donkeys or mules. An extension, the Croydon, Merstham & Godstone Railway, opened in 24 July 1805.

Traffic declined seriously when the competing Croydon Canal opened in 1809. Traffic declined further when the Croydon, Merstham & Godstone closed in 1838 and both lines were abandoned in 1846.

In 1823 William James had proposed the London & Brighton Railway, joining the Surrey Iron Railway near Tooting and using it to Merstham and then a new line to Brighton. Another line was to run from Portsmouth to Rochester. The proposal proved abortive. Another idea for a London to Brighton railway was put forward in 1825 when Sir John Rennie planned a London to Bristol line following a curious route via Brighton, Southampton, Salisbury, Westbury and Bath.

Attempts were also made by Charles Vignoles and Nicholas Cundy, the latter proposing that the Brighton line left the London & Southampton at Wandsworth before striking south. Joseph Gibbs, the London & Croydon Railway's engineer, also set out a plan. In December 1834 Robert Stephenson was brought in to decide the best route and far from choosing between the four, planned his own. A more whimsical proposal was that of John Vallance, who suggested running the whole line in a tunnel and blowing or sucking trains through.

When the proposals came before Parliament, the committee, after hearing evidence, decided that a Royal Engineer be appointed to determine the best plan. Captain Robert Alderson said that apart from Croydon, there were no settlements of over 5,000 on the route from London to Brighton and that it was better to extend the existing Croydon line to Brighton rather than build a completely new railway.

The London & Croydon Railway authorised 12 June 1835 for a line from Corbett's Lane Junction on the London & Greenwich to Croydon. London Bridge was reached over the tracks of the London & Greenwich, but it had its own station on the north side.

On 15 July 1837 royal assent was given to the Act for constructing a line from Croydon to Brighton with branches to Shoreham, Lewes and Newhaven. The first sod was cut on 12 July 1838.

The 41¾-mile-long line left the Croydon line about half a mile south of the present Norwood Junction. It required five tunnels: Merstham, 1,831 yd; Balcombe, 1,1,41 yd, Haywards Heath, 249 yd; Clayton, 2,259 yd; and Patcham, 492 yd. The viaduct over the Ouse Valley was 1,475 ft long with an extreme height of 96 ft. By July 1840 6,206 men, 960 horses and five locomotives were at work on construction.

When the men cutting Merstham Tunnel discovered that there was no beer available nearer than Woodmansterne a distance of at least 2½ miles, they threatened to strike. Eventually boys were paid a halfpenny a trip to fetch the thirst-quenching liquid.

The Brighton to Shoreham section opened on 12 May 1840 and Norwood to Haywards Heath on 12 July 1841. At some intermediate stations trains stopped only if there were passengers to set down or pick up. To be certain of a place on the connecting road coach between Hayward's Heath and Brighton, passengers were required to book their seat on the previous day at London Bridge station, or at one of the eleven coach offices in the City and West End. In the first week 2,483 passengers were carried between London and Hayward's Heath. The London & Brighton Railway was thus the fourth railway to use London Bridge station.

Trains for Brighton had to travel over the rails of four companies before finally reaching their own at Redhill: the Greenwich from London Bridge to Corbett's Lane; the Croydon Railway from Corbett's Lane to Norwood; its own line Norwood to Coulsdon; and the South Eastern Coulsdon to Redhill.

From 21 September 1841 trains ran through to Brighton. On that day the 10.45 a.m. Up drawn by two locomotives consisted of nineteen carriages, five private carriages on wagons and horse boxes with five horses. It only conveyed 146 passengers. Two compartments in the leading carriage of first class trains 'were reserved for servants in attendance on their employers'. The servants were charged second-class fares. Initially third-class passengers were not carried.

The three longest tunnels, Merstham, Balcombe and Clayton were originally whitewashed and lit by gas jets, small gas works being built. It is possible that the dwelling above the north portal of Clayton tunnel may have been provided for the man in charge of the lighting. Tunnel illumination was abandoned by 1849.

David Mocatta was the company's architect and designed an imposing terminus at Brighton, while intermediate stations were built to the same overall design, but given individual treatment regarding the details. Mocatta was one of the first to produce standardised buildings.

On 7 October 1841 the south end of Patcham Tunnel collapsed, but traffic resumed the next day.

An innovation in 1844 was when four Down and six Up trains were provided between London and Shoreham 'without change of carriage or removal of luggage' and that '2nd and 3rd class passengers may go by the same trains, but they are liable to a change of carriage'.

One early chairman of the London & Brighton Company was Rowland Hill, the Post Office reformer. One of his policies was the enforcement of penalties on every breach of a rule. An innovation was excursion trains, which were cheap tickets using scheduled trains.

The first to Brighton left London Bridge on Easter Monday 1844, consisting of thirty-five carriages hauled by four locomotives. Leaving

London Bridge at 8.30 a.m., it arrived Brighton at 12.20 instead of the scheduled time of 11.00 a.m. It is interesting to contemplate how its passengers would have been disgorged as the train would have been too lengthy for the platform. A total of 5,468 passengers were carried to Brighton on that Monday. By 1845 the fastest trains covered the distance of 50½ miles in 90 minutes.

In 1844 the Brighton & Chichester Railway had powers to construct a line from Shoreham to Chichester and sell it to the London & Brighton. It opened to Worthing 24 November 1845; to Arundel, now Ford Junction, 16 March 1846; and reached Chichester 8 June 1846. An interesting feature was the single-track bridge of telescopic design across the navigable Arun. Two men and a boy were able to open the bridge in about 5 minutes, the operation performed by toothed wheels and racks worked by winches.

The *Illustrated London News* of 6 June 1846 stated that the excursion to Brighton 'on Monday last' consisted of forty-four carriages carrying 4,000 passengers, which makes an average of ninety-one passengers in each coach! The present author suggests the total loading was more likely to have been 2,000.

On 27 July 1846 the London & Croydon and London & Brighton amalgamated to form the London, Brighton & South Coast Railway (LBSCR).

Havant to Portsmouth, the last 4½ miles owned jointly with the LSWR, opened 14 July 1847; Wivelsfield to Lewes 2 October 1847; Lewes to Newhaven 8 December 1847; Three Bridges to Horsham 14 February 1848; branches to Hailsham and Eastbourne 14 May 1849; and finally to Deptford Wharf, the latter being the LBSCR's water access, on 2 July 1849. Considerable coal traffic was distributed from there, some going as far as Brighton.

In 1849 an agreement between the LBSCR and the South Eastern Railway (SER) ended friction between them. The SER obtained access to London over the former London & Croydon, from Croydon to Corbett's Lane where the London & Croydon joined the London & Greenwich. In return for running powers over the LBSCR from London Bridge to Corbett's Lane the SER should pay £25,000 and the LBSCR have the use of almost 5 acres adjoining Bricklayers' Arms for a goods depot, to be known as Willow Walk. The SER undertook not to make or work any competing lines to Brighton, Horsham, Chichester or Portsmouth, but complete its line from St Leonards to Hastings and offer the LBSCR running powers.

The LBSCR was keen on gaining these powers as its route from London Bridge to Hastings was 76½ miles compared with the SER's route via Redhill and Ashford of 93 miles. Although the SER line from Ashford to Bo-Peep Junction opened on Thursday 13 February 1851, and the LBSCR extended from its Hastings & St Leonards station to Bo-Peep Junction on the same day, the SER signalmen found difficulty in admitting LBSCR trains to Hastings station, the SER claiming the reason was because a timetable had not been submitted. The matter corrected, on Saturday and Sunday LBSCR trains reached Hastings, and on Sunday evening two locomotives and seventeen carriages and vans were despatched to form the first Up train for the Monday. This was then blocked by an SER engine and some wagons filled with earth. Furthermore the SER lifted the track at Bo-Peep Junction and cut off the gas in the Brighton agent's office at Hastings.

The LBSCR countered this move by providing a bus service from St Leonards to Hastings, but the SER erected a barricade to prevent the vehicle entering the station yard at Hastings. The deadlock lasted several days until reason prevailed and traffic was pooled. With the opening of the direct SER route via Tunbridge Wells on 1 February 1852, net receipts from the Hastings traffic were equally divided. On 11 June 1866 St Leonards, Warrior Square became a joint station, though separate booking offices and staffs lasted until Grouping in 1923.

The Hastings and Bo-Peep tunnels were through clay and sands and as excavation proved difficult, they were built to sub-standard dimensions and without inverts. In 1848 work ceased when it was claimed that tunnelling had taken water from the wells of the houses above. Work was resumed, but the space between the double tracks was less than standard and for many years trains were not permitted to pass in the tunnels.

The LBSCR encouraged commuters between Brighton and London, the chairman at the half-yearly meeting on 24 January 1851 stating that a train ran from Brighton to London Bridge in 1¼ hours, arriving at 10.00 a.m. and departing at 5.00 p.m. Excursionists to Brighton were an important traffic both to the company and to the general public. Sir Richard Mayne, chief constable of the Metropolitan Police, stated it was a positive fact that since the introduction of excursion trains crime had very greatly diminished – though recidivists, perhaps taking advantage of cheap tickets, explored their vocation elsewhere.

In 1851 the new terminus at London Bridge was finished and the company enjoyed huge traffic destined for the Great Exhibition, including foreign passengers using its Dieppe to Newhaven ferry. The transfer of the Crystal Palace to Sydenham in 1852 required a new station there while on 10 June 1854 a branch opened from Sydenham to the Crystal Palace. This proved a goldmine, the line carrying 10,000 passengers each way daily. Handel Festivals, held every three years, were highly popular and audiences regularly exceeded 80,000, with 87,784 attending in 1883.

The Wimbledon–Mitcham–Croydon line following the Surrey Iron Railway for some distance, opened on 22 October 1855. Initially worked by G. P. Bidder, an important civil engineer who had worked with George and Robert Stephenson, in 1856 it was leased to the LBSCR and purchased by that company in 1858, though in 1866 it became a joint line with the LSWR. The line from the Crystal Palace to Wandsworth Common opened on 1 December 1856 and to Battersea Wharf on 29 March 1858.

On 1 February 1858 the LBSCR introduced the first British slip coach working when the 4.00 p.m. London Bridge to Brighton running non-stop between East Croydon and Brighton, slipped coaches for Lewes and Hastings at Haywards Heath. The working timetable contained the instructions:

Before leaving London Bridge the head guard of the Hastings part must see that it is properly secured with the patent coupling, and that the side chains are not coupled, but hung up. He must also see that his rope connection with the Brighton under guard is properly connected.

On arriving near the Haywards Heath Distant Signal, the speed being considerably slackened, the head guard of the Hastings part will first detach his rope communication from the Brighton train, then his coupling, seeing which properly effected the under guard of the Brighton train will give hand signal to the driver to proceed. The head guard of the Hastings train will then brake it gently, and not too suddenly, up to the Station platform. In case anything should prevent the detaching, the guards must give a stop signal to the driver, who must stop at the Station.

The LBSCR was determined to have a station serving the West End so a line from Battersea to Victoria opened 1 October 1860. Because the LBSCR only subscribed half the capital it only owned half the line, the remainder jointly shared with the London, Chatham & Dover and the Great Western, mixed gauge being laid. The rise at 1 in 64 out of Victoria was a handicap for heavily loaded trains. To prevent those living nearby from disturbance, the train shed was extended beyond the platforms and the longitudinal sleepers were initially mounted on rubber.

The East Grinstead Railway ran from Three Bridges opened on 9 July 1855 and was taken over by the LBSCR in 1878.

Initially the ends of LBSCR rails were supported in a special chair, but then in 1847 the locomotive engineer and manufacturer W. B. Adams and R. Richardson patented the fish-plate and by the end of 1857 the line between London and Brighton had been relaid and fish-plated.

The Lewes and Uckfield line opened on 11 October 1858 and purchased by the LBSCR in 1864, while the Lewes and Uckfield Junction line almost parallel with the Keymer branch, enabled trains from Uckfield to enter Lewes from the opposite direction, avoiding Lewes Tunnel. When it opened on 3 August 1868 the old line became redundant.

The line between Epsom and Leatherhead opened 1 February 1859 and worked jointly with the LSWR, as was the extension from Leatherhead to the River Mole where it made a junction with the Leatherhead to Dorking line. A line from Horsham to Pulborough and Petworth opened 10 October 1859 was taken over by the LBSCR in 1862.

On 1 May 1862 New Croydon station opened and was virtually an extension of that at East Croydon. By treating it as a separate station the LBSCR was able to establish a lower fare rate and thus gather more traffic than that from the old station to which the South Eastern Railway was bound to conform. In 1862 the station at Brighton was enlarged at a cost of £92,450.

On 2 March 1863 the West London Extension Railway linked the West End and Crystal Palace line with the London & North Western

Railway and had running powers to Victoria. The additional traffic demanded extra lines from Victoria and these were opened 1 May 1867.

The carriage of Volunteers was an important source of income and on the occasion of the Volunteer Review at Brighton on Easter Monday 1863, nine trains left London Bridge within 2 hours 41 minutes carrying 6,922 volunteers and within 2 hours 50 minutes seven more trains left Victoria with a further 5,170.

The opening of the Hardham Junction to Arundel Junction on 3 August 1863 necessitated a new double-track bridge over the Arun. It had three spans: 30 ft, 90 ft and 70 ft. The central span was movable, and when it was required to be open for river traffic, eight to ten men tilted the central span on to the 70 ft western span. It almost returned by gravity. It took about 30 minutes to open the bridge; for a vessel to pass and then for the span to return. The greatest frustration, in the words of the working timetable, was to 'detach the fishplates and disconnect the signal and track circuit wires and gas and water pipes at the end of the bridge'. It was last opened on 5 April 1936.

When the London Bridge–Waterloo Junction extension of the SER was opened on 11 January 1864, a connection was made with the LSWR by a single line which crossed the circulating area of the main Waterloo station to join the middle road between Platforms Nos 4 & 5. Except for some LNWR trains from Euston to London Bridge via Battersea, for a few months from July 1865 no regular service used this route, which was used for exchanging vehicles and by special trains. When the line was out of use, a section of movable platform was placed across it to allow passengers and luggage to cross at platform level. The connecting line and movable platform were abolished in the 1922 Waterloo rebuilding.

The summer service of 1865 showed an anticipation of the plan, which became, years later, a Southern Electric feature. This was to start trains at standard times. Thirteen of the fourteen down trains left Victoria at 55 minutes past the hour and London Bridge on the hour.

The South London line opened from London Bridge to East Brixton on 13 August 1866 and to Battersea Park on 1 May 1867. To cope with the additional traffic London Bridge was again enlarged and the viaduct approach further widened.

By the end of 1867 the LBSCR was in financial difficulties due to the original capital of £7,700,000 increasing to over £18,000,000 without a corresponding increase in net profits; the average receipt per train-mile down from 7s to 5s. Passenger traffic had increased 60 per cent but as average train mileage increased 170 per cent, average train-mile receipts dropped 40 per cent. A new board of directors reduced passenger train mileage from 3,605,302 in 1866 to 3,312,372 in 1868 and raised the average receipts per train-mile from 4s 10½d to 5s 8¾d.

The Hayling Island Railway opened between Havant and Langston 12 January 1865 and the line completed 17 July 1867. At first the railway was worked by a contractor, but on 25 December 1871 was leased to the LBSCR, the Hayling Railway continuing to own the line until 1923.

The most important feature of the branch was Langston Bridge, a 370 yd long timber trestle with a 30 ft swing span. Regulations stipulated that vessels must not sail through, but must tie up at mooring posts and be warped through. Two railwaymen were required to be present – a signalman to work the box, disconnect and reconnect signal wires, and a length man to remove and replace the locking fishplates and push the span open. Weight restrictions over the bridge limited motive power and for its last seventy-three years it was worked by Terrier class 0-6-0Ts. Latterly spark-arresters were fitted to their chimneys to protect lineside crops.

Turf-cutting ceremonies were often carried out by local dignitaries using ornate spades, but when Lord Henry Gordon Lennox performed the ceremony for the Chichester and Midhurst line on 22 April 1865 he truly acted the part. He took his coat off and used an ordinary spade, though highly polished, as was his ordinary wheelbarrow. The contractor was Dierden & Buxton, but the line failed to survive the financial crisis of 1866. As part of a direct line from London to Portsmouth, the idea was resurrected and the LBSCR opened the line on 11 July 1881, though it was never used by through expresses. Singleton, an intermediate station, had two island platforms as it was convenient for Goodwood Races and so on those occasions was busy.

In 1864 the LBSCR obtained powers to lay a line from East Croydon station to Croydon Central adjacent to the shopping centre. Opened 1 January 1868, due to its proximity to East Croydon usage was light and it closed 1 December 1871. At the request of the town council it reopened 1 June 1886, but was finally closed on 1 September 1890, becoming the site for the town hall.

As a preliminary to the proposed union of the LSWR, LBSCR and the South Eastern Railway (SER) it had been arranged that two of the London Bridge–Brighton expresses should from September 1867 run to and from Cannon Street. On 27 November the three companies signed an agreement to unite. A bill for its confirmation passed the Commons, but was withdrawn when the Lords' Committee insisted on limiting the tolls over the united system to the maximum tariff of the LBSCR. As this would have caused the SER to lose £60,000 annually, the companies withdrew the bill.

The Kemp Town branch opened 2 August 1869. Only 1 mile 32 chains in length, it was a suburban, rather than rural line with up to 36 trains daily. In order to minimise construction cost, it reached the nearest point on the Brighton–Lewes line making the rail distance Kemp Town–Brighton 2¼ miles against the road distance of a mile. The 10-minute train journey would have only been marginally faster than walking. Construction cost of £100,000 was largely taken up by a fourteen-arch viaduct and a 1,024 yd long tunnel. When the main line was electrified in 1933 the branch closed to passengers. During the Second World War the tunnel was used for the safe overnight stabling of electric trains which were steam-hauled over the branch.

Distant signals had the same appearance as home signals and to avoid confusing the two, W. J. Williams had the bright idea of cutting a notch out of the end of the arm. It appeared first at Norwood Junction in August 1872. Other companies gradually adopted the scheme.

Between 1870 and 1875 the LBSCR's gross revenue increased from £1,283,765 to £1,736,868, an increase of 36 per cent which had been earned by an increase of only 29 per cent in the train mileage. From 1 November 1875 saw the first British train to which a Pullman car was attached inaugurated between London and Brighton. Initially six cars were ordered, each costing approximately £6,000 to construct. Parts were sent from the USA and assembled at Brighton. In addition to the ordinary fare, an extra 1s was charged which went to the Pullman Company.

The East London Railway (ELR) was an interesting line. Opened in 1876 from New Cross to Shoreditch it used the Thames Tunnel cut by Sir Marc Brunel and his son Isambard between 1825 and 1843. In 1876 s third-class-only train was run over the ELR from Liverpool Street on the Great Eastern, to Brighton. From 1882 the ELR was run by a joint committee of five companies, including the LBSCR which was offered access to Liverpool Street.

The original station at Portsmouth was some distance from the Isle of Wight ferry and on 2 October 1876 an extension was built from the Town station, where a new high-level platform was created, to the Harbour station.

On 29 March 1877 an agreement was made with the SER to share the London to Eastbourne traffic and thus avoid costly competition. The agreement with the LSWR regarding Portsmouth traffic was renewed, but instead of giving the LBSCR 63 per cent of the receipts, they were to be divided equally.

The LBSCR was the first company to have efficient braking. Initially passenger train braking was only carried out by the engine, tender and brake van or vans. As speed increased, this proved insufficient. In December 1877 the company informed the Board of Trade that it had adopted the Westinghouse air brake and that fifty locomotives and 500 carriages would be fitted.

In the early days of railways there was little or no means of communication between passengers and the railway servants in charge. From 1869 some companies had a cord suspended below the eaves of carriages, but this was of limited use as there was always a considerable amount of slack to draw in before it could sound a warning gong on the tender. Then, by the time the correct tension had been achieved, it may have been too late for the warning to be of use.

The LBSCR locomotive superintendent, Stroudley devised an electrical system which was approved by the Board of Trade in April 1877 and used for the remainder of the company's life. The idea was also adopted by the LSWR and the South Eastern Railway.

In 1878 the Brighton side of London Bridge was becoming overcrowded so to try to avoid costly enlargement, signalling engineers Saxby & Farmer were asked to make suggestions. They proposed extending the platforms, thus allowing each platform road to accommodate two trains simultaneously, and the signalling system was altered to allow each platform to be used for both arrivals and departures.

Safety was assured by giving the arrival signal a lower distant arm. When a platform was free up to the buffers both arms were lowered, but when the line was occupied, but there was room for another train, the distant arm remained 'on'.

Hailsham–Heathfield opened 1 April 1880, and when a borehole was sunk there to tap water it also struck natural gas. The railway used it for lighting and to power a gas engine for pumping. The line between Uckfield and Tunbridge Wells opened on 18 May 1881 and that between Chichester and Midhurst on 11 July 1881.

On 14 October 1881 a Pullman car equipped with electric light started running on Victoria–Brighton trains, this being the first instance in Britain. 1 December 1881 saw the first all-Pullman train to run on the LBSCR, the Brighton Pullman Limited. Four cars were used, electrically lit from eighty Fauré accumulators which were charged at Victoria. Electric communication was provided between passengers and the guard. Mainly owing to the British love of seclusion in compartments over being with others in an open saloon, after some months the Pullman cars were withdrawn; however, they were reinstated on 1882 on weekdays.

The Lewes & East Grinstead Railway opened 1 August 1882, with the branch from Horsted Keynes to Haywards Heath opened 3 September 1883. Two other branches built by the LBSCR in order to prevent the South Eastern Railway from building a line from Tunbridge Wells to Brighton were those from Oxted to Lewes and Hailsham to Polegate. In 1883 Brighton station was enlarged on the same principle as London Bridge. The South Croydon to East Grinstead line constructed jointly with the South Eastern Railway opened 10 March 1884, Oxted tunnel being 2,261 yd long.

The Woodside & South Croydon ran from Woodside on the South Eastern Railway's (SER) Addiscombe Road branch to South Croydon. Although actually promoted by a separate company, it was purchased by the LBSCR and the SER jointly and opened on 10 August 1885. On 27 February 1887 the 384 yd long Bletchworth tunnel near Dorking collapsed and had to be completely relined.

The LBSCR favoured unusually tall signal boxes, and this was not without disadvantages. The signalman could not see the aspect of his signals due to them being situated right overhead; their great height meant that particularly in thick fog a fireman would adopt an improperly hesitant attitude towards carrying out Rule 55 (checking with the signalman to ensure he is aware of the approaching train) when facing the thought of climbing all those steps. In a high wind the tall structure could sway and creak like a sailing ship.

The Dyke branch opened on 1 September 1887, climbed to 400 ft above sea level on a gradient of 1 in 40 for 3½ miles with almost continuous tight reverse curves to a minimum radius of 13 chains in order to closely follow the contours. The only intermediate station, although actually in Hove, was named West Brighton, though the residents of the select district had it changed to Hove in July 1895. Having corrugated iron walls, the timber-framed terminus was less than architecturally fabulous. The refreshment room was an old railway coach with tables and benches outside. The first train, comprising of seven coaches and a guard's van, left at 8.00 a.m. and was hauled by the Terrier class o-6-oT *Piccadilly*.

To accommodate the invited guests from London, the ceremonial train did not leave until noon. It was headed by E class o-6-oT *Orleans*. The Hon. Lady Ponsonby, wife of the company's chairman, declared the line open, the local paper reporting: 'The boisterous condition of the weather precluded a prolonged stay out of doors and the company adjourned almost immediately to the luncheon booth.' The private Golf Club Platform, three-quarters of a mile short of the terminus, provided year-round traffic. The Dyke branch was worked by the LBSCR, which introduced push-pull working in 1905.

The company was incorporated in the SR at Grouping. In 1932 a Sentinel-Cammell railcar worked the service at a running cost of 4½d to 5d a mile. Unfortunately its forty-four seats were too few for summer traffic and after two years it was transferred to the Westerham branch. Latterly a D1 class o-4-2T worked the push-pull service, terminating at Rowan Halt, opened 18 December 1933 half a mile from the junction. During the winter months about half the sixteen daily trains ended at Rowan Halt before returning to Brighton, but the through service was generally in charge of an E4 class o-6-2T. As cars and buses took people to the summit, whereas the railway left them 200 ft below and facing a walk up, the railway lost traffic to its rivals and the branch closed 1 January 1939. When the guard put up the destination boards for the last train before closure, it read 'Journey's end' rather than 'Dyke'.

The line from Hurst Green Junction to Edenbridge opened on 2 January 1888 and was extended to Groombridge 1 October 1888.

Due to a defective water supply, an outbreak of typhoid fever occurred at Worthing in the summer of 1893. It had a serious effect on the LBSCR revenue falling by £15,000 and on 29 August it was believed that there was not a single visitor in the town.

Many railways had a collecting dog and one on the LBSCR died in the autumn of 1891. He was Help, a Scotch collie trained by John Climpson, guard of the evening tidal train from London Bridge to Newhaven. He encouraged passengers and others to donate to the Associated Society of Railway Servants' Orphans fund. The animal wore a silver collar with a silver medal engraved: 'I am Help, the railway dog of England, travelling agent for the orphans of railway men who are killed on duty. My office is at 55, Colebrook Row, London, where subscriptions will be thankfully received and duly acknowledged.' During his lifetime Help raised over £1,000.

In November 1899 the LBSCR agreed to build and maintain the mile-long branch to Hellingly Asylum north of Hailsham. Traffic consisted mostly of coal, food and clothing. As the asylum had its own power station, in 1903 the line was electrified and taken over by the East Sussex County Council. The 14 hp electric locomotive could haul two wagons. The line also possessed a twelve-seater tramcar for patients, visitors, attendants and officials. Passenger traffic ceased in 1931 and goods in 1959.

Brighton expresses were relatively slow, the fastest being the City Limited, taking 65 minutes for an average speed of 46.6 mph. Ahrons compared this to an LNWR fish train booked from Tebay to Preston at 47.7 mph, saying: 'Better a dead mackerel on the North Western than a first-class passenger on the Brighton.'

In 1895 one Hastings express was described in a letter to *The Times*:

It was a light train running on a lovely afternoon, and there was no snow or rain, no head wind or fog. We swept on so rapidly that the speed could not alarm the most timid. We did not scamp a single stoppage, and yet we steamed into Victoria at 5.30 so proudly that I felt sure we must have arrived unexpectedly early. The time-table (a work of fiction!) indeed, made us arrive at 4.37, but this I saw must be merely a printer's error. Is there another line in the world that would dare to run such a train at the break-neck speed of 74 miles in 200 minutes?

In 1898 Rous-Marten, in his annual bulletin to the International Railway Congress, reported:

With reference to the work of the London, Brighton and South Coast Railway I have again little of interest to relate. The booked speed is poor, and in my experience much time was lost by signal checks or otherwise. Travelling by the train known as the Isle of Wight special express from London Bridge, the time lost to Portsmouth Harbour (86¾ miles) was no less than 64 minutes! The engine was not blameable for the loss, which was due to defective traffic arrangements along the line. It is curious to note that the time of the London, Brighton and South Coast's fastest run, *viz.:-* London to Brighton (50½ miles) in 65 minutes, is exactly the same as it was in 1857, forty years ago!

The LBSCR was also parsimonious regarding the quantity of luggage passengers could carry free of charge. Ahrons wrote that the company

... scrupulously weighed every particle of luggage with the same scientific exactitude as the modern provision shops weigh tea and margarine (inclusive of paper). The fine-art avoirdupois proclivities of London Bridge and Victoria would have done credit to the troy methods of a dispensing chemist in the poison business. Consequently there was naturally insufficient time for the process. The company seemed to expect the long-suffering public to attend the place of execution hours beforehand so that due time should be provided for their satellites to extract excess shekels for a few extra pennyweights of luggage.

Due to congestion on the Croydon to Redhill line used by the LBSCR and the SER, an independent line avoiding Redhill was built from north of Coulsdon station, crossing over the original line and running parallel with the Down line to join the LBSCR main line at Earlswood. It required three tunnels: Covered Way, 417 yd through the ground of Cane Hill

Asylum; Merstham, 2,113 yd; and Redhill, 649 yd. The new route, often called the Quarry Line, opened 1 April 1900.

In contrast to the care made for Queen Victoria's travel when she was alive, her funeral train arrangements from Gosport to Victoria were chaotic. The plan of the train had been made out for when it arrived at Victoria and it had been overlooked that it would need to reverse at Fareham. As a result everything at Gosport was back to front and mourners had problems finding the correct carriage.

LSWR and LBSCR officers blamed each other for the 8-minute delay in departure, while a further 2 minutes were lost at Fareham. The queen disliked high speed and stipulated a maximum of 40 mph during daylight and 30 mph at night. As King Edward abhorred unpunctuality, the LBSCR obliged, 4-4-0 No. 54 *Empress* making a very fast run to Victoria to make up the 10 minutes and actually arriving 2 minutes early. It is believed that a maximum speed of 75 mph was attained down Holmwood Bank.

On 26 July 1903, B4 4-4-0 No. 70 *Holyrood*, heading the Pullman Limited consisting of three cars and a brake van, ran the 50 miles 73 yd Victoria to Brighton in 48 minutes 41 seconds, averaging 63.4 mph the maximum of 90 mph being reached near Horley. It returned in 50 minutes 21 seconds, averaging 60.8 mph with a maximum of 85 mph.

On 1 March 1905 the Sunny South Express began running between Liverpool and the south coast, worked by the London & North Western to Willesden where an LBSCR engine took over.

Suburban electric tramways were making inroads into LBSCR receipts, so it was decided to electrify the line between Peckham and Battersea Park using the overhead system with high-tension single-phase alternating current, the arrangements for power distribution being simpler than those for direct current; this also had the advantage of avoiding dangerous ground-level conductor rails. Time proved that the LBSCR was right in choosing the overhead AC system; modified to 25 kw, it is now the standard.

In view of the broad/standard-gauge controversy, it is most surprising that the Board of Trade did not establish a standard electrification system because it was obvious that sooner or later overhead and conductor rail systems would meet.

Materials for the LBSCR electrification were supplied by Allgemeine Elektricitats Gesellschaft (AEG) of Berlin. Later it was decided to carry electrification into London Bridge and Victoria and adapt the line Battersea Park to Selhurst and Peckham Rye to West Norwood. Total length of electrified line was sixty-two miles.

Eight three-coach trains were constructed by the Metropolitan Amalgamated Carriage & Wagon Co Ltd, Birmingham. The 63 ft 7 in. long by 9 ft 3 in. wide motor coaches contained a guard's and motorman's cubicle and luggage compartment and eight third-class compartments, the total weight being 54 tons. Trailers weighing 30 tons had nine first-class compartments. Total seating for a three-car train was 74 first and 144 third class. They were in a livery of umber brown for the lower sides and cream for the upper.

To protect from possible leakage from the collector bows, the timber bodies were covered in aluminium with double floors packed with slag wool over Uralite and aluminium, earthed to the underframe. Each motor coach had four 115 hp Winter Eichberg motors, each pair served by a 220kW transformer with contactors which enabled current to be supplied at 450, 580, 640 or 750V. The roof at the driving end was lowered to mount two collecting bows (one for each direction of running) raised and lowered by compressed air. Repair shops were at Peckham Rye and four-wheeled petrol rail-motors used for maintaining the overhead.

Power at 6,700V 25Hz was generated by the London Electric Supply Corporation's plant at Deptford and supplied to the railway from a switch station at Queen's Road. Victoria to London Bridge came into operation 1 December 1909; journey time for the 8 miles 51 chains with nine intermediate stations was 24 minutes – 12 minutes less than steam trains.

Electrification proved a wise move. In steam days over 8 million passengers had been carried on the South London line in 1902, but tramway competition reduced this figure to less than 4 million in 1909; however, in the first year of the electric trains the number of passengers rose to 4,500,000. The system was known as the 'Elevated Electric' due to much of the original section being carried on viaduct or embankment. This trade name was proclaimed in large green-and-white enamelled signs on station frontages. To aid economy, coasting marks consisting of a small square blue plate with a white St Andrew's Cross indicated where motormen should cut off the current. Blue figures 2, 3 or 6 were displayed on platform lamps indicating stopping places for trains of varying lengths.

The three-coach sets proved uneconomical – too short in rush hours and too long in quiet periods. The first-class trailers were withdrawn, adapted for steam haulage and given central lavatories and used on Brighton workings. Driving trailers converted from bogies suburban sets were coupled to motor coaches to form two-coach units of sixteen first- and 132 third-class seats which ran in the slack period, but were coupled to two others to form a six-coach train for the rush hours.

Electrification from Battersea Park to Crystal Palace opened 12 May 1911 and Peckham Rye to West Norwood 1 March 1912. Opening of the latter was to have been on 1 June 1912, but due to the coalminers' strike, the inauguration was bought forward to economise on locomotive coal. Loading gauge restrictions through Crystal Palace tunnel demanded narrower coaches, thirty motors coaches and thirty trailers being built by the Metropolitan Amalgamated Carriage & Wagon Co. Ltd at the LBSCR's carriage works at Lancing. They were 57 ft 7 in. long and 8 ft wide. Four 150 hp Winter Eichberg motors were installed. A three-coach set offered forty-eight first- and 170 second-class seats. In peak hours two sets were coupled. Between December 1909 and June 1912 the sparks effect gained the LBSCR almost 14 million extra passengers.

Numbered head codes were used:

1 Victoria–Crystal Palace
2 Victoria–Streatham Hill
3 Victoria–Norwood Junction
4 London Bridge–Crystal Palace
5 London Bridge–Streatham Hill or Victoria
6 London Bridge–Norwood Junction

In 1914 work started on electrifying lines to Coulsdon & Smithson Downs and Sutton via Selhurst, but the outbreak of the First World War in August 1914 put a stop to any importation of material from Germany, and it was not until 1922 that work was restarted. It was not completed before Grouping.

In common with many other railway companies, in the early twentieth century push-pull trains were favoured. This was a great timesaver and also avoided signalmen having to make signal movements for an engine to run round. When a driver was in a vestibule at the end of a train, controls to the engine were air-operated.

On 1 July 1908, the enlarged Victoria station was formally opened. Suburban traffic was transferred from the west to the east side of the station, the direction from which most of it came. On 1 November 1908 a new train of first-class only Pullman was introduced. Called the Southern Belle, it made two journeys daily between Victoria and Brighton in exactly an hour. Second class was abolished on suburban services from 1 June 1911 and on all services 1 June 1912.

On 24 June 1913 H1 class 4-4-2 No. 39 *La France* (later renamed by the SR *Hartland Point*) carried the French president from Portsmouth Harbour to Victoria. In addition to a sparkling livery, the coal in its tender was whitewashed!

To celebrate their coronation, on 30 June 1911 King George V and Queen Mary gave a fete for 100,000 London school children. Ninety-six trains conveyed the youngsters to the High and Low Level stations at Crystal Palace, and also Penge and Sydenham Hill.

25 June 1913 saw the day service between Victoria and Paris speeded to almost 8 hours due to the French State Railways reducing the journey by 20 miles and the placing in service on the Newhaven–Dieppe crossing of *Rouen* and *Paris*, both capable of reaching 24 knots. On 12 September 1915 third-class Pullmans appeared on some trains.

During the First World War, apart from moving troops the LBSCR was responsible for sending to France from Newhaven and Littlehampton munitions and stores. 19,750 special trains arrived at Newhaven made up of 866,021 wagons, 336,153 carried munitions and 529,868 stores. A large number of wounded soldiers were cared for at Brighton, 233 ambulance trains arriving, while 445 ambulance trains travelled to other LBSCR stations. Despite the war, the LBSCR continued to issue tickets to the continent via Newhaven–Dieppe.

Brighton Works produced various items for paravanes and 9,000 four-pronged grapnels. Those manufactured elsewhere had failed the 5 cwt test on each arm, but those made at Brighton were perfect. 10,000 Mills hand grenades were produced and a chassis part for a Handley-Page aircraft. A new ship's rudder and post was made in six days.

In February 1916 an electric train from Crystal Palace to Victoria failed to stop at Gipsy Hill, so the guard applied the Westinghouse brake. When he went to have a word with the motorman he found the driving compartment empty. A search was made and his body found in Crystal Palace Tunnel. Furthermore, a wedge which could have been used to secure the controller was discovered in the motorman's compartment.

Six of the LBSCR's passenger fleet were used as hospital ships or for troop transport, while six of its cargo ships were used by the government. 34.6 per cent of the company's men enlisted and of the 5,635, no less than 532 were killed. A war memorial was set up at London Bridge station and the L class 4-6-4T No. 333 was named *Remembrance* and bore bronze tablets engraved: 'In grateful remembrance of the 532 men of the L.B.S.C.R. who gave their lives for their country 1914–1919.'

IO

LBSCR ACCIDENTS

On 2 October 1841 a derailment occurred just north of Hayward's Heath, killing four passengers and two company employees. The train engine had six wheels while the pilot was a four-wheeler, and due to wet weather the road gave way under the weight of the locomotives, which were travelling at over 30 mph even though a watchman warned them to reduce speed. The jury believed four-wheeled engines were unsafe, but the Board of Trade after investigations concluded:

> Four-wheeled engines are rather more unsteady and subject to oscillatory movements and especially to vertical movements, which, in extreme cases, may lead to jumping off the rails, while, on the other hand, six-wheeled engines are thought to be less adapted for going round sharp curves; and if constructed with outside bearings which are generally used with this description of engine, to be more liable to fracture their axles than four-wheeled engines with inside bearings.

A deodand of a shilling was levied on the engines. A consequence of the accident was that a set of trailing wheels was added to the 2-2-os.

On 6 June 1851 a passenger train was descending the incline between Falmer and Lewes when, shortly before the underline Newmarket Arch, the tender and engine left the rails, crossed the Up line, demolished the parapet wall and fell 25 ft to the road, dragging a second- and a third-class carriage, killing three passengers and the fireman, the driver dying three days later. It was believed that the accident was caused by the ten-year-old Jimmy Boakes having placed a sleeper across the line. The lad was acquitted for it was improbable that he could have moved such a heavy weight, but curiously, exactly a year later, on 6 June 1852, he was killed by lightning within a short distance of the bridge.

The area was again in the news on 3 October 1859 when a goods train of forty-five wagons was climbing the gradient of 1 in 80 from Lewes to Falmer when the firebox exploded, fatally injuring the driver. Behind the engine was a wagon loaded with hops and behind that a cattle truck containing two cows. The banking engine at the rear continued propelling and forced the cattle van over the hop wagon on to the engine. When the van was lowered and the cows released, they quietly grazed on the embankment, none the worse for their adventure.

On 25 August 1861, primitive signalling and human frailty caused in Clayton Tunnel the worst British railway disaster to date. Three trains left Brighton for Victoria at 8.28, 8.31 and 8.35 a.m. with sixteen, seventeen and twelve coaches respectively. The line was worked on the time interval system, a minimum of 5 minutes being stipulated between each train. Since 1841 the tunnel had been equipped with a telegraph system between signal boxes at both portals. This meant that a signalman would be aware of a train entering the tunnel, and if it broke down before emerging he would be aware of it.

The distant signals were Whitworth's patent, and when a train passed over, a treadle automatically placed it at danger. Should the arm have failed to operate, an alarm bell rang in the signal box.

Henry Killick was on duty at the South box, and as Sunday marked the change of shift from day to night duty, he worked a continuous shift of 24 hours instead of the regulation eighteen, in order to allow him one free day a week.

The 8.28 sounded the alarm bell when the signal failed to work. Unfortunately Killick did not immediately respond and as the 8.31 approached he waved his red flag as the engine passed his box. He than used the telegraph to Signalman Brown at the North box to inquire if the tunnel was clear. Brown, overlooking that Killick had sent two 'Train in tunnel' messages, saw the 8.28 emerging and signalled 'Tunnel clear'.

The driver of the 8.38 seeing the distant signal now placed at danger, braked, but Killick believing the tunnel clear, waved his red flag so Driver Gregory opened his regulator.

Unfortunately Driver Scott of the second train, had glimpsed the red flag and brought his train to a halt inside the tunnel and started to set back to find out what was wrong. Driver Gregory's engine on the third train smashed into the second with such violence that it was thrust forward 50 yd. Twenty-three passengers were killed and 176 seriously injured.

John Lynn, one of the passengers, had the good sense to make an exit through the tunnel's south portal and run over Clayton Hill to the north end where he was able to prevent a train from London entering the tunnel and causing further mayhem.

At the subsequent Board of Trade inquiry Captain Tyler recommended that an interval of space, rather than of time, should be observed but the block system was not universally applied throughout the system until 31 December 1874. This accident resulted in a travelling porter being placed on the rear of each tender to watch for any breakaways, or mishaps.

Relatively few railway accidents were caused by speed, an exception occurring on 29 May 1863 on the 5.00 p.m. Brighton to Victoria. Near the foot of the 1 in 126 gradient just before Streatham, Craven 2-4-oT No. 131, travelling bunker-first at an estimated speed of 70 mph at the head of sixteen coaches, oscillated violently and left the track, dragging the train with it. After bouncing along the ballast for 224 yards, the locomotive rolled over, its dome struck a rail and the boiler exploded. The driver, a lady and two members of the Grenadier Guards were killed and fifty-nine injured.

An unusual accident occurred on 26 March 1865. The Gloucester Road bridge, Croydon, was being replaced by a wider construction and a locomotive and chains were deployed to demolish the brickwork of two small side arches. As men were loosening the bricks preparatory to the locomotive being used the bricks fell, burying six workmen, three of whom were killed.

A collision at New Cross on 23 June 1869 was unusual for it cost the LBSCR a staggering £74,010, even though there were no fatalities and no broken bones. A goods train, overrunning signals, collided with an excursion train containing 600 passengers, 360 of these claiming for personal injury. Many accepted the sum offered by the company, but 126 took to litigation although this was not necessarily money well spent. One passenger who claimed £5,000 was awarded £10; another asking for the same sum was awarded £125; a claimant for £3,000 received £250 and one for £1,500, £250.

On 1 May 1891 an accident occurred at Norwood Junction which, although there were no fatalities, had far-reaching consequences. A bridge of cast-iron girders failed and this caused the Board of Trade to circularise all the railway companies. Every bridge on the LBSCR was examined and repairs and renewals cost the company almost £100,000.

On 19 December 1899 in dense fog a passenger train standing in Bermondsey station was struck by another killing two passengers. Four days later also in fog, the Up Continental boat train stopped at Wivelsfield was run into by an express from Brighton, five passengers were killed.

An unusual accident occurred at Stoat's Nest (Coulsdon) on 29 January 1910 when a wheel shifted on its axle, causing the train to be derailed and killing five passengers and two others waiting on the platform. Forty-two were injured.

On 18 April 1918 an accident occurred in Redhill Tunnel to an ammunition train. An Up goods train became divided in the tunnel and the signalman failed to notice the train had passed incomplete. Another train was allowed to enter the section, struck the wagons and derailed them. A Down munitions train ran into the wreckage and twenty-six wagons were destroyed. The tunnel was cleared and reopened in only 40 hours.

LBSCR LOCOMOTIVES, COACHING STOCK & STEAMER SERVICES

Before 1 March 1844 the Brighton company possessed its own locomotives, many of the company's early four-wheelers being of primitive design, not dissimilar to those of the LSWR, but from that date the Croydon, SER and Brighton companies had joint locomotive and carriage stock. Thirty-one London & Brighton Railway engines had been handed to the Joint Committee but when the Joint Committee was dissolved 31 January 1846, the Brighton Company took fifty-one of the committee's engines. Its first new locomotives were 2-2-2 well-tanks designed by John Gray in 1852 while in 1854 0-6-0 goods engines appeared. In 1862 Craven's so-called Standard 2-4-0 appeared, though hardly any parts were interchangeable. Standard-class No. 150 was the first LBSCR engine to have a brick arch in its firebox enabling the use of coal rather than coke. In September 1863 Craven produced two 2-2-2s with 7 ft diameter driving wheels, the largest used by the company. In January 1864 Nos 172 and 173 appeared, the first engines on the line to be fitted with cabs and later No. 173 was the first to be painted in Stroudley's standard yellow. In 1864 twelve large 2-2-2s were built by Robert Stephenson & Co. but a few months after they were delivered, four were repurchased by the makers to fill a rush order for the Egyptian Government.

In 1866 the LBSCR ordered six 2-2-2s from Dodds & Son of the Holmes Engine & Railway Works, Rotherham. Due to the company going into liquidation, only two were finished: No. 127 *Norwood* and No. 128 *Croydon*, maker's Nos 69 and 70. Curiously, the works was not linked to a railway with the result that the locomotives had to be drawn over fields and roads to the River Don, placed on barges and drawn upriver until they could be placed on rails.

In October 1869 Sharp, Stewart supplied 2-4-0T No. 96. Originally named *Kemp Town*, it was later removed from the branch, sent to Hayling Island and suitably renamed. Stroudley later gave it a cab of his own design, added a small saloon to the back of the engine plus an additional set of wheels making it a 2-4-2T. A speaking tube provided communication between the inspector and the footplate. Renamed *Inspector*, it was used by the engineer when inspecting permanent way, bridges, etc. Craven retired at the end of 1869, leaving the company with no less than seventy-two different types of locomotive out of a stock of 233.

He was replaced by William Stroudley, formerly works manager at Cowlairs on the Edinburgh & Glasgow Railway and later locomotive and carriage superintendent of the Highland Railway. On the LBSCR he let his predecessor's engines wear out and replaced them with his own neat designs using standard parts as far as possible. In March 1885 he read a paper before the Institution of Civil Engineers setting out some of the problems he faced.

> This railway system offers some peculiarities, when compared with its neighbours, in having no less than 90 miles within the Metropolitan area, 15 of these having three or four lines of rails. Some of the lines have heavy gradients, and curves as small as 6½ and 7 chains radius; there are ninety-four junctions, and twenty terminal stations and from some of these latter, the line rises with gradients of from 1 in 64 to 1 in 80. These features, together with a crowded passenger traffic moving at irregular intervals, over about twenty hours of every twenty-four, cause the working to be very difficult. Some of the engines are attached to as many as sixteen trains in one day; the loss of time in running on and off, and in standing waiting, tending to increase the cost of working, as compared with those railways having more continuous lines. The great distance from the collieries also renders fuel costly.

Stroudley's first engines for the LBSCR were two 0-4-2Ts which appeared in December 1871 and two C class 0-6-0s, Nos 84 and 85. At the time, the latter were the largest goods engines in the country. For economy, some of the exhaust steam heated water in the tender. In October 1872 the A class 0-6-0Ts, nicknamed Terriers, appeared. Designed for working the East London Railway with severe gradients and light rails, they weighed only 24 tons 7 cwt. It is interesting to record that of the fifty built, about half were sold on second-hand to other railways including two to the LSWR which required something light for the Lyme Regis branch, while the Weston, Clevedon & Portishead Railway also acquired two, and when the line closed in 1940 these became GWR property. In 1875 the New South Wales Government Railway built eight of the same design.

On 25 November 1873 the first of the D class 0-4-2Ts appeared. About 50 of the 125 were adapted as motors to work push-pull trains. In November 1874 the E class 0-6-0Ts for goods traffic appeared. In due course eleven of this class were rebuilt as 0-6-2Ts and designated E1/R to work the North Devon & Cornwall Light Railway.

In December 1874 Stroudley built G class 2-2-2 express engine No. 151 *Grosvenor*, with 6 ft 9 in. diameter driving wheels. In 1875 *Grosvenor* was sent to the Newark brake trials to work a train fitted with a Westinghouse vacuum brake, but with the compressed air system proving better it was this which was adopted by the LBSCR. Three engines of the G class were sold to the Italian State Railways in 1907.

As the D class 0-4-2Ts proved steady at high speed, Stroudley decided to use the dimensions on a main-line engine. The D2 0-4-2 tender engines appeared in September 1876 with 5 ft 6 in. wheels. They were specially designed for working fast fruit traffic between Worthing and London and express and fast fish trains between Newhaven and London. They also appeared on excursion and heavy stopping passenger trains. The D2s were followed by similar express engines, the D3 class, with 6 ft 6 in. wheels. Despite predictions that the large-diameter leading wheels would cause them to derail, they were found to traverse curves successfully at high speed.

In June 1882 class C, large goods 0-6-0s appeared, while at the end of 1882 the B or Gladstone class 0-4-2s saw the light of day. These were the most powerful engines for their weight, at only 38 tons 14 cwt, of which 28 tons 6 cwt was available for adhesion. B class No. 189 *Edward Blount* was shown at the Paris Exhibition of 1889 and won a gold medal. Following the exhibition's closure for a few weeks it ran trials on the Paris, Lyons and Mediterranean Railway between Paris and La Roche in competition with the SER's No. 240. While supervising the preliminary arrangements for these tests, Stroudley contracted a violent chill; followed by other complications, it ended fatally in Paris on 20 December 1889.

In the 1890s B class 0-4-2 No. 186 *De La Warr* worked a through special from Brighton to Birmingham over the LNWR. Later, that engine and No. 198 *Sheffield* were converted to burn liquid fuel using Holden's system.

Stroudley's use of coupled wheels at the front of an engine was rather at odds with other locomotive engineers who favoured a pony truck or bogie at the leading end, but Stroudley explained to the Institution of Civil Engineers:

> By placing the coupled wheels forward, where the greatest weight is, the hinder part of the engine may have small wheels, the base be shortened, and the use of heavy cast-iron weights at the back of the engine be dispensed with. It is found that an engine runs much more smoothly when the centre of gravity is kept well forward. The large leading wheels pass over the points, crossings, etc, very easily; causing less disturbance than small ones. They pass round curves without shock, or oscillation, which is no doubt owing to the small weight upon the trailing wheels, as it is the trailing wheels that have the most influence in forcing the leading flanges up to the outside of a curve.

Stroudley never designed a bogie locomotive, considering that for LBSCR conditions it was costly to construct and contributed enormously to dead weight.

Another of Stroudley's ideas was that one set of men should look after one engine and apart from exceptional circumstances none other than the regular crew should work it. The driver's name was painted in the cab above the firebox of the engine in his charge.

Stroudley, mindful of the safety of firemen, curtailed the height of a tender so that, if of ordinary stature, he would not foul the loading gauge.

Stroudley in his March 1885 paper argued that it was:

> ... a great advantage to keep separate engines for drivers. I have always believed that if an engine was made as carefully as possible,

it would respond to the attention it got afterwards; that the driver would be proud of its appearance and of the duty he could get out of it; and doubly proud to be able to perform a great duty with a small amount of expense.

It was to be found that the same man would not take care of another engine, should he have to work one for a time, as he did his own; and those engines which had unfortunately to be entrusted to several drivers deteriorated in quality, consumed more coal, and got dirty and out of repair much more rapidly than those which were appropriated to particular men.

He was of the opinion that it was better for a railway company to spend more capital and have more engines, so that one locomotive could be retained for each driver, as the total cost for stores and maintenance would in that case be less.

Robert J. Billinton replaced Stroudley, taking office on 13 January 1890. The son of a railway contractor, his previous posts had been at locomotive works. In May 1870 he was appointed Stroudley's assistant until 1874 when he was assistant to S. W. Johnson at Derby, where he appreciated the Midland Railway tradition of small locomotives and light trains. His first design was the D class 0-4-4T which appeared in 1892 followed by C2 class 0-6-0s in 1893. In 1894 he produced E3 class 0-6-2 radial tank and in 1895 the B2 4-4-0s; altogether 282 engines of Billinton design were built at Brighton.

In 1902 experiments were made using oil fuel on locomotives as it had the advantage of eliminating ash disposal and fire-cleaning work. Milburn's system was adopted. Oil burning proved unsuccessful with the four tank engines and they were converted back to coal in 1903, but oil burning on the eight tender locomotives lasted until 1904 when lower-priced coal supplies made it uneconomic.

Billinton died aged fifty-nine in November 1904 and in January 1905 was succeeded by Douglas Earle Marsh. Starting locomotive work at Swindon under William Dean, he was appointed assistant works manager in 1888. He then progressed to being Henry Ivatt's assistant at Doncaster in 1896.

At the LBSCR Marsh changed the startling yellow livery to dark umber, passenger engines being lined with gold leaf for those working principal express engines while those on less important duties were lined with yellow. Goods engines were black. Locomotive names were largely abolished.

As rail motors were in contemporary favour, Marsh ordered two four-wheeled petrol units from Dick, Kerr & Co. and two bogie vehicles from Beyer, Peacock & Co., two of the five the company ever built for a British railway. The horizontal boiler was almost entirely placed within the steel cab, only the smoke box protruding. The coachwork, with forty-eight seats, was made by the Electric Railway & Tramway Carriage Co. (Dick, Kerr). Lighting was by gas; control wires from rear compartment to the locomotive were carried outside the roof. The engines were detachable from the passenger body.

The rail motors proved to be a white elephant as they were underpowered for the steep Dyke branch for which they had been intended so worked between Portsmouth and Chichester, but inadequate when heavily loaded as they usually were. As on other railways, these rail motors were found to be somewhat inflexible and a better solution was to use push-pull trains and small tank engines such as the Terrier 0-6-0T and D class 0-4-2T with the result that both the rail motors were withdrawn in 1909.

The two petrol railcars had reversible seating so that passengers could always face the direction of travel. As with the steam railcars, they were replaced by locomotive-worked push-pull trains.

The company urgently needed a large express engine and the H1 4-4-2 appeared, virtually a copy of some working on the Great Northern Railway. The first appeared in December 1905. No. 39 was temporarily christened *La France* to celebrate a visit of the French President in 1909, but all were later named by the Southern Railway.

The C3 class of large 0-6-0s appeared in 1906 and the 4-4-2T I1 class in September 1906 shortly followed by slightly modified versions the I2, I3 and I4 classes. The I3 class were the first tank engines used in Britain on express passenger work. They were fitted with superheaters and the running of Nos 23 and 26 on the Sunny South Express between Rugby and Brighton on alternate days revealed the economy brought by superheaters when compared with the working of LNWR engines on the alternate days.

In December 1910 Marsh produced an even larger engine 4-6-2T No. 325. Marsh retired from the LBSCR aged fifty at the end of 1911 and was appointed consulting engineer to the Rio Tinto Co. until 1932. Marsh had improved many of Robert Billinton's engines by fitting them with larger boilers.

Marsh was succeeded on the LBSCR by Lawson B. Billinton, Robert's son. He began at Brighton Works as a pupil under his father, becoming a draughtsman and then inspector. He had been responsible for the oil fuel experiments and express engine trials. In 1907 he was appointed assistant district locomotive superintendent at New Cross, then rising to chief superintendent.

His first new engine appeared in 1913 as a goods 2-6-0 while in April 1914 the first member of the L class 4-6-4T appeared. Three were named, but only *Stephenson* and *Remembrance* retained their names in Southern Railway days.

Until the 1870s the locomotive livery was Brunswick green, lined black and white with dark red underframes. In 1870 Stroudley introduced a dark mustard yellow known as Stroudley's Improved Engine Green, with olive-green edging, white, black and vermillion lines and claret underframes lined in white, black and vermillion. Stroudley's goods engines were olive green. His successor, Billinton, continued with this scheme. In 1905 Marsh reduced the cost of locomotive painting by using for express engines umber lined with gold, passenger tank locomotives the same as express but lined out in orange. Goods engines were a dark olive-green until 1911 when changed to black lined out with crimson.

Brighton locomotive works opened in 1852, the location not favouring expansion. In 1901 workshops were opened at Newhaven for the steamers thus relieving the pressure on Brighton.

Carriages

In 1848, LBSCR third-class carriages, as opposed to those running in Parliamentary trains, had no roofs and some even had no seats, sections of a carriage being divided by an iron rail. Third-class covered accommodation was provided by 1850, but seats were hard and the windows small, a policy adopted to make third class unattractive and thus drive passengers to patronise a higher class. Sir Allen Sarle, who became secretary and general manager in 1886, recollecting early days, said: 'The old idea of management was to charge as much as you dare and give as little as you knew how.'

In 1848 the LBSCR carried more second-class than third-class passengers:

1st class passengers	469,000
2nd class passengers	1,160,000
3rd class passengers	856,000

In 1896, the figures were:

1st class passengers	1,724,000
2nd class passengers	2,946,000
3rd class passengers	45,810,000

The difference the LBSCR brought to life was startling. In pre-railway days coach travel from London to Brighton cost a guinea inside or 12s outside but with the coming of the LBSCR one could travel all over the company's system from Sunday morning until Saturday night for the modest sum of £3, or for £60 you could do it for a year.

The LBSCR's gauge was originally 4 ft 9 in., the extra half-inch allowing vehicles to run with greater ease.

One good thing about the LBSCR was that it was one of the first English companies to adopt an efficient continuous brake: by June 1879 it had 54 locomotives and no less than 513 carriages equipped with the Westinghouse air brake.

Passenger communication with the guard was another feature in which the LBSCR was well ahead of the northern companies. The latter clung to the obsolete cord communication where a passenger had to read a lengthy notice fixed in the compartment and having digested that, had to lean out of the window and haul in a few yards of slack cord, often drawing a blank. The LBSCR provided an electric bell in each compartment which communicated immediately with the guard's van. According to *Punch*, one of the first-class patrons of the line, on the earliest appearance of the new apparatus, rang the bell for a whisky and soda. What he actually got *Punch* did not state; possibly it was a 40 shilling fine.

In 1876 third-class passengers from the less affluent areas of Bethnal Green and Shoreditch were carried between the Great Eastern Railway's station at Liverpool Street and Brighton. Stroudley's third-class coaches were used, these probably carrying a greater number of passengers per ton than any other contemporary railway.

On 1 November 1875 the LBSCR inaugurated an express with the Pullman car *Jupiter*. This left Victoria at 10.45 a.m. and ran the 50½ miles non-stop in 70 minutes. It only carried first-class passengers. The Pullman cars introduced had closed vestibules rather more suited to British weather than those with open platforms imported from the USA.

In October 1881 the LBSCR was the first British railway company to introduce electric lighting for carriages, power being supplied from batteries charged from a shore line.

The first vehicle to be equipped was the Pullman drawing room car *Beatrice*, equipped with a thirty-two-cell Fauré battery and twelve Swan lamps. The light was only a little brighter than that of gas and much less steady, while the carbon-filament lamps were fragile and unreliable, nevertheless in December 1881 all the vehicles of the Victoria–Brighton Pullman Express Limited were similarly equipped. In 1883 Stroudley devised an improved system using a belt-driven generator in a van feeding accumulators offering a light far superior to the dingy oil lamps of the northern lines.

Stroudley experimented with a three-axle coach with the central axle placed on a laterally sliding frame, connected by radial rods to a pair of pivoted tracks carrying the outer axles. The trial proved that it was not advantageous to adopt the arrangement generally. One success was Stroudley and Rusbridge's patent emergency communication system, operated by a pull-out knob set in a conspicuous position on the compartment partition. This system remained in use until SR days.

Billinton was responsible for the introduction of lavatory carriages on the LBSCR, with steel underframes. He oversaw the construction of a new carriage, paint and trimming shop at Preston Park, Brighton, and the enlargement of the locomotive works. His carriages had higher pitched roofs, four-wheeled coaches were replaced and gas or electric lighting was installed. The LBSCR never had any corridor coaches.

Generally until 1903 carriages were varnished mahogany, or a bright red-brown with red ends, but in 1897 some coaches were painted experimentally with green lower panels and underframe, with white upper panels. In 1902 a complete train of suburban coaches was painted with olive-green lower panels and Improved Engine Green upper panels.

In 1906 the company adopted a passenger livery of umber lower panels with ivory white above.

The first telephone on a British train was in 1910 when the LBSCR carried out a trial between Horley and Three Bridges.

In 1920, coaches fitted with a chain communication cord which rang a bell in the guard's compartment and driver's compartment were distinguished by contact boxes at the ends of the coaches being painted red. Those which additionally applied the continuous brake had the contact boxes painted black.

Goods wagons were painted light grey.

Lancing carriage works opened in 1912, covering about 66 acres. New housing proved unnecessary as employees who had previously worked at Brighton preferred to remain in the town as it offered the opportunity to make a supplementary income by letting rooms in the summer, so workers travelled from Brighton to Lancing in the unadvertised 'Lancing Belle'.

LBSCR Steamer Services

In conjunction with the London & Brighton trains, from 6 April 1844 the General Steam Navigation ran a packet every Wednesday and Saturday that went Shoreham–Brighton–Dieppe; this company had from June 1825 run steamers working Newhaven–Brighton–Dieppe.

In 1847 the LBSCR formed an independent company, the Brighton & Continental Steam Packet Co., though as the South Eastern Railway objected to the LBSCR subscribing towards the company it was dissolved and the Newhaven–Dieppe service taken over by Maples & Morris, which had opened the route in 1851. As the fares were cheaper than those via Dover, the vessels were crowded.

In 1862 the LBSCR obtained parliamentary powers to operate its own steamer service from Newhaven to Dieppe jointly with the Western Railway of France. Services from Littlehampton to St Malo opened 1867, and services from 1870 to Honfleur and Jersey belonged solely to the LBSCR. *Paris II*, which was first used in 1875, was a handsome vessel, but rather slow. At the beginning of every trip a sovereign was placed in a cupboard at the top of the engine room platform and was given to the firemen if the passage was made in under 5 hours. It was not until March 1888, when she was almost thirteen years old, that she crossed in 4 hours 50 minutes – her first time under 5 hours. Also in 1875 two screw-driven cargo vessels were placed in service.

In 1878 the *Brighton* and *Victoria* became the first steel vessels in the LBSCR fleet and also had the first steam steering gear. In 1888 the *Rouen III* and *Paris III* were the last new paddle steamers added to the fleet, subsequent vessels propelled by twin screws. Until 1881 all the jointly owned vessels sailed under the British flag, but that year the cargo ships flew the French flag and the passenger ships the British. The next improvement was the *Brighton* of 1903, which had three turbine-driven shafts.

12

THE SOUTH EASTERN
RAILWAY

When the London & Brighton Act received royal assent on 15 July 1837, it was the view of Parliament that London should have only one entrance from the south. This meant that the South Eastern Railway's (SER) start to Dover was roundabout. It had to run over 1¾ miles of the London & Greenwich between London Bridge and Corbett's Lane; 7¾ miles of the London & Croydon from Corbett's Lane to Jolly Sailor; 5 miles of the London & Brighton from Jolly Sailor to Stoat's Nest; and then 6½ miles over its own line from Stoat's Nest to Earlswood Common (Redhill). Although the route was not a beeline, it had the advantage that, being longer, the company could charge higher fare. The most noticeable feature of this roundabout line was that the 46 miles to Ashford were practically straight and dead level and that extensive cuttings and embankments were not required to achieve this. Although officially known as the South Eastern Railway, some official publications referred to it as the 'Dover Railway' or the 'London & Dover Railway'.

Its engineer was William Cubitt, who in 1817 had invented the treadmill, which was then immediately installed in most English prisons.

Although Sunday was generally observed as a day of rest, bricklayers had to be employed at the 1,327 yd long Bletchingley Tunnel on that day because it was essential that excavations made on Saturdays were supported as soon as possible. Construction of the tunnel was unusual in that bricks for lining it were actually made at the top of each working shaft, rather than from being brought in from elsewhere.

SER permanent way consisted of double-headed 71 lb/yd iron rails laid in cast-iron chairs with ash keys. Worn double-headed rails were not turned. Cubitt was one of the first to use transverse sleepers, the Board of Trade inspector noting:

> The peculiarity of Mr Cubitt's construction consists in using transverse triangular sleepers, between 8 and 9 feet in length, with the vertex of the triangle undermost, which renders them much easier to arrange by the process technically termed packing, than the more usual forms either of a rectangular section or of half spars round at top but flat at bottom.

The line opened from Reigate (Redhill) to Tonbridge on 26 May 1842 and to Ashford on 1 December 1842. The principal stations were well designed, with the main platforms reached by loops from the through roads – ideal for allowing non-stop boat trains to overtake slower trains. The line was extended to a temporary station at Folkestone on 28 June 1843, when the opening special conveying the directors and guests covered the 82 miles in 2 hours 40 minutes, including five stops. The fastest regular trains averaged a speed of 29.6 mph, almost three times the speed of a mail coach. The company adopted the policy of relatively low fares to create traffic from an area which might not otherwise have attracted many passengers.

The Foord viaduct, of nineteen arches, each with a 30 ft span, with piers only 6 ft wide, had to be completed before Folkestone was reached on 18 December 1843. Between Dover and Folkestone were four significant tunnels: the Martello 530 yd; Abbot's Cliff 1,933 yd; Shakespeare 1,392 yd and the short Archcliffe tunnel, just west of Dover Town station and opened out in SR improvements of the twenties. Between Abbot's Cliff and Shakespeare tunnels was a sea wall 30 ft wide at the base and 50 to 70 ft high. The line opened Folkestone to Dover Town station 7 February 1844, one unusual feature of the line being that it actually cost less than expected.

The temporary station at Dover consisted of wood and tarpaulin and the cash-strapped SER transferred it physically to Maidstone for that opening on 25 September 1844.

With the line opened to Dover, the Duke of Wellington became a regular traveller to London and the news of his death reached London by 'private message of the telegraph of the South Eastern Railway'. In due course, the SER charged his estate £90 for assisting with the funeral arrangements.

Third-class passengers were not allowed to terminate at London Bridge, but had to detrain at New Cross. SER rules forbade smoking and the offering of gratuities.

Folkestone Harbour, built by Thomas Telford in 1809, was purchased by the SER in 1843, the year the steeply graded harbour branch was opened to goods traffic, it not being passed for passenger use until 31 December 1848. As the harbour station was 111 ft below the level of the main line, the branch had an average gradient of 1 in 36 with a maximum of 1 in 30. Heavy trains require four engines, heavy engines not being permitted due to the limitations of the swing bridge over the entrance to the inner harbour.

As early as 14 June 1843 the SER ran a day trip to France.

Most of the original SER stations had platforms staggered, rather than opposite each other. This was for safety, as in the days before footbridges passengers crossed the tracks behind the train they had just left. To prevent them being mown down by a train on the other road, they were required to be accompanied by a railway servant.

Initially Bricklayers' Arms was the SER's West End station, used by Princess Alexandra of Denmark when she arrived on 7 March 1863 for her marriage to the Prince of Wales. She had arrived at Gravesend by sea, then travelling by special train to Bricklayers' Arms and by coach to Paddington before travelling by rail to Windsor. The opening of Charing Cross in 1864 diminished the importance of Bricklayers' Arms.

The SER and London & Brighton opened a joint Italianate style London Bridge station in 1844, but a few years later, unable to agree on an enlargement, in 1863 two adjacent stations were built, the SER's being designed by Samuel Beazley.

The branch from east of Paddock Wood to Maidstone opened on 25 September 1844, passengers on the first day being offered free travel. The branch was equipped with the electric telegraph, the SER being one of the first companies to adopt it, two years later using it on all its lines.

The Canterbury & Whitstable Railway was the first steam-powered passenger and goods line in the south of England, though due to inclines the greater part of the distance was worked by cables and stationary engines, only the last 2 miles being locomotive-worked. With George Stephenson as engineer, it opened 3 May 1830, almost four months before the Liverpool & Manchester Railway. The 0-4-0 *Invicta* was driven by the company's locomotive engineer, Edward Fletcher, later to become locomotive superintendent of the North Eastern Railway. *Invicta*, built by George Stephenson's son Robert at their new locomotive works, was the first engine to have outside cylinders at the front end and therefore was the direct ancestor of most subsequent locomotives. Robert took over the position of Canterbury & Whitstable engineer from his father and was anxious to do so because London, easily accessible from Canterbury, was where his future wife, Fanny Sanderson, lived.

The official journey time of 40 minutes for covering the route of 6 miles was about the same as that by stagecoach, but from 1831 when the fare was reduced from *9d* to *6d* the railway won on price. Unfortunately *Invicta* failed to maintain the 12 mph average on its section of the line and the trip actually took 70 minutes.

As on 19 March 1832 the railway ran a train at a reduced fare, it could be considered the first company to operate an excursion train. It was also the first to issue season tickets as 'family' and 'personal' tickets were available from 25 March 1834.

In 1832 the company built and opened Whitstable Harbour, the first example of a railway building and operating a port.

The line was leased by the SER in 1844, that company purchasing it in 1853. In 1845 the SER abandoned stationary engine working and used locomotives throughout.

In due course, what was thought to be the last train on the line ran on 29 November 1952, but then the disastrous Kent coast flooding of 1 February 1953 rendered it necessary to reopen the branch in order to send coal to Whitstable until main-line connections could be reopened.

The first special train for Kent hop-pickers ran in 1844 and these trains became a regular summer feature. A farmer would notify hop-picking families, giving details of date, train time and destination. Up to 30,000 people worked in the fields for several weeks, and this meant that luggage vans were added to the train. Men normally left at the end of the first weekend to return to their regular jobs, leaving the women and children to pick.

Due to poor financial circumstances, fewer hoppers' specials ran to Kent than returned, some being unable to afford the fare down and having to walk. For instance, in 1880 nearly 19,000 were carried down, but over 22,600 returned.

In 1940, as the Blitz had started, children were evacuated straight from the hop gardens to the Midlands and North without returning home, one train running from Marden to Birmingham and another from Wateringbury to Warrington.

Special trains were run at weekends for the friends of hop-pickers, and these visitors could number 40,000. As late as 1952, 4,442 pickers and 23,000 friends travelled in fifty-six special trains. The traffic ended in 1960 when some hops were imported and there was less demand for hops grown in Kent.

On 14 October 1844 a fire started at New Cross works in the loft of the engine shed, then used as a paint shop. It was caused by the spontaneous ignition of the vegetable black in the paint. As it happened, the fire was witnessed by King Louis Philippe. He had intended returning to France from Southampton, but on arrival there found that a violent storm prevented him travelling by this route and so travelled via New Cross and Dover.

The SER engineer from 1844 to 1851 was Peter William Barlow, who favoured rails supported on short, independent cast-iron longitudinal sleepers with integral chairs, the line kept to gauge by transverse iron bars. When 61 miles of track had been relaid using this method, the directors disagreed with him; he resigned 10 July 1851 and was succeeded by Thomas Drane, who reverted to traditional creosoted timber cross-sleepers.

The branch from Tonbridge to Tunbridge Wells opened on 20 September 1845, including the 254 yd long Colesbrook or Southborough Viaduct. The line from Ashford to Canterbury opened 6 February 1846; to Ramsgate Town 13 April 1846; and to Margate Sands 1 December 1846. By rail the latter was 101¾ miles from London Bridge, yet only 64 as the crow flies.

The Thames & Medway Canal from Gravesend to Rochester had opened in 1824 and a single track railway was laid along its towpath and on staging through the tunnel. At 3,946 yd, the canal tunnel was the second longest in England while the 35 ft from the bed of the canal to the top of the arch and a width of 26 ft 6 in. made it by far the largest. It was the tallest in order to accommodate a sailing barge with its mast stepped.

From 10 February 1845 the company ran six trains illegally daily, as power to run at railway was not granted until 31 July 1845 when it became the Gravesend & Rochester Railway. In 1846 it was purchased by the SER for £310,000 and double track laid.

Average speeds on the SER in May 1847 compared favourably with those of other companies:

Railway	Avg. speeds incl. stops	Avg. speeds excl. stops	Avg. distance between stops	No. of passengers trains daily
LSWR	22.4 mph	30.24	5.5	101
LBSCR	20.03	28.94	5.17	43
SER	22.11	28.55	7.12	54

The SER reached Reading on 4 July 1849 and from 1856 the LSWR exercised running powers from Wokingham to Reading. There was no real competition with the GWR to carry passengers to London as the SER route was 68¾ miles, the LSWR route 43½ miles and the GWR route 36 miles.

The Rye and Ashford line opened 13 February 1851, a swing bridge provided across the River Rother near Rye, but in 1903 the river authority agreed that it could be replaced by a fixed bridge. A branch to Rye Harbour opened March 1854.

Angerstein Wharf, built by John Angerstein, opened in August 1852 at the end of a mile-long branch from Charlton Junction, and both line and wharf were leased to the SER, which bought them in 1858.

The SER was up to date with new inventions. In 1852 it ran a telegraph wire from the Royal Observatory at Greenwich to Lewisham station so that at noon and 4 p.m. the telegraph needle would offer the exact time to all its stations.

On 15 May 1855 three crates containing bullion worth £14,000 were sent from London to Paris, but when they were unlocked on arrival it was found that lead shot had been substituted. The robbery should have been discovered before the boxes arrived in Paris, as when they were weighed at Boulogne one crate was found to be underweight and the other two overweight.

No culprit was discovered, but over a year later Edward Agar was arrested for cheque fraud and sent to a prison hulk on the Thames.

When he discovered that a portion of the takings from the gold robbery had not been passed to his girlfriend by his co-conspirator William Pierce, a furious Agar revealed that Pierce, an ex-railwayman, had made duplicate keys for the bullion van and with the assistance of the guard, James Burgess, swapped the gold for lead en route to Folkestone. Pierce was sentenced to only two years' imprisonment, while William Tester, the roster clerk who arranged for Burgess to be guard on the train, and Burgess both received fourteen years' transportation to Australia for being in breach of trust.

The SER was a pioneer in installing the block telegraph and by the 1850s it was in operation throughout between London and Dover, almost forty years before it became a legal requirement for a passenger line.

The SER issued a rulebook in 1857 which stated that before a train was allowed to leave on a single line it had to be ascertained by telegraph that the line was clear; then the telegraph clerk wrote out a pass that the stationmaster signed and the driver carried with him, surrendering it at the other end.

All trains ascending the incline out of Folkestone Harbour were to have a 'harbour brake-van' attached behind and when descending coupled next to the engine. In the vicinity of London, trains ran in the same direction on parallel lines and the temptation to race was great – this was strictly prohibited. Smoking was banned both for employees and passengers, and the proprietors of refreshment rooms were not allowed to sell cigars or tobacco. Stationmasters were expected to inspect toilets daily in order to remove any unseemly writing or drawing. A rule stated: 'If an Engine-driver or Stoker be not required for his full time on the line, he is to employ the remainder of his time in the shop, under shop rules, and at *any work* the foreman may give him.'

The company introduced slip coach working in May 1859, when the 12.20 p.m. express from London Bridge to Ramsgate and Margate introduced a slip at Canterbury.

An attempt to reach the West End was the London Bridge & Charing Cross Railway. Authorised in 1859, it was financially supported by the SER and amalgamated with it in 1863. St Thomas's Hospital was on the route, and although only a sixth of an acre of the hospital grounds was required, the hospital authorities required the railway to purchase the whole site for £750,000, notwithstanding that the company's whole capital was only £800,000. The arbitrator assessed the sum to be paid at £296,000. This enabled the hospital to erect new buildings opposite the Houses of Parliament.

Having paid the cost, on 21 January 1862 the company applied to the hospital to give up possession and was refused. The railway workmen then forced open a gate into the hospital grounds and claimed ownership, the hospital replying by seeking an injunction. Eventually a compromise was reached whereby the railway could use the land it required, the hospital itself being able to continue until July 1862 when the last patients were removed.

The railway was also responsible for the removal and reinterment of over 7,000 corpses from the burial ground of St Mary, Lambeth. Their removal to Brookwood was a welcome business for the LSWR.

Charing Cross station, designed by Sir John Hawkshaw, opened to local traffic for Greenwich and mid-Kent trains 11 January 1864, to North Kent trains on 1 April 1864 and for main-line trains on 1 May 1864. It is London's most central terminus and convenient for the West End. Every train leaving Charing Cross crossed the Thames three times: first when it left, then when it called at Cannon Street (opened 1 September 1866), and finally when it left Cannon Street to call at London Bridge. It certainly perplexed strangers who thought they had found a seat facing the engine.

A train ran every 5 minutes, with 3.5 million passengers annually travelling just between the two stations. The journey took only 7 minutes, the fares comparing favourably with the horse bus which took longer: first class 6*d*; second 4*d* and third 2*d* whereas the bus fare was 3*d*.

The Charing Cross–Cannon Street loop meant that every Up train fouled every Down train leaving Cannon Street and could require the movement of thirty to forty levers by signalmen.

Cannon Street station designed by Sir John Hawkshaw, was larger than Charing Cross and twice the size of King's Cross. Opened on 1 September 1866 it was 189 ft wide, 685 ft long and 106½ ft high. It had nine roads and five platforms, one with a double carriage road for entrance and exit. Eight roads were for regular use and the ninth for reserve stock. Some 31 million bricks and 2,050 tons of wrought and cast iron were used in its construction. The two imposing towers at the river end contained water tanks for the hydraulic lifts. The City Terminus Hotel at the road end of the station was designed in French and Italian style by E. M. Barry and converted to railway offices in 1931. Trains approached Charing Cross over a five-span 700 ft bridge over the Thames consisting of continuous girders carried on plain iron columns. The bridge had five roads: two for Charing Cross, two for the eastern lines and one for general purposes.

Saxby & Farmer installed the sixty semaphore signals worked by two signalmen, a booking clerk and a telegraph clerk. The signalmen had no chance to experience the locking frame, and when the station opened such was the confusion that C. W. Eborall, SER manager and superintendent, gave orders that the interlocking be taken out. Fortunately for safety, within 24 hours and before the interlocking was removed, the signalmen had become accustomed to the frame so it was retained.

Cannon Street had a triangular approach from the Charing Cross line and until the end of 1916 most trains reversed at Cannon Street before continuing to Charing Cross. The sides of the triangle proved too short for the longer trains required and it was sometimes completely blocked by trains fouling each other. By 1902 13.5 million passengers used the station annually, principally City commuters. Third rail reached Cannon Street on 28 February 1926. In 1956 the 190 ft span train shed was removed and the eight platforms extended across the circulating area, while a new one was built below the building that was formerly the hotel.

A ticket collector in the gentlemen's toilet pounced on unwary patrons and demanded a ticket. Many inspectors were also employed to weigh passengers' luggage and obtain payment for every ounce over the free allowance.

In 1866 the service inaugurated between Charing Cross and Cannon Street took 7 minutes and this brief time of seclusion in a compartment was valuable to certain ladies and gentlemen who were not unknown to practise vice; a first-class ticket was cheaper than paying for a hotel room.

The station at Waterloo Junction (simply 'Waterloo' from 7 July 1935), adjacent to the LSWR's Waterloo station, opened 1 January 1869, and the shorter distance between stops reduced the number of compartments with the blinds down when occupied by certain ladies, while the completion of the Circle Line on 6 October 1884 saw the short-distance traffic by other users reduce further. The practice of running Charing

Cross trains into and out of Cannon Street ended as a First World War economy measure 31 December 1916.

On 5 December 1905, the beam of the train shed at Charing Cross collapsed. Passengers were cleared from the platforms just in time before two outer roof bays and the windscreen at the river end also fell. The station wall supporting the bays crashed through the wall and roof of the adjoining Avenue Theatre, then under reconstruction. Two of the thirty men repairing, glazing and painting the station roof were killed as was one of W. H. Smith & Son's bookstall employees and three of the men working in the theatre. Until the structure was made safe, traffic was diverted to Cannon Street.

At the Board of Trade inquiry Sir John Pringle found that the disaster was caused by the weight of staging causing a tie rod to fail at a weld made when the roof was erected *circa* 1863.

The train shed was replaced by a low ridge-and-furrow roof and reopened on 19 March 1906. This roof was in turn was supplanted in 1990 by Embankment Place, an office complex. The seven-storey hotel faced the Strand. Third rail reached the station 28 February 1926.

From 20 June 1863 the SER and the London, Chatham & Dover inaugurated a jointly operated mail service between Dover and Calais while on 10 August 1865 expensive competition ceased when all income from traffic via Dover or Folkestone was divided. In 1866 the SER proportion was 64 per cent, but as the Chatham company carried more traffic, in 1872 it was agreed to divide receipts equally.

In 1863 the SER opened a new station at London Bridge designed by Samuel Beazley. Three years later AB signal box was opened to work it. Built by Saxby & Farmer built of timber on iron piers it spanned the tracks. It was worked by the SER and controlled Brighton, Crystal Palace and Greenwich trains in addition to those of the SER. During the 18 busiest hours it dealt with a train on an average of one every 1½ minutes.

The London Bridge area was a bottleneck as trains proceeding into Cannon Street from London Bridge had to cross the path of those coming out to go to Charing Cross and vice versa. The sides of the triangle were so short that an empty stock train from Charing Cross to London Bridge direct could block all entrances and exits to and from Cannon Street.

On 19 July 1860 the Sittingbourne & Sheerness line opened King's Ferry Bridge, available for both road and rail traffic. Until its construction communication between Sheerness and the Medway towns and London was by water. By the turn of the century the bridge needed replacement, and in 1902, as permission had been granted to dispense with the movable span of the Medway Bridge at Rochester, the SER sought powers for the new King's Ferry Bridge to be fixed. The Admiralty successfully opposed this scheme on the grounds that the Swale provided an alternative approach to Chatham Dockyard. The new bridge, opened in 1904, had a Scherzer lifting span. The railway collected road tolls until 1929 when they were bought out by Kent County Council.

In 1864 Sir Edward Watkin became a director of the SER. For some time the SER had wanted him on the board, but there was no vacancy until that year. Rising rapidly, Watkin became deputy chairman in February 1865 and chairman in 1866. Aged twenty-six, Watkin was secretary to the Trent Valley Railway, then assistant to the London & North Western's general manager; in 1854 he became general manager to the Manchester, Sheffield & Lincolnshire Railway which later extended to Marylebone and became the Great Central Railway. He had dreams of a Channel Tunnel, so becoming chairman of the SER and then the Metropolitan Railway gave him control of a potential line from Manchester to France. Following the death of C. W. Eborall, general manager on 19 December 1873, the board decided that Watkin should take over most of his duties.

On 3 February 1868 the SER opened to goods traffic the 24 miles from St Johns on the North Kent line to Tonbridge, reducing the distance by 12½ miles and avoiding the congestion experienced north of Redhill. Due to slipping of cuttings and embankments the line was not opened to passenger traffic until 2 March 1868. Chelsfield on this line was the nearest station to Halstead Hall, the home of Edith Nesbit from 1871 to 1874. It was the station there and the nearby tunnel that formed the background to her novel *The Railway Children*.

The SER planned a faster route from London to the Channel ports: New Cross to Chislehurst opened 1 July 1865, to Sevenoaks 2 March 1868, reaching Tonbridge 1 May 1868. Construction was not easy: tunnels were needed at Polhill (2,610 yd), Sevenoaks (3,454 yd), plus great lengths of high embankment and several substantial brick bridges.

Safety was improved when on 24 January 1866 C. V. Walker, the telegraph superintendent, tested an electrical communication between passengers and the driver and guard, the Board of Trade officially approving it on 2 January 1869. In 1870, the first annual accident report by the Board of Trade said:

> The South Eastern, having regard to its mileage and gross receipts, takes the lead among the 'no accident' companies and the London, Chatham & Dover, deserves also to be specially referred to ... But it is worthy of observation at the outset - though I do not wish to lay too much stress on the experience of a single year - that the South Eastern and the London, Chatham & Dover Railways, on which no accidents have needed investigation, are worked by the telegraph block system.

By 31 December 1873 all the 355 miles of double track was on the block system. When the Act of 1889 passed and made interlocking, the block system and continuous brakes for passenger trains compulsory, the SER reported that 237 locomotives and 23 per cent of its carriages had the vacuum brake.

In 1868 Watkin introduced workmen's tickets from Plumstead, Woolwich and intermediate stations to London at 4*d*. They were found to lose the company revenue, so were discontinued after 1 October 1874.

In 1868 when the Regulation of Railways Act stipulated that a smoking carriage must be attached to every train containing more than one carriage of each class, most railways labelled the carriage 'Smoking', but the SER labelled the others 'Non-smoking'.

In 1869 the SER had 243 locomotives of which forty-five were in the reserve stock. Its carriages were replaced on average every twelve years and wagons every fifteen. It ran twenty-three trains daily between London and Dover compared with only five daily by the French railway between Boulogne and Paris.

In 1870 the Post Office paid the SER £200,000 for its telegraphs. A line proposed under Greenwich Park was opposed by the Astronomer Royal, fearing possible vibration might interfere with the Observatory. The solution was that the SER agreed to pay the cost of any practical experiments to determine the effect of the tunnel. This was never pursued and Maze Hill to Charlton opened 1 January 1873, and Greenwich to

Maze Hill 1 February 1878, which involved the closure of the existing Greenwich station, the original terminus of the first railway out of London.

On 9 October 1874, 3½ miles of double track line were opened from Sandling Junction to Hythe and Sandgate. In 1876 powers were obtained for an extension from Sandgate to Folkestone Harbour and had it been built, would have obviated the harbour incline. The SER also operated the horse-worked Folkestone, Sandgate & Hythe Tramway. Although construction began in 1889, the first section from the Sandgate School terminus to Hythe sea front and the railway-owned Imperial Hotel was not opened until 18 May 1891. The remaining section into Hythe proper and Red Lion Square depot was opened 6 June 1892. The SER, which had a financial interest in the line, purchased it outright in 1893, changing its name to the non-geographical order of Folkestone, Hythe & Sandgate.

There were five-single deck cars painted in SER carriage lake pigment. The line was closed during the First World War, and when reopened in Whitsun 1919, ex-Army mules were used until horses could be purchased. The mules were not a success, proving obstinate and wilful. Sandgate Urban District Council was concerned over the poor state of the track, and as motor bus competition was increasing the line closed 30 September 1921.

On 11 March 1875, the SER offered a grant of £20,000 towards trials to test the possibilities of a Channel Tunnel on the condition that the Chatham company would subscribe the same amount.

In April 1875 the SER officially announced the union of the SER and the London, Chatham & Dover Railway (LCDR), but the following month differences arose because the proposal was a fusion of net receipts, whereas the LCDR wanted it to be based on gross receipts. The scheme was aborted.

On 1 March 1876, for the first time at Folkestone Harbour trains could actually run alongside the steamers and allow passengers to pass directly from one to the other. A new pier was created at Folkestone and completed in May 1883.

On 10 April 1876 the East London Railway opened from New Cross to Shoreditch, offering access to Liverpool Street and creating a link between railways north and south of the Thames. The company owned no rolling stock, but its services were operated by other companies. On 1 April 1880, the SER worked sixteen trains daily between Addiscombe Road and Liverpool Street.

In March 1877 the Granville Express was inaugurated between London and Ramsgate Town, Down on Fridays and Up on Mondays.

Excavating Weybridge cutting *circa* 1836. Wheelbarrows loaded with spoil were hauled up the timber runways on a rope attached to a horse on the flat ground at the top. When the runways were slippery with mud, there was plenty of opportunity for accidents. (Painting by J. Absolon)

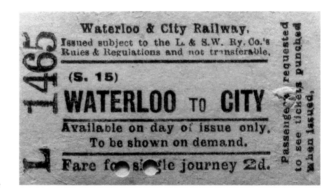

Waterloo & City Railway ticket.

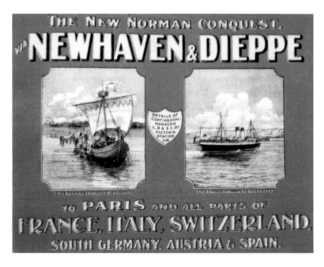

Poster *circa* 1910 advertising the LBSCR's Victoria–Paris service via Newhaven.

LBSCR poster *circa* 1910 advertising the Southern Belle.

LBSCR poster *circa* 1912 advertising weekend breaks on the south coast.

Above: SR 1936 poster promoting Southampton docks.

Below left: SR poster depicting 4-6-0 King Arthur class No. 853 *Sir Richard Grenville* heading the Golden Arrow Limited.

Below right: 1933 poster advertising the Bournemouth Belle.

Left: SR poster advertising house removals using a container.

Below left: The cover of *Walks in North Devon* by S. P. B. Mais, published by the SR.

Below right: The most famous SR poster of 1936, copied from a photograph taken in 1924.

Postcard depicting Barnstaple Town station, with the 1 ft 11½ in. gauge Lynton & Barnstaple Railway on the left and the standard gauge Ilfracombe branch on the right.

Publicity shot of a Lynton & Barnstaple train at Collard Bridge taken before the public opening.

An Adams 415 class 4-4-2T at Waterloo before the station was rebuilt.

LSWR E10 class 4-2-2-0 No. 370. As the driving wheels are not coupled it is referred to as a 'double single'.

LSWR T14 class
4-6-0 No. 443.
Its impressive
appearance belied its
hauling capabilities.

Right: An early
aircraft racing T14
class 4-6-0 No. 443.

Below: No. 395, an
S11 class 4-4-0. The
inside-framed bogie
tender is seen to
advantage.

Stroudley Terrier 0-6-0T No. 39 *Denmark*.

L.B. & S.C.R. and L. & N.W.R. Liverpool to Brighton Express passing Wandsworth.

LBSCR 4-4-0 No. 210 at Wandsworth hauling a through Liverpool–Brighton express.

The Southern Belle hauled by 4-4-2 No. 425 *Trevose Head* passing Star Lane signal box between Coulsden and Merstham *circa* 1912.

H1 class 4-4-2 No. 40 heads the four-car Southern Belle. Notice the headcode.

4-4-2 No. 422 *North Foreland* leaving Victoria in 1921. D3 class 0-4-4T No. 380 right and a 0-4-2T left.

H1 class 4-4-2 No. 40 blows off steam through its safety valves at Victoria *circa* 1910.

4-6-2T *Bessborough*, a tank engine designed for hauling express passenger trains.

A busy scene at Cannon Street.

SECR express passenger 4-4-0 No. 504.

D class 4-4-0 No. 482.

4-4-0 No. 730 leaves Shakespeare Tunnel, Dover.

SECR 4-4-0 No. 769 travelling at 60 mph near Grove Park.

D class 4-4-0 No. 145 on the Hastings 'Car Train' *circa* 1905.

D class 4-4-0 No. 591 at Charing Cross heads a train to Dover. A 4-4-0 and 0-4-4T are on the left.

Early long-boiler SER locomotives.

2-2-2 No. 13, one of the first batch of Sharp, Roberts engines built for the SER in 1842.

A restaurant car express to Portsmouth in 1924, hauled by H15 class 4-6-0 No. 475.

The Golden Arrow hauled by King Arthur class 4-6-0 No. 798 *Sir Hectimere.*

A Golden Arrow jigsaw depicting Lord Nelson 4-6-0 No. 853 *Sir Richard Grenville.*

L1 class 4-4-0 No. 1758 and D1 class 4-4-0 No. 1145 at Bickley with London–Paris wagon-lits and a Pullman car *circa* 1937.

Waterloo in wartime.

Waterloo in 1947.

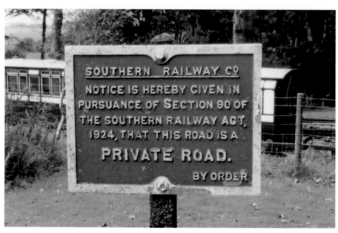

An SR 'Private Road' notice at the narrow gauge Woody Bay station, with preserved Lynton & Barnstaple Railway coaches in the background.

Conveying first-class passengers only, the proprietor of the Granville Hotel at St Lawrence-on-Sea, a resort adjacent to Ramsgate, arranged with the SER to run this express for weekend visitors, advertising it in *The Times* as the Granville Private Express. In reality it was available for ordinary first-class passengers and the word 'private' was omitted from public timetables. The following year third-class passengers were carried and the title disappeared in the summer of 1927.

On 1 June 1878 a junction was made with the LCDR at Blackfriars giving the SER access to the Metropolitan Railway and the Great Northern Railway and allowing the SER to operate a service to Finsbury Park and Alexandra Palace, while in exchange the Great Northern was granted running powers to Woolwich.

In 1881 Sir Edward Watkin had a dream to connect the SER with the Northern Railway of France. That year trial excavations started in the neighbourhood of Abbot's Cliff and Shakespeare Cliff and over in France, near Sangatte. The general public was generally against anything liable to make Great Britain easier to attack, so in April 1882 the Board of Trade, probably urged by the War Office, obtained an injunction that tunnel works should cease as they infringed the Crown's foreshore rights.

In 1881 the SER purchased the nominally independent Hundred of Hoo Railway, which ran from Hoo Junction on the North Kent line across the Isle of Grain to Port Victoria, the complete line being opened 11 September 1882. The SER cleverly named its harbour Port Victoria, which was situated opposite the LCDR's port of Queenborough. The railway-owned timber-built Port Victoria Hotel was leased to Messrs H. & G. Simonds, whose brewery was at Reading, the other end of the SER's system. Although Port Victoria was 10 miles shorter from Charing Cross than the LCDR's route from Victoria, due to the ferry link the shorter route was not popular. The one thing in favour of Port Victoria was privacy, and so Queen Victoria and Kaiser Wilhelm graced the rickety pier, the last royal train carrying the king and queen of Norway on 12 October 1913. The ferry closed in 1916, as did the Port Victoria pier in 1916. The anticipated continental ferry traffic never materialised, though it was used by some Thames excursion steamers.

Queenborough Pier was damaged by fire on 19 July 1900, and until January 1901 passengers were landed at Port Victoria and freight at Tilbury. Day boats then returned to Queenborough, but night boats continued to use Port Victoria until rebuilding was completed in May 1904.

Port Victoria proved useful when on 17 December 1922 a vessel en route to Ridham Dock struck King's Ferry Bridge and prevented closure of its lifting span. On 27 December 1922 a ferry service was inaugurated between Port Victoria, Sheerness and Queenborough. This was withdrawn 1 March 1923 when King's Ferry Bridge was reopened for pedestrians. In 1931 the pier at Port Victoria was declared unsafe to run trains along, and a timber platform constructed at its landward end.

In 1906 the SECR introduced a steam-railcar service, four new halts being opened to serve villages and another for workers at the Uralite factory. When the Admiralty depots near Sharnal Street expanded, traffic was so heavy that even when the rail motor drew a trailer there was insufficient capacity; in January 1908, ordinary trains were run.

On 14 May 1932 a line was opened from Stoke Junction to Allhallows-on-Sea, and most of the trains were diverted there and through expresses run to London. It failed to develop as a popular resort due to the Thames mud, but bore sufficient traffic for the line to be doubled in 1934, the terminal platform being converted to an island. The Grain oil refinery, opened in 1951, swallowed Port Victoria. Port Victoria has now become the deep-water container seaport Thamesport, and the single-track line is now one of the most intensively used freight lines in England.

When the Hawkhurst branch was built, Holman Stephens, later to become the light railway king, oversaw its construction.

On 31 May 1894 Sir Edward Watkin resigned as chairman and was succeeded by Hon. James Byng, who had been chairman from 1855 to 1866 when displaced by Watkins. Byng resigned on 24 January 1895 and was succeeded by Sir George Russell, who died 7 March 1898. H. Cosmo O. Bonsor was then elected. William Wainwright, carriage and wagon superintendent, died on 21 May 1895 and was succeeded by his son Harry S. Wainwright.

In 1898 the SER opened extensive sidings at Gravel Lane, Southwark to store a dozen trains during off-peak hours. About the same date a goods yard was created between Hither Green and Grove Park stations.

On 1 January 1899, in anticipation of parliamentary powers, the SER and the LCDR worked under a joint committee, net receipts being divided 59 per cent to the SER and 41 per cent to the LCDR. The joint committee consisted of four members from each board. Bonsor of the SER was chairman, with the Rt Hon Aretas Akers-Douglas of the LCDR as deputy.

13

SER ACCIDENTS

On 28 July 1845, adhering too strictly to a safety policy caused an accident. When the evening train from Dover arrived at Tonbridge the last coach was shunted off, but inadvertently the tail lamps were not transferred to the last vehicle. After the train left, a light engine was sent after it with the missing lamps. Unfortunately the driver believed it was the locomotive head lamps that he was carrying, so was unaware that the train he was trying to catch lacked tail lamps. Too late he saw it stopped at Penshurst; he telescoped three coaches, injuring about thirty passengers. On board the train was the line's resident engineer, P. W. Barlow, plus Robert Stephenson and three medical doctors; the latter were able to help the injured. When the driver was brought to trial, he was found not guilty.

On 26 March 1846, 0-6-0 No. 121, hauling a coal train of nine wagons on the Canterbury–Whitstable line, was derailed at Bogshole when an embankment collapsed under its weight. The driver, fireman and brakeman were badly injured. No. 121's chimney was embedded in the earth and the locomotive was recovered when a temporary track was laid to enable horses to haul it to the main line.

On 28 June 1857, the 9.15 p.m. from Strood was stopped at Lewisham and the second guard sent back with a red lamp to prevent a rear-end collision. The driver of the 9.30 p.m. from Beckenham failed to observe the warning and ran into the rear of the 9.15 p.m. The brake van of the stationary train was forced on to the adjacent open third-class carriage, killing twelve. The accident was caused through the driver ignoring the distant signal. The Board of Trade inspecting officer criticised the weakness of the uncovered carriages and the unequal height of the buffers. He said that the use of open carriages and cattle trucks for conveying passengers was objectionable and unsafe. Driver Thomas Perry and fireman Edward Whiffen were charged with passing a danger signal.

On 16 December 1864 the rails in Blackheath Tunnel were slippery and brought a ballast train to a halt. An express ran into its rear, killing five platelayers who were in the brake van.

The company's worst accident occurred near Staplehurst on 9 June 1865. The Beult Viaduct consisted of cast-iron trough girders resting on brick piers. The longitudinal timber baulks, which lay in the girders and supported the rails, were being replaced. Work was being carried out between trains, and by the afternoon only one of the baulks remained to be changed. Foreman John Benge planned to do this between the Up train at 2.51 p.m. and the Down train at 4.15 p.m.

John Wiles protected the Up line and was supposed to place a detonator every 250 yd from the viaduct up to 1,000 yd, where he was to place two detonators and station himself with a red flag, but Benge posted him only 554 yd from the viaduct and supplied only two detonators, which he was told not to use unless it was foggy – it was a bright and sunny afternoon.

Unfortunately Benge overlooked the Up Folkestone Boat Express, known as the 'Tidal' as its timing varied with the tides that governed the Folkestone Packets, which could only berth at certain states of the tide. He believed it was due at Headcorn at 5.20, whereas it was actually due at 3.15.

When the express approached at 50 mph the new timbers had been set in place, but not the rails.

When the driver spotted Wiles' red flag he tried to stop, but in such a short distance this was impossible with his train of thirteen vehicles. Unfortunately the guard failed to see the red flag, and when he heard the brake whistle he applied the ordinary screw brake. Only when about 250 yd away did he realise the urgency and apply the Cremar's patent brakes fitted to the leading van and the first two coaches.

The locomotive, tender and leading van crossed the timber baulks, but the engine's weight, not being supported on rails, caused a cast-iron girder to snap. The first coach came to rest at a perilous angle supported by the van coupling, but the next five tumbled into the stream. Ten passengers in these coaches died and forty-nine were injured, the latter taken to houses in Staplehurst.

In the leading coach was Charles Dickens, reading the manuscript of *Our Mutual Friend*; he mentioned his experience in the postscript he added to the novel.

> On Friday the Ninth of June in the present year, Mr and Mrs Boffin (in their manuscript dress of receiving Mr and Mrs Lammle at breakfast) were on the South Eastern Railway with me, in a terribly destructive accident. When I had done what I could do to help others, I climbed back into my carriage – nearly turned over a viaduct, and caught aslant upon the turn – to extricate the worthy couple. They were much soiled, but otherwise unhurt … I remember with devout thankfulness that I can never be much nearer parting with my readers for ever, than I was then, until there shall be written against my life, the two words with which I have this day closed this book:- THE END.

And writing to Thomas Mitton, a friend he penned:

> Suddenly I came upon a staggering man covered with blood (I think he must have been flung clean out of his carriage) with such a frightful cut across the skull that I couldn't bear to look at him. I poured some water over his face, and gave him some to drink, and gave his some brandy, and laid him down on the grass, and he said, 'I am gone', and died afterwards.
>
> Then I stumbled over a lady lying on her back against a little pollard tree. With the blood streaming over her face (which was a lead colour) in a number of distinct little streams from the head. I asked her if she could swallow a little brandy, and she just nodded, and I gave her some and left her for somebody else. The next time I passed her she was dead.

Unfortunately for Dickens, he was not travelling alone but with his mistress of seven years and also her mother; his image as a family man had been a fiction since 1858 when he separated from his wife.

Although Dickens was not physically hurt, he never really recovered from his experience and died aged fifty-seven on 9 June 1870, the fifth anniversary of the disaster. The SER presented him with a piece of plate as an acknowledgement of the help he rendered to the injured.

On 12 January 1877 a slip at the southern end of the Martello Tower Tunnel blocked the Folkestone to Dover line. 60,000 cu. yd of earth fell into a 116 ft deep cutting, killing three men. Single-line operation began on 12 March 1877 and ordinary working resumed on 30 May 1877.

One of Ramsbottom's Ironclad 2-4-0s, No. 268, when in charge of the 5.55 p.m. empty stock from Charing Cross to Gravesend on 6 August 1883, had an exciting journey. Between Dartford and Greenhithe a donkey strayed on the line and was killed, this causing a delay of 30 minutes. Then, soon after restarting, a passenger-carrying balloon drifted below treetop height towards the line along which a goods train was travelling behind a Cudworth 0-6-0. Just when the balloon was about to strike it, a gust of wind lifted the balloon and basket clear of the line and deposited the occupants in a nearby field. The balloon, with its two passengers, had been launched some hours earlier from Tunbridge Wells Common.

On 9 October 1894 a goods train struck a horse-drawn cart loaded with hop-pickers on a private level crossing between Canterbury and Chatham. Seven were killed and eight injured. The fault lay with the horse-driver.

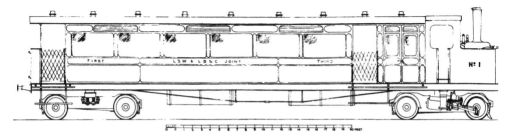

LSWR and LBSCR Joint steam rail-motor No. 1.

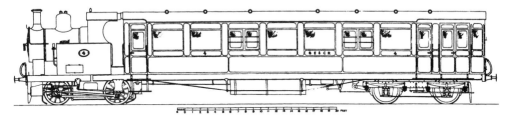

SECR steam rail-motor No. 4 showing its horizontal boiler.

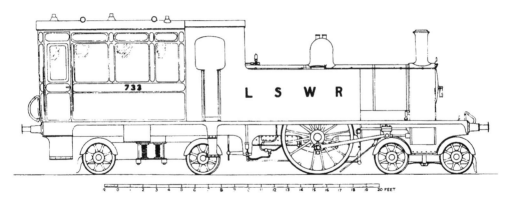

Drummond's locomotive and saloon No. 733 'The Bug'.

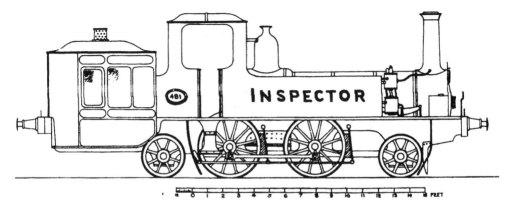

Stroudley's ugly *Inspector*.

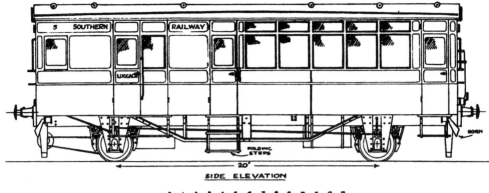

SIDE ELEVATION

SCALE IN FEET

SR No. 5, a 50 hp Drewry petrol-driven twenty-six-seat railcar of 1928. In 1934 it was sold to the Weston, Clevedon & Portishead Light Railway for £272.

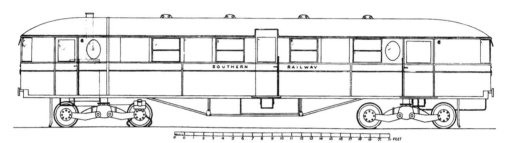

SR Sentinel railbus, built in 1933 for the Brighton–Dyke branch. Although it had phenomenal acceleration and was capable of 61 mph, its light construction caused its frame to break in 1933 and it soon became a financial liability. Suitable for one-man operation, water and coal were fed automatically.

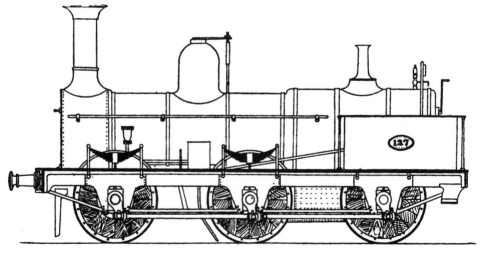

SR 0-6-0 No. 127, unusually fitted with Mansell wheels which were a feature of carriages rather than locomotives.

The original timber drawbridge of 1846 across the River Arun at Ford.

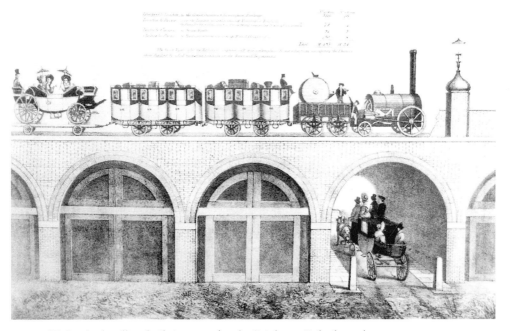

SR Sentinel railbus built in 1933 for the Brighton–Dyke branch.

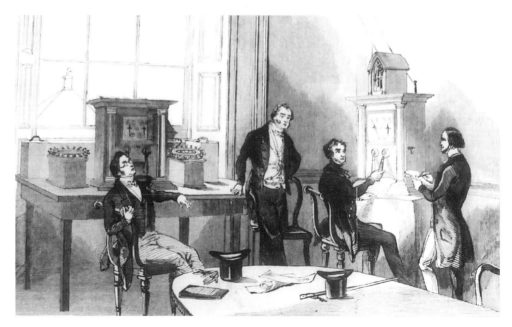

An early use for the LSWR telegraph was for a chess match on 10 August 1845 between two men in Portsmouth and two others at Vauxhall.

Folkestone Viaduct, 1844.

The new racecourse station at Epsom Downs, 1865.

The Bricklayers' Arms terminus of the SER, 1844.

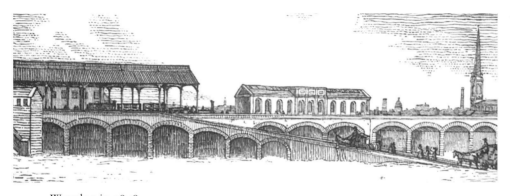

Waterloo in 1848.

Cannon Street in 1866.

The SER station at London Bridge in 1844.

The original LBSCR London Bridge station in 1846.

The SER London Bridge station, 1851.

The new LBSCR terminus at London Bridge in 1853; part of the SER station is on the left. The horse buses left to right are named *Chelsea*, *Favorite* (*sic*) and *Atlas*.

Above left:
Hop-pickers leaving
London Bridge
station for Kent at
midnight, 1891.

Left: The temporary
entrance to Charing
Cross, 1864.

Below: The smoky
archway to the
temporary entrance
at Charing Cross,
1864.

Charing Cross under construction in 1864.

Collapse of a roof girder at Charing Cross, 5 December 1905. The man killed is seen centre, on a stretcher.

The Staplehurst accident on 9 June 1865, which involved Charles Dickens.

The Bricklayers' Arms signalman at work, 1844.

The signal box at Bricklayers' Arms in 1844: the signal to/from London Bridge, right, marked 'LB'; that to/from Bricklayers' Arms, left, the signal marked 'BA'.

London Bridge AB signal box in 1866. The signal arms are marked with the initials of the lines to which they refer.

The interior of the AB signal box at London Bridge in 1866. The signalman on the right is working Saxby's frame, while the booking boy on the right is using the telegraph.

The LCDR PS *Princess Imperial* when new in 1864.

An LBSCR advertisement in the *Illustrated London News* of 28 August 1915.

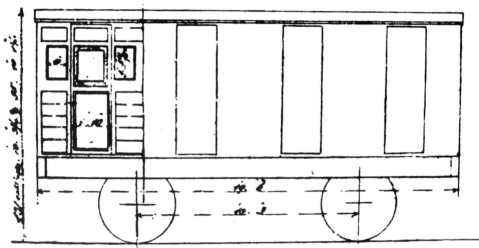

Above: An SER third-class coach *circa* 1850.

Below: An SER third-class bogie carriage built in 1880, before most other railway companies introduced bogie coaches.

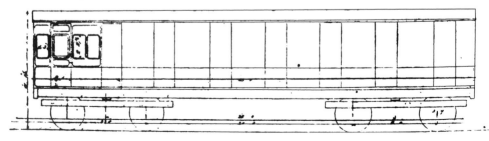

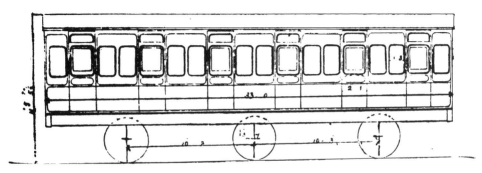

An SER six-wheel coach of 1887.

An unwelcome notice which sometimes appeared at Lynton in the summer.

Lynton & Barnstaple Railway Co.

The Lynton Station Water Supply has failed, and the public are requested to refrain from using the Station lavatories.

By Order.

An advertisement showing S15 class 4-6-0 No. 515, converted for the Scarab oil-burning system. Cost of conversion was £501 0s 7d. It entered traffic as an oil-burner in September 1921, but oil fuel proved twice as expensive as coal and it was re-converted back to coal in October 1921. During the General Strike of 1926 it again burnt oil from 12 June to 17 December.

OIL BURNING
for
LOCOMOTIVES

Locomotive of the L.S.W. Rly. fitted with the Scarab Oil Burning System.

THE SCARAB OIL BURNING SYSTEM

can be fitted to any type of locomotive. Existing engines can be converted quickly and easily. The system is simple and fool-proof. The maximum boiler efficiency and the greatest possible fuel economy are assured with smokeless combustion.

The Scarab System can also be applied to all types of stationary boilers, furnaces and steam road wagons.

THE SCARAB OIL BURNING CO. Ltd.,
28, CHARLES STREET, HAYMARKET, LONDON, S.W.1.
Telephone: Regent 4822, 4823.   Telegrams: "Esscarabel, Piccy, London."

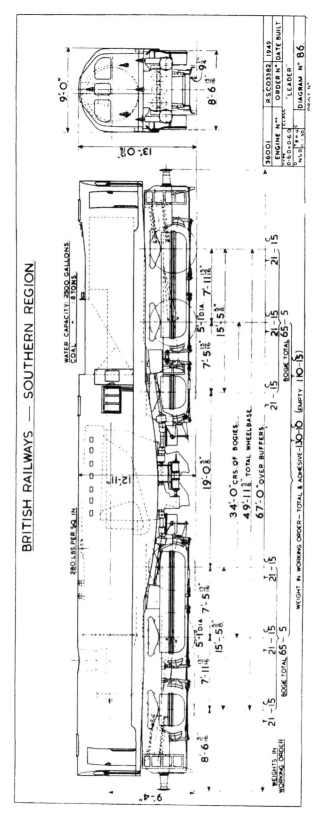

Drawing of the 0-6-0 + 0-6-0 Leader locomotive.

14

SER LOCOMOTIVES, COACHING STOCK & STEAMER SERVICES

By 1842 the London & Greenwich, the London & Croydon, the London & Brighton and the SER were all running over the London Bridge to Corbett's Lane section and in May 1842 it was decided to pool rolling stock, but then with extensions opening away from the Metropolis, on 12 April 1845 the locomotives were divided between the companies. All the engines received by the SER were standard products of the various locomotive builders.

James Anson Cudworth was appointed locomotive superintendent on 22 May 1845 and set up a locomotive works at Ashford which was fully opened in 1853.

An Act of 9 & 10 Vic cap 56 of 1846 authorised the construction of a locomotive, carriage and wagon works at Ashford to replace its works at New Cross. The works opened in 1847 on a 26½-acre site in the fork between the Dover and Hastings lines. In 1850 the carriage and wagon department occupied premises on the opposite side of the Hastings line.

There was an adequate supply of unskilled labour available locally, workmen with higher skills being brought from the North of England. The company built a housing development Alfred Town, named after Alfred, Duke of Connaught, who had a residence nearby. The name did not prove popular and in due course the railway settlement became known as Ashford New Town. Back-to-back houses with ground-floor and first-floor flats surrounded a green. Skilled workers enjoyed terrace houses, while large villas were provided for the manager and other railway officers. A central bath house was surmounted by a huge water tank and flanked by a shop and public house, the Alfred Arms. The SER also provided a library, reading room, a school and a Provident Savings Bank. Shareholders, by voluntary subscription, paid for a church. In the 1860s new houses were of superior quality and had Dutch gables. The locomotive superintendent was supplied with a mansion. Rents were based on the means of the tenants.

As the works expanded during the latter part of the nineteenth century, private builders constructed the necessary dwellings, though when the South Eastern & Chatham Railway closed the former London, Chatham & Dover Railway's Longhedge works in 1900, the company provided 126 houses for workers moved from Battersea.

In June 1850 the SER signed a contract with Robert Stephenson & Co. for ten express 4-2-0s under the 1849 Crampton patents in which the single driving wheels were sited behind the firebox and attached by coupling rods to an intermediate wheel-less shaft. No. 136 *Folkstone* (*sic*) was exhibited at the Great Exhibition in Hyde Park and awarded a gold medal.

The SER carriage and wagon superintendent was R. C. Mansell who in 1848 patented an improved carriage wheel. Around an iron central boss, the wheel was formed from sixteen teak segments. Hydraulic pressure forced these on the inner face of the tyre. On each side a securing ring was fixed in the tyre groove and bolted together by nuts and bolts. The system was adopted by other railways and by 1874 20,000 sets of Mansell wheels were in use in Britain, and no failure was ever reported.

The first engine constructed by the SER in its own shops was a vertical-boilered four-wheeled tank engine Coffee Pot No. 126. It was capable of conveying seven passengers 'with a moderate quantity of light parcels'. Although construction had begun at Bricklayers' Arms in September 1848, it was completed at Ashford in September 1850.

Until 1899 when the SER was amalgamated with the London, Chatham & Dover Railway just over 400 locomotives had been constructed at Ashford. In 1851 five members of the Bulldog class were received from R. Stephenson & Co. They looked like 0-6-0Ts with the centre set of wheels missing and replaced by a dummy shaft. Intended for the steeply graded and severely curved Folkestone Harbour branch, they suffered from lack of adhesion and at times all five were required to draw just one train up to the main line. Following withdrawal in March 1877, one Bulldog, No. 153, was used as a stationary boiler provided steam to power a timber hoist at Ashford Works. It was fired on a mixture of coke, sawdust and odd bits of wood. On 23 September 1881 sparks from its chimney ignited nearby seasoned timber. Before the fire brigade arrived, the entire timber yard was alight, and the Carriage & Wagon Works buildings threatened by sparks. A sudden thunderstorm saved the situation but in the excitement no one thought of the water level in No. 153's boiler which ran dry and the engine had to be scrapped.

In 1853 the Hastings class 2-4-0s were the first to appear from Ashford. The 118 class 2-4-0s appeared in 1857 and continued to be built until 1875. The design was better than similar engines built by other companies as there was an excellent distribution of weight on the wheels, due largely to the long firebox with sloping grate which allowed the trailing axle to be arranged beneath it. In due course they were relegated to the Reading branch and E. L. Ahrons in *Locomotive and Train Working in the Nineteenth Century* wrote:

> Reading to Redhill is 46¼ miles, and the fastest train appeared to average about 4 miles an hour, with occasional spurts to five. I know that this is not far from the mark, because I once tried it myself, and decided to walk if ever I had to go that way again.

In 1861 Cudworth's 2-2-2 Mail engines appeared, and for their dimensions they were amongst the finest express engines in Britain. They consumed an average of only 21.34 lb of fuel per mile on trains of which the mean weight was 142.3 tons running at an average speed of 44.15 mph, which is excellent considering the severe nature of the road to Dover. It was not unknown for them to cover the distance of 26½ miles between Tonbridge and Ashford in 26 minutes.

Working the Tidal Express to Folkestone with ten coaches, an engine left Cannon Street and covered the 70 miles in 85 minutes. In November 1885 No. 203 slipped to a standstill in Sevenoaks tunnel with a heavy express. A stop for signals had been made before entering the tunnel and a start on the greasy rails had proved too much for the single driving wheels. As a result Stirling removed all surviving members from main-line express duties and replaced them with locomotives with coupled wheels.

Some of Cudworth's engines were equipped with his patent coal-burning double firebox, a long, sloping grate having a central mid-feather partition. The two grates were fired alternately, so one had a bright fire while coal was burning through on the other. It was thus possible to burn coal slack, a much cheaper fuel than coke. Its construction was more complicated and when in 1858 the Midland Railway brought in the brick arch and the Birkenhead Railway invented the deflector plate, these gave the same results of burning coal smokeless – hitherto coke had been used – with less expensive construction. In due course Cudworth fireboxes were altered to ones with a brick arch and deflector plate.

The double-framed 2-4-0s of 1857 and 0-6-0s of 1869 brought full standardisation. In the mid-seventies the express locomotives were too small for the heaviest expresses and Cudworth was unwilling to design something larger.

Although standardisation has very many advantages, if carried too far it produces defects such as a reluctance to alter a standard when heavier and more powerful engines prove necessary. It was this that caused Cudworth's downfall, as he was still using 16-inch cylinders when other companies had changed to 17, or even 18 inches.

To obviate this situation, and in a bid to force Cudworth to retire so that his son could take over the post, in 1875 Sir Edward Watkin commissioned John Ramsbottom, Cudworth's London & North Western counterpart, to prepare a design. The ten 2-4-0s designed by Ramsbottom appeared in 1875. Cudworth told the chairman that he believed the grate area was too small for heavy main-line duties and suggested that one of the 118 class in good condition would be better. Time proved him right. As Cudworth's nose had been put out of joint, he resigned 14 September 1876.

The SER had carried standardisation to a greater degree than most other British railways. Of the 258 locomotives there were no less than 124 almost identical 2-4-0 passenger engines together with 53 standard goods engines.

Cudworth was replaced by Alfred Watkins, Sir Edward's son. Cudworth's three 0-6-0Ts for working the Folkestone Harbour incline appeared in 1877 after his retirement. Mansell took charge of the locomotive department and in 1877–8 nine Mansell 0-4-4Ts of the

144 class appeared. Used principally on London to Greenwich trains, they were nicknamed 'Gunboats'.

Alfred Watkins in turn was replaced on 28 March 1878 by James Stirling from the Glasgow & South Western Railway. Watkins' retirement was forced as one of the terms of employment was that no outside business activities were permissible and he had stood for and been elected to Parliament as member for Great Grimsby in the summer of 1877.

Stirling introduced larger and improved versions of his Scottish classes, his first, in 1878, being O class 0-6-0s of practically the same design as those he built for the Glasgow & South Western Railway. Stirling was one of the pioneers of the inside-cylindered 4-4-0 and those of the A class constructed 1879–81 were the first SER tender engines with bogies.

The Cudworth 0-4-4WTs steamed badly when condensing in tunnels, so on 13 April 1880 Stirling wrote to the Metropolitan Railway requesting the sale of two or three of their standard 4-4-0Ts. It agreed to sell three brand-new machines to the SER at £2,150 each, which was £200 more than the purchase price from Beyer, Peacock & Co. When the twelve condensing Q class 0-4-4Ts entered service, the Metropolitan engines were transferred to Tonbridge, but on 26 September 1883 they were sold back to the Metropolitan Railway for £1,900 each.

Stirling's F class 4-4-0s appeared in 1883. In 1889 No. 240 of this class was taken into the Ashford paint shop to be prepared for the Paris Exhibition. Painted umber and named *Onward*, all its metalwork was highly polished. It won a gold medal at the exhibition and so impressed the French that it made trial runs over the Paris, Lyons & Mediterranean Railway with Stroudley 0-4-2 No. 189. The latter was found to be lighter on fuel which was briquettes, but No. 240 reached a maximum speed of 78½ mph while No. 189 was unable to match this speed as it was extremely rough riding.

Stirling noticed that a large amount of local work, particularly in the London area, was carried out by locomotives running tender-first, a procedure uncomfortable for their crews. As mentioned above, in 1880 his Q class 0-4-4Ts appeared and by 1897 it formed a class of 118 engines. Some were fitted with low chimneys and condensing apparatus for working through the Metropolitan Extension tunnels to Wood Green on the Great Northern Railway. In the tunnels the exhaust steam was returned to the left-hand tank from where warm water was supplied to the boiler by means of a pump. The usual connection between the two side tanks did not exist, thus the water in the right-hand tank remained cool. Steam reversing gear was applied to nearly all SER locomotives. The earlier engines had the actuating cylinders inside the cab, sometimes taking up valuable space, but in the later engines they were placed at the front of the driving splasher in a vertical position so as to act directly on the reversing shaft.

In 1880 Stirling classified most of the locomotive stock.

Class letter	Details of locomotives
A	Stirling 1879-81 bogie passenger class.
B	Cudworth Mail singles; Stirling 1888–9 express passenger 4-4-os.
C	Rebuilds of the 1851 Folkestone class.
D	Wilson 1857 2-4-os.
E	Cudworth 118 class 2-4-os.
F	Stirling 1883–98 express passenger 4-4-os.
G	Cudworth 1863–4 0-4-2WTs.
H	Cudworth 1867–9 0-4-2WTs.
I	Cudworth standard 0-6-0 goods.
J	Cudworth 1866 0-4-4WTS.
K	Folkestone Incline tanks Nos 152/3/4.
L	Ramsbottom Ironclads.
M	Mansell Gunboat 0-4-4Ts.
N	Mansell goods 0-6-0 Nos 59/70/150.
O	Stirling standard 0-6-0.
P	Metropolitan 4-4-0Ts Nos 299, 300/1.
Q	Stirling standard 0-4-4Ts.
R	Stirling standard 0-6-0T.

The SECR and the SR continued with the same system for classes originating at Ashford Works, rebuilds or modified versions denoted by a suffix number.

In 1893 the directors, concerned at the cost of coal supplies, asked Stirling to investigate the possibilities of using oil. On 26 October 1894 he said that an inspector had visited the Great Eastern Railway and travelled on an oil-burner, finding it smelly, exuding greasy smuts and extremely complicated to fire. Stirling believed using oil would show no benefit. The directors, still not convinced, asked for an O class 0-6-0 to be converted. No positive steps were taken because following the formation of the SECR Stirling retired and was replaced by Harry Wainwright.

Wainwright decided to convert B class 4-4-0s Nos 454/9, with Holden's patent oil firing system. Extensive trials were run for two months and were found to be a success. No. 459 caught fire at Bricklayers' Arms shed in July 1902 and was sent to Ashford for firebox repairs and a repaint. No. 459 was re-converted to coal in June 1904 and No. 454 in February 1905. They had cost 12 per cent more to run than their sister engines and were more troublesome to maintain. Wainwright delegated most of the design work to his chief draughtsman, Robert Surtees, and his team.

Timekeeping improved over the years. The average lateness tables for the summers of 1878 and 1898 being:

	Passenger trains	Goods trains
June 1878	16.25 minutes	34 minutes
June 1898	3.75 minutes	13.5 minutes

The cost of working the SER was extremely low at 4.65 pence per mile when the figure for the London, Chatham & Dover was 4.80*d*, the LBSCR 5.58*d* and the Great Western 6.74*d*. Of the better-known lines only the Great Northern 3.94*d* and the Midland 4.12*d* could run cheaper services than the SER.

On 1 January 1899 the SECR locomotive stock comprised 459 ex-SER engines and 215 from the LCDR. To avoid having two locomotives carrying the same number, LCDR engines were re-numbered following the SER series. Thus LCDR No. 1 became SECR No. 460.

In Cudworth's time SER engines wore a green livery, a relic of the locomotive pool maintained by the London & Brighton, London & Croydon and the SER. Stirling introduced chrome green. Tank and goods engines were black.

Early passenger carriages were of primitive design and not unlike those of the LSWR and LBSCR. A one-off coach of interesting design was exhibited at the Great Exhibition in 1851. Some 44 ft in length, it was built to Adams' patent and consisted of two four-wheelers coupled to form a rigid frame. In order to allow it to round curves, the wheels had lateral play. The total of eighty passengers were accommodated in four first- and four second-class compartment while another compartment was allowed for the guard and luggage. Second- and third-class passengers were not provided with carriage lighting until 1852.

A particularly striking feature of a long SER train was that hardly any two carriages were alike as to size, height or contour. Third-class passengers enjoyed hard wooden seats and partitions so low that when a man sat down with his back to one of them, his head nearly collided with the back hair and best hat of the female in the next compartment. E. L. Ahrons in *Locomotive and Train Working in the Nineteenth Century* remarked that:

> The carriage floor was constructed on the atmospheric principle, and when the train was moving a violent gale frequently raged in those latitudes which lay below the seats. There were usually two oil lamps of about half candle-power to each carriage, and as there were four compartments, the allowance of light was 0.5 lamp per compartment. The centre of each lamp was immediately above one of the backboards or partitions.
>
> But as the South Eastern was always well to the forte in regard to mechanical appliances for rolling stock, an occasional oil lamp was apparently constructed on the sight-feed lubricator principle and delivered about one drop of oil per minute on the passengers. The drawback to the arrangement was that the only means of regulating the feed of oil was to knock the lamp out into its roof casing by means of an umbrella.
>
> There was, however, a silver lining even to the South Eastern clouds. There was one feature in carriage construction in which this line took the lead, namely, the use of solid Mansell wheels with wood centres, which were invented on this railway. But only some of the carriages had the added glory of Mansell wheels, and the average passenger as a rule knew nothing of, and cared less about their special merits, since they did not help to make the partitions and seats less hard.
>
> Mansell, the carriage and wagon superintendent, perhaps unwisely saw that the carriages were built of teak which meant that the design was out of date before the bodies were worn out. First

class saloons built in 1849 were still in use in 1899, their doorways being only 1 ft 8 in. in width.

Ahrons continued:

> The first-class fare for any distance above 20 miles was considerably more than most of the carriages were individually worth. The fare from London to Dover, for instance, was estimated by competent statistical authorities who used this railway to be approximately equal to the value of four complete South Eastern coaches of average quality. On the other hand, it must be stated that the South Eastern to its credit was one of the very earliest railways to introduce lavatories into second-class main-line carriages, and this improvement took place at about the same time that the Midland fitted them up in their main-line third-class stock.

The SER had a deliberate ploy in making its third-class carriages deliberately uninviting in order that passengers would be encouraged to purchase second-class tickets. Seventy-three drainage pipes were let into the floor of some third-class coaches to facilitate cleaners swilling away spittle expectorated by passengers. In 1851, when the SER commenced building its own carriages, opposing seats were only 16¾ inches apart. The SER could provide some luxury – in 1860 wealthy invalids could use a carriage with a movable bed and fully equipped lavatory.

The ploy to inveigle third-class passengers to use better accommodation did not meet with success as between 1862 and 1865 the demand for third-class accommodation increased and 186 four-wheeled carriages had to be constructed. In 1865 new close-coupled trains were built for the Greenwich line, the SER being one of the first companies to adopt this scheme, necessary to avoid longer trains taxing the platform accommodation. Although the seats were not upholstered, comfort was improved by leaving a distance of 1 ft 8 in. between the seats. D. T. Timins wrote in the *Railway Magazine* that 'ten corpulent persons would have split any of the carriages into fragments'.

In 1872 the first six-wheeled third-class coaches were constructed for the SER and these were blessed with larger windows.

Another experimental vehicle appeared in the early 1880s at a time when railways constructed wooden coach bodies. This had its panels covered with nickel plate. It was hoped this would avoid the expense of painting, but the corrosive London atmosphere would not allow this, so it had to be painted.

In the same era, some six-compartment six-wheelers and seven-compartment bogie coaches were constructed prior to the appearance of Wainwright's high-roofed bogie coaches with their distinctive guard's 'bird-cage' lookout at the brake ends. In the late 1880s third-class rolling stock was fitted with upholstery when it was possible to do so without too great a reduction in the space between the seats. In practice it was found that bogies were not desirable on suburban trains due to their greater weight and the difficulty some locomotives experienced in drawing away from a station.

The SER was a pioneer of communication between passengers and railway servants and in 1865 used Walker's electric bell system, the alarm sounding on an average of approximately once every three and a half weeks.

By 1888 there were eight expresses each way between London and Dover, the best averaging 47 mph over the non-stop run.

In 1892 a train of Pullman-type first class drawing room cars with open platforms at the ends, was built in the USA by the Gilbert Car Manufacturing Company of Troy.

In the 1897 the SER constructed an eight-car set of first, second and third quasi-Pullman cars. They had a centre corridor with closed vestibules and gangway connections. The underframes were of composite construction with solebars of steel and remainder wood. Gould automatic centre-couplers joined the coaches. Dynamos were used for the electric lighting while a stove in each vehicle provided hot water heating. Clerestories were placed over all sections containing passengers, but on the brake-thirds the luggage compartments had plain roofs with raised lookouts for the guards. This up-and-down effect rather spoilt the outline of a fine train. Referred to as the American Car Train it worked on the Charing Cross to Hastings service. Despite offering luxury, the train was not generally popular, the public complaining that the carriages were too warm, or too draughty, or afforded poor privacy. The result was that these cars were taken over by the Pullman Company which dispersed them for use on various trains.

Early carriages were a rich brown, the family colour of the Duke of Wellington, the duke being Warden of the Cinque Ports. Between 1870 and 1880 coaches had flesh-tinted upper panels and brown for the lower, but Stirling changed this to a dark reddish-brown. The American Car Train was painted lake with gold ornamental panels below the waist.

Old coaches were used for the hop-pickers' trains, the paint peeling off and much of the upholstery tattered or very thin. In 1893 so many hop-pickers invaded Tonbridge Down platform one September evening that they overflowed on to the track and the stationmaster refused to permit entry of the train they hoped to catch. This so annoyed the gathering that they attempted to burn down the waiting room. Order was only restored when mounted police charged along the Down platform and made several arrests. Until the First World War a special hand-cart was kept at the police station to trundle any hop-pickers to the cells if the officer at the station ticket barrier considered them unfit to travel.

SER Steamer Services

The SER secured powers to run steamer services in 1853. The SER used Folkestone–Boulogne for continental traffic and due to shallow water at Boulogne used paddle steamers. This design also had the advantage that they could be brought alongside a pier, or could get away faster, saving 5 minutes at each pier. A further advantage was that there was less vibration.

15

THE LONDON, CHATHAM & DOVER RAILWAY

John Rennie, engineer to the Central Kent Railway proposal of 1838, laid out a line from London Bridge to Dover passing through Lewisham, Gravesend, Rochester and Maidstone, at which point it was to diversify: one branch to Ashford and Folkestone and the other to Canterbury and Sandwich. Although the SER initially decided to take over this plan, in the event the SER reached Folkestone via Reigate and Tonbridge. The North Kent line was built via Gravesend to Strood and then it occurred to two of Rennie's assistants –T. R. Crampton, the locomotive engineer, and one Morris – that it would be an economic proposition to build a shorter line from Strood to Canterbury. Local landowners formed a company and were supported by the enthusiasm of the contractor George Burge, who had invested considerable capital in Herne Bay and had purchased Folkestone Harbour for £10,000 and then sold it to the SER for £18,000.

Parliamentary powers for constructing the East Kent Railway (EKR) were obtained in 1853. As insufficient financial support was not forthcoming, Burge became alarmed and was bought out by Crampton and Morris. Morris retired and Crampton persuaded the contractors Samuel Peto and his brother-in-law Edward Betts to join him.

In 1855 the EKR obtained powers to extend from Canterbury to Dover. The sections were opened as follows: Strood–Chatham 29 March 1858; Chatham–Faversham 25 January 1858; Faversham–Canterbury 9 July 1860; Canterbury–Dover Town 22 July 1861 and Dover Town–Dover

Harbour 1 November 1861. Between London and Strood the SER was to transmit the EKR traffic. In 1859 the EKR changed its name to the London, Chatham & Dover Railway.

The Strood–Dover line had significant engineering features. The four-span bridge over the Medway, designed by Joseph Cubitt, originally had an opening span, but as there were no demands for it to be opened it was eventually fixed. The line through Rochester and Chatham was expensive as it required valuable property and the construction of three tunnels: Fort Pitt, 1,200 ft in length; Chatham, 795 ft; and New Brompton, 2,685 ft. Other tunnels were at Selling, 1,188 ft, and Shepherd's Well, 7,128 ft. A considerable portion of the line was on gradients of 1 in 132 or steeper.

Not having its own line to London, the EKR in 1856 sought a bill for running powers over the SER from Strood to Dartford and then constructing its own line through Lewisham to link with the West End & Crystal Palace Railway at Battersea and then into Victoria by the Victoria Station & Pimlico Railway. The EKR reached Victoria 1 December 1860, though in 1859 the company had changed its name to the London, Chatham & Dover Railway (LCDR). The LCDR was one of the few railway companies to possess its own printing works; these were situated at Victoria.

The Strood–London route suffered as much from gradients as that from Strood to Dover. The line see-sawed from Strood to Penge mostly at 1 in 100. Penge tunnel, 6,600 ft long, passed through London clay which, although treacherous to work with, provided material for the 33 million bricks required to line the tunnel. It was constructed to sub-standard dimensions which for seventy years restricted the type of stock permitted.

In 1862 the LCDR secure the contract for carrying mails between Dover and Calais, whereas hitherto it had been worked by an operator who used the SER. After June 1863 mails were a joint operation with the SER and in 1865 pooling arrangements were made with the SER to cover all continental traffic via Dover and Folkestone. Competition did not cease as an allowance was made to each company for every passenger carried. When the extension at Dover to the Admiralty Pier was opened in 1860 a paper recorded:

> It is generally a moot point whether the express from Charing Cross or Victoria shall be first alongside the steamer at Dover. The fact

has been noted by the idlers on the pier, who have devised a new form of gambling, and bets are freely laid as to which train shall be first past the post. The difference in actual mileage from London is comparatively nothing, and the betting is accordingly even. When signals have fallen on both tracks the excitement becomes intense. The S.E.R. has a clear run in by the shore and when the train shoots out of the tunnel the backers of the Charing Cross are jubilant; but, as often as not, Victoria suddenly shoots round the corner and wins, like a well-ridden thoroughbred, by a short head.

A significant event occurred on 27 February 1865. The LCDR inaugurated two trains daily between Victoria and Blackfriars, enabling 'artisans, mechanics and daily labourers both male and female' going to and from work to travel for only a penny. They were required to hold a weekly season ticket, costing a shilling, to be purchased not later than the Thursday in the week before use. To prevent misuse, the holder was required to state name, address and occupation and also those of the employer. The morning train from each end started at 4.55 a.m. and arrived just before 6.00 a.m. On five days a week the evening train left at 6.15 p.m., but on Saturdays at the earlier hour of 2.30 p.m. No luggage could be carried, but a basket of tools or implements of labour not exceeding 28 lbs could be taken.

Shareholders held differing views on these cheap trains, one complaining that receipts would not pay for the coke, while another believed it 'highly creditable to be the first to run these trains' and suggested others be put on later for the benefit of clerks and other workers.

The chairman James Staat Forbes explained:

The company was described as a great destroyer of house property in London, and was charged with turning the working man out of his habitation. To meet this state of feeling it was thought advisable to make a graceful concession on the part of the company; they therefore volunteered to run cheap trains for the benefit of workmen, and a clause was inserted in the Act of Parliament for that purpose. That Act fixed both the hour at which the trains should be run, and the fares to be charged, and the company had strictly adhered to the Act in these particulars. He believed those trains would be successful and prove both beneficial to the working classes and advantageous to the company.

This Act created a precedent, and whenever a railway sought powers to demolish urban housing Parliament insisted on the provision of workmen's trains.

A temporary station at Ludgate Hill opened on 21 December 1864 and a permanent replacement on 1 June 1865, its platform on the first storey. Accommodation was provided for the heavy passenger traffic expected on completion of the High Level Crystal Palace Railway and Upper Norwood. There were two booking offices at Ludgate Hill, on one side for suburban stations and on the other side for main-line and continental trains. The station only dealt with passengers, goods traffic being accommodated on the Surrey bank at Blackfriars Bridge. The sensitively sited Ludgate Hill bridge was designed by Joseph Cubitt and F. T. Turner, joint engineers to the LCDR.

The Crystal Palace High Level branch from Peckham was brought into use on 1 August 1865; its construction required Crescent Wood Tunnel, 362 yd in length, and Crystal Palace, 430 yd.

LCDR finances were far from healthy, and in December 1864 a circular noted:

The position of the company having recently been the subject of much misrepresentation, the board think it incumbent on them to afford some information to the proprietors without waiting until the general meeting in February.

The authorised capital of the company is, in the opinion of the board, sufficient to complete all the company's works, including the junction with the Metropolitan, discharge all their liabilities and leave a surplus to meet demands for additional rolling stock and siding accommodation for increased traffic.

An arrangement has been made with the South Eastern, subject to confirmation by Parliament, by which the traffic of their whole system will, on payment of adequate tolls, obtain access over the Metropolitan Extension lines to Ludgate Hill station and thence over the City Junction to the Metropolitan at Farringdon Street and the Great Northern and Midland and King's Cross. The arrangement also embraces the provision of additional accommodation at Farringdon Street for the South Eastern, at their cost, upon land already acquired by this company.

The recent traffic receipts of the Metropolitan Extension have been represented as discouraging and tending to preclude any hope of adequate return upon the capital expended. Such representation is, in the judgment of the board, without any foundation; and it must be obvious to the proprietors that any opinion formed on the basis of existing traffic must be fallacious. The Metropolitan Extensions were designed to convey passengers, goods and minerals between the Great Northern, Midland, Great Western and Metropolitan, the south of London, the Kent coast, the South of England and the Continent. Therefore, until the last important link in this chain of communication is completed none of this vas traffic can be brought upon the lines of the company.

The failure on 10 May 1866 of Overend, Gurney & Co.'s bank following the tightening of credit had a severe effect on the LCDR. The contractors Peto & Betts had its liabilities secured against debentures issued by the LCDR (in lieu of payment for work, contractors had been given debentures at 75 per cent discount), thus the LCDR in turn went into receivership due to its reliance on that firm to finance its extensions.

An application was made in Chancery for the appointment of a receiver and manager, so Forbes, the manager, and W. E. Johnson, secretary, were jointly appointed. The directors assigned to certain creditors the rolling stock, plant and movable chattels, to prevent their seizure by special creditors.

The half-yearly report issued that summer explained to shareholders that the causes of the trouble were:

a) The delay in the completion of the Metropolitan Extensions and the City and Victoria station works beyond the period originally fixed, which had thus postponed the receipt of income and aggravated the amount of interest;
b) The increased cost of the Metropolitan and City lines;
c) The state of the money market;
d) The very heavy working expenses required for the efficient conduct of the traffic, coupled with the incompleteness of the line.

A sequel to this was the Arrangements Act of 1867, which granted exceptional powers for raising capital, provided for the claims of creditors and debenture holders, gave a moratorium of ten years, and allowed for the creation of three classes of debenture stocks.

The scheme proved satisfactory and receipts were £168,175 in 1866, £219,842 in 1867 and £231,062 in 1868. The LSWR was rewarded for having advanced money for the Metropolitan Extensions when from 3 April 1866 its trains from Kingston via Clapham ran to Ludgate Hill.

The Great Northern Railway was similarly rewarded for its £300,000 by being allowed to inaugurate, from 1 March 1868, a service to and from Victoria via Brixton.

The line from Nunhead on the Crystal Palace branch to Greenwich was opened as far as Blackheath Hill on 18 September 1871 and reached Greenwich Park 1 October 1888.

Holborn Viaduct station opened on 2 March 1874 with four platforms, each 400 ft in length. On 1 August 1874 a low-level station, Snow Hill, opened at the foot of a 1 in 39 incline. Renamed Holborn Viaduct Low Level, it closed 1 June 1916. Holborn Viaduct Hotel opened 17 November 1877.

Holborn Viaduct, although on one of London's main arteries, was so hidden by the hotel that a casual passer-by almost missed its existence. Inside, it was quadrilateral with a very narrow neck and the sides were bounded by walls that hid most of the daylight that might reach the station. From the south of London it was easily the nearest City station and also nearest to the main northern termini of Euston, King's Cross and St Pancras and so was very convenient for passengers from the north of England travelling to the continent.

The Franco-German War affected the LCDR's continental traffic, with receipts down £28,000 in the second half of 1870, but when it was over traffic increased considerably. Due to a shortage of rolling stock on the French railways, the LCDR and the SER each loaned the Northern Railway of France twenty passenger coaches to accommodate the Anglo-French traffic.

In 1871 some 70 lb/yd iron rails were replaced with 84 lb/yd steel rails. At the end of 1873, when the first Signal Arrangements Return was made, all its 134 miles of double track were equipped with the block system while by 1889 all signal boxes were fitted with interlocking.

W. R. Sykes who had been appointed the LCDR's signalling engineer in 1863, devised the 'lock-and-block' whereby the block instrument could be interlocked with the signals. Train wheels activated treadles to prove that trains had passed through a section and signals placed at danger before a further train could be accepted. Four Board of Trade inspectors, Captain Tyler, Colonel Yolland, Colonel Rich and General Hutchison were greatly in favour of a trial which took place at three consecutive boxes. Shepherd's Lane, Brixton and Canterbury Road. By September 1881 the line was so equipped to Faversham and to Dover by June 1882. In November 1883 Sykes installed fifty electrically operated shunting signals at the LDCR part of Victoria station, actuated by a small switch.

In 1874 the price of coal increased. This affected the LCDR in two ways: it increased running expenses of its locomotives and also reduced domestic consumption and as the Great Northern and the Midland conveyed coal over the LCDR to their depots in south London paying a toll for every ton carried, these tolls fell by £11,733 for the first half of 1874.

The Midland started running trains to Victoria on 1 July 1875. As mentioned earlier, in 1875 the SER and the LCDR almost amalgamated.

On 15 May 1876 boat expresses were run to and from Sheerness connecting with the Flushing steamers, a station being provided on Queenborough pier reached by extending the existing branch.

In 1878 the LCDR brought into service the PS *Calais-Douvre*. In an attempt to combat seasickness it had twin hulls with the paddle wheels in between and its fore and aft ends were identical. Her speed was a relatively slow 13 knots and her coal consumption proved excessive. Although popular with travellers, she was withdrawn in 1887.

The failure of the SER and LCDR to combine led to renewed competition, one line being the Dover to Deal railway, the first sod being cut by Earl Granville, Lord Warden of the Cinque Ports, on 29 May 1878. Despite requiring the cutting of the 1,425 yd long Guston tunnel, the line opened 15 June 1881.

The LCDR attempted to capture some of the passenger traffic on the Thames at Gravesend, and to this end on 10 May 1886 opened a line from Fawkham to Gravesend West Street where a pier was erected, thus scoring over the SER, whose station was some distance from the river. It was not successful as the London, Tilbury & Southend Railway's fare at a halfpenny a mile retained most of the traffic and only a few steamers used the LCDR's pier.

Also on 10 May 1886 St Paul's station, renamed Blackfriars 1 February 1937, was opened, reached by a seven-road bridge with five spans. The opening of St Paul's caused Holborn Viaduct to lose traffic.

In 1885 the LCDR put forward a bill for a union with the LBSCR, but the latter objected. A greater legal fight started in 1886 with the SER regarding the Continental Agreement. The SER claimed that Queenborough was outside the agreement as it did not lie between Margate and Hastings. The LCDR complained that Shorncliffe (now Folkestone West) was in Folkestone and not outside the agreement.

On 2 February 1886, regarding Queenborough, Mr Justice Chitty gave judgment in favour of the LCDR and in due course the verdict on Shorncliffe was also in favour of the LCDR.

1889 saw the introduction of a Club Train leaving London at 4.15 p.m., the French connection due in Paris at 11.15 p.m. First class only, with rolling stock supplied by the International Sleeping-Car Company, a supplementary fare of 16s was charged. It ran at a loss.

Associated with the Calais harbour improvements in 1889 was the declaration by the French government that French mails could only be carried in vessels built in France, flying a French flag with French owners and a French crew. It was ironic that in addition to the LCDR losing this traffic, as the Nord Railway had insufficient craft, initially some of the LCDR ships were borrowed.

By 1889, eighty-one engines and 44 per cent of LCDR coaches had been fitted with the Westinghouse brake.

On 1 July 1892 the line between Nunhead and Shortlands opened, giving an alternative to the line through Penge Tunnel which was sub-standard in width and required special rolling stock.

In July 1894 a bill was passed giving authority to the LCDR and the SER to enter into a pact for sharing competitive traffic not covered by the Continental Agreement. The measure came into force on 1 January 1895 and because there was no longer any competition, fares rose on some routes.

Legal measures to unite the two companies began in 1899, and from 1 January 1899, in anticipation of Parliament granting powers, the two systems were worked as one. The South Eastern and London, Chatham &

Dover (Working Union) Act received royal assent on 1 August 1899. The two companies retained a separate existence but were under the South Eastern & Chatham Railway Companies Managing Committee (SECR). This comprised nine members under a chairman, who was the SER chairman, and a deputy, who was the LCDR chairman. Revenue was pooled and divided 59 per cent to the SER and 41 per cent to the LCDR.

Accidents

Due to its efficient signalling, the LCDR was generally free of serious accidents, so its sobriquet of 'Undone, Smash 'em & Turnover' was inappropriate. The worst accident occurred at Sittingbourne on 31 August 1878. A heavily laden excursion from the Kent Coast to London struck goods wagons from a Down train which were destined for Queenborough. The Up line was signalled Clear for the passenger train, but the guard pulled the wrong lever and sent the wagons to the Up line in front of the express The driver reversed his engine and braked. The ensuing collision derailed the engine and tender but the first two thirds and the first-class coaches were smashed, resulting in five deaths and forty injuries. It happened due to lack of interlocking between points and signals.

On 31 August 1891 an accident occurred at Ramsgate with an empty train; had it been full the accident would have been disastrous. A train of Great Northern Railway coaches left Margate to form an Up return excursion and was hauled by a LCDR engine running tender first. The GNR coaches were fitted with the vacuum brake. The LCDR engine was dual fitted, but unfortunately had no vacuum pipe at its front end so was unable to operate the brakes. Even more unfortunately, the driver was unaware of this fact.

The approach to Ramsgate station was through a tunnel on a descending gradient of 1 in 75. The train ran out of control and crashed through a wall into the street. The crew jumped clear, but a hawker in the street was killed by the falling wall and others were injured. The engine crossed the road, passed through a shed and dropped into a saw pit.

16

LCDR LOCOMOTIVES, COACHING STOCK & STEAMERS

When opened in 1858 the EKR was worked by contractors' engines and six 2-2-2s hired from the Great Northern Railway. The first new engines were long-boilered Cramptons, some 2-4-0s and others 4-2-0s, the latter having old-fashioned bogies without side-play. When William Martley, formerly the GWR's locomotive superintendent for south Wales, became locomotive superintendent in 1860, he rebuilt most of them as ordinary 2-4-0s with inside cylinders and double frames. Engines merely bore names, but when William Kirtley, nephew of Matthew Kirtley of the Midland Railway, became superintendent in 1874, he added numbers on buffer beams and the rears of tenders, the names being removed when the engines were again rebuilt, the LCDR being short of cash.

In 1861 six 2-4-0s were purchased from the Dutch Rhenish Railway; these had been built by Sharp, Stewart in 1856. Also in 1861 two 0-4-2 mixed traffic engines constructed by Sharp, Stewart & Co. as part of an order for the Glasgow & South Western Railway to the design of Patrick Stirling. They were named *Brigand* and *Corsair*, but these appellations had nothing to do with the operations of the LCDR in extracting excessive fares from their passengers. The names came from Daniel Gooch's first two broad-gauge tank engines, Martley having been one of Gooch's pupils.

In 1862 five 4-2-0s were built by Stephenson's to the Crampton design of having the driving wheels set towards the rear of the firebox and a gap of 15 ft 2 in. between the centre of the bogie and the driving wheel centres. The inside cylinders drove a wheelless crank axle to which coupling rods connected with the driving wheel. Proving unsuccessful, Martley rebuilt them with a pair of wheels on the crank axle and substituting outside for inside frames. These were some of the earliest engines in the country of this wheel arrangement with inside cylinders. They carried out most of their work on continental mail expresses between London and Dover.

There was also a class of 2-4-0s some built by Sharp, Stewart & Co. and a similar class by Peto, Brassey & Betts. Both had Cudworth's patent fireboxes with long sloping grates and mid-feather partitions.

In 1863 0-4-2 side tanks appeared, the LCDR being one of the first lines in the country to use tank engines for suburban work. In 1866 0-4-2WTs came on the scene with an Adams' radial truck 11 ft 9 in. behind the last set of coupled wheels. That same year six fine goods 0-6-0s were supplied by John Fowler & Co. In 1866 the 0-4-2T Scotchmen appeared, so called because they were named after Scottish rivers and islands. They were Archibald Sturrock's Great Northern design.

The period from 1869 to 1870 saw three 2-4-0s constructed by the LCDR at its own Longhedge Works. The first was named *Enigma*, Martley stating that it was a puzzle how the engine ever reached completion, work on it having been stopped so frequently due to lack of finances.

Almost without exception LCDR express engines had 6 ft 6 in. driving wheels, whereas the SER favoured a 7 ft diameter. Nevertheless, the speed of LCDR expresses was generally higher than that of the SER owing to the absence of the 60 mph speed restriction on the latter line.

In 1873 the larger 0-4-2T Albion class appeared. They were principally employed on the service from Victoria to Moorgate Street, then onwards over the Metropolitan Extension to Wood Green on the Great Northern and Hendon on the Midland. They also worked on the Crystal Palace service. In order to equalise expenses, just as LCDR engines worked to Wood Green and Hendon, so Great Northern and Midland engines worked to Victoria.

Martley's last engines were the Europa class, four being built in 1873 by Sharp, Stewart and two in 1876 at Longhedge. They worked the continental mails between Victoria and Dover for many years. They also headed the Victoria to Queenborough Pier boat expresses.

These six engines were the only LCDR engines fitted with the Westinghouse brake.

That the LCDR was not generally loved by its passengers is shown when in 1877 the MP for Whitstable, referring to the LCDR, stated in the Commons:

> Its trains are formed of unclean cattle trucks propelled at snail-like speeds with frequent stops of great length by Machiavellian locomotives of monstrous antiquity held together by pieces of wire, rusty bolts and occasionally by lengths of string, which clanked, groaned, hissed and oozed a scalding conglomeration of oil, steam and water from every pore.

In 1878 the time allowed for the 74 miles from Herne Hill to Dover was 94 minutes, making an average speed of 47¼ mph, a good performance by the Europa class considering that only 18 miles were easier than 1 in 200. Trains averaged ten to twelve coaches. The main train started from Victoria, but a tank engine worked a portion from Holborn Viaduct to Herne Hill, where it was attached to the Victoria portion.

Dover expresses were equipped with the Westinghouse brake, whereas the seaside expresses had to manage with handbrakes until the end of the 1880s.

Foxwell, in *Express Trains*, published in 1888, wrote:

> The little Chatham and Dover is to be praised for the spirited way which it runs over its hilly route. But during a great part of the year it is wasting its substance on the seven Dover expresses, while duplicates of these are running at identical times on the South Eastern. These 14 Dover expresses merely divide, and do not breed, any Continental traffic; for none of them are third-class, and the fares are excessive.

William Kirtley's first engines were 0-4-4Ts, and when they appeared they were the most powerful passenger tank engines in the country. For forty years they worked the Metropolitan services from Victoria to Moorgate Street and to Midland and Great Northern stations as well as those to Crystal Palace.

In 1877, 4-4-0s appeared. Only occasionally did they haul the fastest trains, chiefly being utilised on the heavier seaside trains to Margate and Ramsgate. They ran between Herne Hill and Margate at an average speed of 43.8 mph. On two occasions in 1896 one of Kirtley's later 4-4-0s ran the 78 miles between Victoria and Dover in the remarkable time of 83 minutes, giving an excellent average speed of 56½ mph while it must be remembered that there were difficulties in getting up speed in the crowded London suburban area and the Rochester curve had to be taken easily.

Early carriages were four-wheeled vehicles, later ones being 25 ft in length with four compartments, second-class coaches being the same dimensions but with five compartments.

About 1875, Messrs Mann operated a Palace Car between Victoria and Dover. It contained four sections: drawing room saloon, smoking saloon, small family saloon and a honeymoon compartment for two.

When the LSWR, LBSCR and the SER companies chose the electric bell for passengers to raise the alarm, the LCDR used the emergency cord system, awkwardly running it along the bottom of its coaches, passengers having to grope through a hole in the floor – perhaps a difficult task if you were being assaulted.

LCDR Steamers

In 1862, steamers were purchased for the Dover–Calais service. In 1875, the Queenborough–Flushing route to the continent offered an overnight crossing with the hope that passengers could fall asleep on the quiet Thames before the possible roughness of the North Sea.

17

THE SOUTH EASTERN & CHATHAM JOINT COMMITTEE

As noted before, the working union between the SER and the LCDR came into operation on 1 January 1899 in anticipation of parliamentary sanction, which was obtained on 1 August 1899. Alfred Willis was appointed general manager and H. S. Wainwright was locomotive, carriage and wagon superintendent. One result of the union was the introduction of through expresses from Victoria to Hastings via Sevenoaks.

The Sheppey Light Railway opened from Queenborough to Leysdown on 1 August 1901 and was absorbed on 3 October 1903.

London Bridge to New Cross was widened in 1902, and the low-level station at London Bridge reconstructed to be used by passenger trains again. A new station opened 1 October 1902 at Southwark Park just east of the site of the original Corbett's Lane Junction and at the same location as Commercial Docks opened July 1856 and closed 1 January 1867. Southwark Park station closed 15 March 1915.

The Purley–Kingswood branch was extended to Tattenham Corner on 4 June 1901 when a station with six platforms and three middle roads was erected to cater for the Epsom race traffic. On 1 June 1902 the Crowhurst–Bexhill branch was opened.

On 17 July 1903 Chislehurst Tunnel was closed due to a new tunnel under construction causing damage. Due to the union of the two companies, the alternative route could be used. The tunnel was reopened on 3 November 1903. The new tunnel was part of the widened lines between St John's and Orpington, these works completed June 1905. It enabled heavy trains between Victoria and Dover to use the more easily graded SER route east of Orpington and heavier locomotives could not be utilised as many of the underbridges on the Chatham route were of light construction.

In July 1904 Dover became a port of call for the Atlantic liners and the railway was able to offer increased accommodation.

The through service between the Great Northern line and Victoria via the Metropolitan Extension was discontinued on 1 October 1907, the corresponding Midland service being withdrawn 1 July 1908.

In connection with the Cunard liners, in 1912 special continental boat expresses were run between Fishguard Harbour and Dover Pier, thus offering passengers for the continent a faster journey than if they remained on the steamer. As the last sailing to France from Dover was at 10.30 p.m., a train only ran if this connection could be made.

In August 1912 Ben Adams, driver of B class 4-4-0 No. 34, working one of these trains, was severely reprimanded and fined two pounds for running from Redhill to Ashford in 44½ minutes instead of the booked 52. He said: 'It was such a lovely evening with all the signals showing for miles ahead that I let the old girl have her head.'

In 1911 the decision was made to concentrate locomotive building and repair at Ashford and close the former LCDR works at Longhedge. On 1 May 1911 the Flushing night service was transferred from Queenborough to Folkestone.

Dover Marine station with two island platforms each 700 ft in length and 60 ft wide, was opened in December 1914. Its customs room was 360 ft long with 530 ft of benches for baggage. The station was rapidly finished in order to cater for ambulance trains. Two vessels and six hospital trains could be dealt with simultaneously. From December 1914 until February 1919 4,076 hospital ships containing a total of 1,260,506 wounded, and 7,781 hospital trains were dealt with at Dover. Some ambulance trains from Dover travelled to Sidcup where a large hospital was set up, others going on to Charing Cross. Forces' leave trains and mail used Victoria. During the First World War 14,871 special Forces' leave trains ran from Dover or Folkestone to Victoria and vice versa, while military mail was dealt with at Victoria and carried to Folkestone, requiring the use of about thirty covered goods wagons each night. Civil mail to and from the continent travelled via Southampton. In 1918 Cannon Street was closed to passengers outside the rush hours and used for the transfer of goods trains from the Midland and Great Northern railways.

Being so close to Westminster, during the First World War Charing Cross kept a special train constantly ready for VIP journeys usually consisting of a Pullman car and brake composite. It made 283 trips. From late October 1914 a lookout was posted on Hungerford Bridge to watch for Zeppelins, and if one was spotted no trains were allowed on the bridge.

On 19 December 1915 abnormally high rainfall caused a landslip near Warren Halt between Folkestone and Dover, in some places the line moving as much as 160 ft. The strata at Folkestone Warren are soft chalk on blue clay – this proved an unstable combination and at exceptionally wet periods watchmen were posted. On 19 December 1915 at about 6.50 p.m. a railway watchman heard a rumbling near the east portal of the 1,596 ft long Martello Tunnel. Aware that an Ashford to Dover train was due, he summoned help from soldiers at a nearby sentry post. Imaginatively they tied red flags round oil lamps and walked along the subsiding line towards the tunnel.

While still in the tunnel, the driver saw these makeshift warning lights and brought it to a standstill outside. The 130 passengers on board felt the coaches moving on the shifting ground, the train ending up looking like a fairground rollercoaster. Passengers walked back through the tunnel to Folkestone Junction station. Near Folkestone Warren Halt, a strip of land almost half a mile in width moved towards the sea, the halt itself shifting 53 yd.

The signalman at Abbot's Cliff signal box was alerted by a platelayer who warned him to stop all trains. Minutes later he reappeared to warn him to leave the box as the cliff was moving. It was just as well he did for within moments the box was swept away. The train was recovered within a few days but damage to the line was so serious – and as during the First World War the railways came under the control of a government unwilling to spend money and manpower repairing the line – nothing was done and it remained closed for the rest of the First World War and only reopened on 11 August 1919 at a cost of £250,000. 82,000 yd of earth and chalk had to be removed.

The SECR proved a vital link in the war effort, possessing the two shortest cross-Channel routes, and with valuable links at London with the Great Northern, Great Eastern, Midland, London & North Western and Great Western railways, while there was an additional junction with the Great Western at Reading using a line which avoided London. The company served Woolwich Arsenal, other munitions works, ports and dockyards. Large numbers of wounded and refugees arrived at Dover and when that town was full they were received at Folkestone. On 14 October 1914, 26,000 Belgians landed in just one week.

A new military port was created at Richborough from where 9,644 barges were taken across the Channel right into the French canals serving the battlefields. As Dover and Folkestone were under strain, Sir Eric Geddes, former North Eastern Railway manager, was appointed to assess the transport situation. He recommended the expansion of the new port at Richborough which eventually had 65 miles of track. By 10 February 1918 a roll-on, roll-off train ferry operated from Richborough to Calais and Dunkirk carrying various war supplies including locomotives, rolling stock, tanks and heavy guns on their own mountings. The three train ferries each carried ten Railway Operating Division 2-8-0s or fifty-four wagons. The train ferry proved a much faster method than loading by crane. In the inter-war period the SR missed an opportunity to utilise this rail link.

During the First World War some former running lines were used for stabling – for example the Greenwich Park branch was closed to passenger traffic and used for holding wagons loaded with war material awaiting inspection. The line between Welling and Bexleyheath was worked as a single line while the other roads held coal wagons and following the landslip between Folkestone and Dover, the undamaged section was used for stabling over a hundred wagons of explosives in Shakespeare Tunnel.

Some vessels from the company's fleet became seaplane carriers or minesweepers, while its workshops made shell parts, ambulance stretchers and railway wagons for the war effort. Some 5,222 employees joined up and 556 gave their lives.

On 24 September 1918, disaster overtook the troop ship *Onward* in Folkestone Harbour. Shortly after the servicemen disembarked, smoke was spotted issuing from the ventilators and the alarm was given. Despite rapid action by naval firefighting teams the blaze quickly spread throughout the ship, and to save the harbour installations it became necessary to open the seacocks. As *Onward* filled with water and settled on the harbour bed, she developed a severe list which increased until she was lying on her port side with the funnels and mast protruding across the harbour.

SECR 0-4-0ST No. 313 had been used by the port authorities to haul wagons of equipment clear of the blazing vessel and had been left standing just clear of the vessel's bow when the cocks were opened. As *Onward* listed away from the quay, the mooring ropes parted and one became entangled around No. 313. The wire slowly dragged No. 313 towards the harbour, and but for the presence of mind of her crew, who severed the wire with a cold chisel, she would probably have ended up aboard the scuttled ship.

In due course salvage operations were carried out, *Onward* not only having to be floated but returned to an even keel. To achieve this, compressed air was pumped in while four locomotives on the quay, two 0-6-0s and two 0-6-0Ts, exerted a steady pull and succeeded in dragging her upright.

As early as 1903 the SECR realised the benefits to be gained from electrification and obtained powers for carrying this out, but it was unable to raise the necessary capital. In September 1919 Alfred Raworth reported to the SECR board proposing the elimination of steam by the use of electric locomotives. To minimise the number of substations required it selected the third and fourth rail system at 3,000 volts. In 1920 this was amended and 1,500 volts DC delivered through a third rail. The Trade Facilities Act of 1921 enabled the Treasury to guarantee for twenty-five years the principal and interest on £6½ million, of which £5 million was for the actual electrification and the balance for the power house. For efficiency, the Electricity Commissioners ruled that power be obtained from the London Electric Supply Corporation.

At the end of 1922 the route length of the SECR was 638 miles, 65 of this being single, 573 double, 40 miles with a third track, 29 miles with a fourth and 23 miles with over four tracks. During its existence it had improved punctuality, strengthened bridges, installed heavier rails and replaced shingle ballast with Kentish stone.

Accidents

A curious mishap occurred in March 1900 to the Whitstable Harbour to Canterbury West coal train. As William Atkins, a farm worker, had missed a passenger train and did not wish to wait an hour and a half for the next, he begged the guard for a lift in his van. In due course the train stopped to set Atkins down, the guard taking the opportunity to move forward and join the engine crew on the footplate.

Unfortunately, as the train moved off Atkins stumbled and his thick leather belt lassoed the van's coupling hook. He managed to get his legs over a buffer, but was unable to free himself and his shouts for help were unheard until the train stopped at Canterbury. In due course the driver and guard were severely reprimanded and fined £4 each.

In October 1912 a similar incident occurred. As the Maidstone West to Bricklayers' Arms goods was leaving the sidings at Paddock Wood, Shunter Percy Brown was collecting his pole from across the front buffers of the engine just when the 'Right away' was given. In his haste he slipped on a greasy sleeper and fell, his leather belt catching in the engine's coupling hook. His shouts were not heard but the signalman at Tudeley spotted him and showed a red light. The incident inspired the company to issue a circular warning employees of the danger of wearing thick belts.

The first fifteen years of the SECR passed without an accident involving the death of a passenger, but on 25 October 1913 three were killed when two passenger trains collided in dense fog at Waterloo Junction station.

On 21 August 1922 the guard waved a train off from Gravesend and the driver opened up without checking that the signals were clear. He struck the rear of a train at Milton Range Halt, fatally injuring three of its passengers.

On 27 December 1922 a ship collided with the Swale opening bridge at Sheerness and put it out of use. Both railway and road communication between Sittingbourne and Sheerness was closed until partially restored on 1 October 1923, and fully on 1 November 1923.

18

SECR LOCOMOTIVES, ROLLING STOCK & STEAMERS

As there was a serious shortage of locomotive power early in 1900, the company purchased five 4-4-0s built by Neilson, Reid & Co. which had been intended for the Great North of Scotland Railway. In May 1900 the first of Wainwright's engines, a C class 0-6-0, appeared. At the end of 1900, fifteen R1 0-4-4Ts appeared in an improved R class. In 1904 Ashford constructed H class 0-4-4Ts.

Wainwright's D class 4-4-0s first appeared in 1901, some built by private builders and others constructed at Ashford. In 1915, his E class 4-4-0s emerged with Belpaire fireboxes, smaller wheels and larger cylinders.

Wainwright designed two rail motors for use on the Sheppey Light Railway and the Hundred of Hoo branch. Initially No. 1 had 'Sheppey Light Railway' on the cant rails, but this was soon painted out and replaced with standard SECR lettering. Kitson & Co. constructed the engine units and the Metropolitan Carriage & Wagon Co. the carriage portions. They entered traffic in 1904. In 1905 six more were built, Kitson's providing the 0-4-0T engines, which had their boilers in the normal position, and Oldbury Carriage & Wagon Co. supplying the carriage portions. Unusually for rail motors, they had Belpaire fireboxes. Initially the engine units were painted lake to match the coachwork, but they were soon given the locomotive green and the dome covers polished brass. All doors were recessed and footsteps for low-level platforms fixed. The cars were electrically lit. The Oldbury cars had drop lights fitted with three bars to prevent passengers leaning out as clearance on some lines was limited. In addition to the branches mentioned above, rail motors also ran on the Sandgate, Hayes, Westerham and Dungeness branches.

Around 1911 the services worked by rail motors were changed and they began to be seen between Ramsgate and Birchington, Deal and Minster, Bickley and Orpington, and Appledore and New Romney. Traffic on some branches grew, causing rail motors to be replaced by ordinary trains. No special trailers were constructed but if necessary an ordinary six-wheeled coach was attached.

All rail motors were out of service by late 1914, having been superseded by push-pull trains worked by P class 0-6-0Ts. The rail motors were stored away, some in a siding at Sidley and others in a tunnel outside Greenwich Park station. All were broken up between 1917 and 1923, the coach portions being converted to push-pull sets.

H. S. Wainwright retired in November 1913 and was replaced by E. L. Maunsell, who had been locomotive superintendent of the Great Southern and Western of Ireland.

Ten L class 4-4-0s had been ordered from the German firm of Borsig. They were delivered in May 1914 and the contract stated that they were on three months' trial before payment. The period expired on 8 August 1914, four days after war was declared! Payment was not made until 1920, when the bill was settled with interest. These engines had arrived just in time because the SECR was desperately short of locomotives and to help with the war effort had to borrow fifteen E class 2-4-0s from the Great Northern, fifteen B class 0-6-0s from the Hull & Barnsley and six K8 2-8-0s from the Great Eastern.

As runs were under 80 miles, Maunsell decided that only two designs were necessary: a 2-6-4T for express passenger working and a 2-6-0 for goods. With this in mind he designed the N class 2-6-0s, which were so successful that in the post-war period, to alleviate unemployment, locomotives of this design were built at Woolwich. His other class, the K 2-6-4T, were similar, but as they proved unsteady they were rebuilt as U class 2-6-0 tender engines.

In May 1899, Craven Bros supplied several trains of eight four-wheeled close-coupled coaches electrically lighted including the tail lamps. After experiments were carried out, the teak livery of the LCDR was abandoned and all passenger vehicles were painted in the SER claret.

On 21 March 1910 Pullman cars were introduced on the Dover Continental expresses. Under Wainwright, although there were corridors to lavatories, there were no gangways between coaches. Following his resignation, new stock built in 1921 for its continental trains had corridor stock for the first time.

Steamer Services

As the SER had no parliamentary powers to run steamer services, in August 1845 a subsidiary company, the South Eastern and Continental Steam Packet company, was formed to run steamers from Dover and Folkestone to Calais, Boulogne and Ostend. In 1853 the SER obtained the necessary powers and purchased eight of the continental company's vessels.

In 1896 it was decided to withdraw the small ships, some over thirty years old, from the night services and replace with those of modern design. The three new ships, with triple expansion engines capable of 19.65 knots, were extremely economical. By 1898 the Northern of France ran the morning mails, the LCDR taking the midday and night services. With the fusion of the SER and LCDR in 1899, the old boats were laid aside and only the modern ones retained.

As the Parsons turbine proved economical the SECR ordered the turbine steam *Queen*. On her trials she steamed at 21.76 knots and could be brought to a dead stop in 1 minute 7 seconds. She gathered way from rest more quickly than the paddle steamers. The result was that four more were ordered, while in 1911 two larger vessels joined the fleet.

There is no record of passengers being lost in accidents to railway steamers on the Dover or Folkestone routes, which is excellent considering that many journeys were made in storm or fog.

19

THE SOUTHERN RAILWAY

The Railways Act of 19 August 1921 stated that the railways of Great Britain were to be amalgamated into four groups. Each new company would have constituent companies and smaller absorbed companies.

The SR had five constituent companies: the LBSCR, LCDR, LSWR, SER and the South Eastern & Chatham Railway Companies' Managing Committee – though the latter should not have been included as it was not a company with stockholders.

Each company held a special meeting to approve the proposal, the LBSCR on 16 November 1922, the LSWR the following day. The SER and LCDR accepted on 13 December 1922 after considerable opposition.

Statistics of the Principal Companies

LSWR

Total length of single track, including sidings: 2,382 miles
Locomotives: 931
Coaching vehicles: 4,061
Goods vehicles:14,563

LBSCR

Single track: 1,265
Locomotives: 615

Coaching vehicles: 2,604
Goods vehicles: 10,357

SECR
Single track: 1,302 miles
Locomotives: 724
Coaching vehicles: 3,805
Goods vehicles: 11,461

IOWCR
Single track: 35 miles
Locomotives: 9
Coaching vehicles: 47
Goods vehicles: 322

Subsidiary companies allocated to the SR were the Bridgwater; Brighton & Dyke; Freshwater, Yarmouth & Newport; Hayling; Isle of Wight; Isle of Wight Central; Lee-on-the-Solent; London & Greenwich; Mid-Kent (Bromley to St Mary Cray); North Cornwall; Plymouth & Dartmoor; Plymouth, Devonport & South Western Junction; Sidmouth; and Victoria Station & Pimlico undertakings.

In 1923, parliamentary powers were obtained to acquire the 1 ft 11½ in. gauge Lynton & Barnstaple Railway – being narrow gauge, it was outside the 1922 Act. The SR also obtained powers to hold jointly with the London, Midland & Scottish Railway the Somerset & Dorset Joint line, as joint lines were also outside the Act.

The last lines to be absorbed were the Lee-on-Solent and the Freshwater, Yarmouth & Newport. The former had liabilities exceeding £14,000 which the SR did not wish to take over. The cases came before the Railways Amalgamation Tribunal and the SR was ordered to take over these lines. The Brighton & Dyke line went to the Court of Appeal and the SR had to take it over.

The SR commenced business on 1 January 1923. It had 2,178 miles of first track, 4,175 miles of running line, 1,205 miles of siding, 2,281 locomotives, 7,500 passenger vehicles, 36,749 wagons, 41 steam vessels and 11 hotels. It took over 56.8 route miles of third-rail electrification from the LSWR, 24.6 miles of overhead from the LBSCR and 1.5 miles of the Waterloo & City tube.

In 1923 the SR took over 464 vehicles for use in electric trains:

LBSCR	South London line stock	30
	Crystal Palace stock	104
LSWR	3-coach motor sets	252
	2-coach motor sets	48
Waterloo & City tube cars		30

The first board meeting of the SR, held on 4 January 1923, saw eight directors from the LSWR, five from the LBSCR, five from the SER and five from the LCDR. Sir Hugh Drummond, the LSWR's chairman, was elected the SR chairman.

Sir Herbert Walker (LSWR), Sir Percy Crosland Tempest (SECR) and Sir William Forbes (LBSCR) retained their positions by being appointed joint general managers. The last two soon retired and from 1 January 1924 Sir Herbert Walker was in sole charge. R. E. L. Maunsell (SECR) was appointed chief mechanical engineer and A. W. Szlumper (LSWR) chief engineer.

The SR was divided into three sections, Western, Central and Eastern, formed from the LSWR, LBSCR and SECR respectively.

The LSWR had been the first railway in Britain to adopt the automatic telephone system when in 1921 a fifty-line system was installed at Waterloo and in 1923 a 300-line system was provided at Southampton Docks.

An immense floating dock at Southampton, capable of lifting a ship of 60,000 tons, was opened by the Prince of Wales on 27 June 1924.

The amalgamation brought improvements, one being that in January 1924 a start was made on removing the divisions between the Brighton and Chatham side of Victoria. During the latter half of 1924, serious complaints were made of overcrowding and late-running trains. This resulted in management placing an advertisement in the principal daily papers stating what had been done in the First World War and the difficulties which the company had subsequently faced. This satisfied the public and complaints died out. The chairman, Brigadier-General the Hon. Everard Baring, explained at the annual general meeting on 27 February 1925 that one reason for the crowded trains was that hundreds of carriages had to be withdrawn from service in order to be converted for electric traction. Regarding late running he said that 93 per cent of trains had arrived on time or less than 5 minutes late and only 2 per cent over 5 minutes late. He also said that the company carried 26 per cent more passengers in 1923 than in 1913, and as an example of what the SR could do, a rugby match at Twickenham brought 30,000 spectators who had to be carried there during the Saturday rush hour.

In 1912 the SECR had started to strengthen its main-line bridges and the SR continued this work to allow the use of Maunsell's new King Arthur class 4-6-0s, which weighed 81 tons against the 51 tons of the 4-4-0s hitherto used on the continental expresses.

Electrification was proceeding with the line from Balham, through Streatham Common, Selhurst and East Croydon to Coulsdon North, and that from Selhurst through West Croydon and Wallington to Sutton opened on the overhead system on 1 April 1925. Train sets used consisted of a bogie motor luggage van without passenger accommodation (they were nicknamed 'milk vans'), set between two leading and two trailing coaches; the end of each outer vehicle had a driving compartment. Some were in SR green livery and others in the former LBSCR umber brown. Power at 6,700V AC single-phase, 25Hz, came from the London Electric Supply Corporation, fed in at New Cross Gate and conveyed to Gloucester Road Junction, Croydon. As the LBSCR had envisaged that in due course the line to Brighton would be electrified throughout, the overhead system was the best choice, whereas third rail was better for just a suburban system.

At the AGM in February 1925 the chairman observed that the company used two different electric traction systems – overhead on the Central Section and third rail for the Western and Eastern Sections – and as the systems were not interchangeable, the matter would need to be resolved. The solution announced on 9 August 1926 was the replacement of the overhead AC system by the DC third rail, on the grounds of the latter's ease of installation and low cost of construction and maintenance. It was decided that the planned extension of the elevated electric would go ahead but in due course the twenty-one motor vans for this would be converted into 27-ton bogie goods brake vans and the coaches suitably altered for third rail use. Alternating current trains were gradually withdrawn, the last running at 12.30 a.m. on 22 September 1929.

It was also resolved to adopt the LSWR standard of three-coach motor sets (motor car plus trailer plus motor car) and two-coach trailer sets. This offered three possible formations: a single three-coach train; two three-coach units coupled, or two three-coach units with an intermediate trailer unit. All three-coach motor units were close-coupled with side buffers and screw couplings only at the outer ends. Motor bogies had two nose-suspended, self-ventilated 275 hp motors. The controller handle was of the hold-down pattern.

With the abolition of the Elevated Electric, the SR, keen on recycling, used some of the girders formerly supporting the overhead wire as signal gantries, while others were used for roofing a new locomotive shed at Ryde, Isle of Wight, and others became lighting standards at carriage sidings. An erstwhile train shed from Exeter Queen Street was moved to become a drying shed for concrete castings manufactured at Exmouth Junction.

On 12 July 1925 electrification in the Western Section was Claygate to Guildford, Raynes Park to Dorking, and Leatherhead to Effingham Junction. Power came from Durnsford Road at 11,000V, three phase, 25Hz and substations converted it to direct current at 600V. Also on 12 July 1925 the Eastern Section started work on electrifying Victoria to Orpington, Holborn Viaduct to Herne Hill, Loughborough Junction to Shortlands (Catford Loop) and Nunhead to Crystal Palace (High Level). Power was obtained from the London Electric Supply Corporation.

An interesting proposal in 1925 was the Southern Heights Light Railway, a single-track light railway to be operated by standard SR electric stock. Powers lapsed in 1931.

By July 1925 the bridge-rebuilding programme enabled King Arthur class 4-6-0s to be used from Victoria to Dover via Tonbridge, while a year later they could work to Brighton, Eastbourne and Worthing.

Two light railways were opened in 1925, the first being that between Totton and Fawley which was opened 20 July 1925, the other being the North Devon & Cornwall Junction between Torrington and Halwill, which opened 27 July 1925.

In the autumn of 1925 the SR inaugurated a 1,000-line automatic telephone system. One advantage of this was that the operating superintendent could speak to all his divisional officers almost before the end of the morning peak and discover any delays.

One feature of the SR was the upgrading of stations, and at the SR's AGM on 26 February 1926 the chairman announced that forty-nine stations had been entirely reconstructed or substantially improved since the last meeting and work on forty others was in hand.

Colour-light signalling from Holborn Viaduct to Elephant & Castle was brought into use on 21 March 1926. It was the very first installation of four-aspect signalling in the world, the double-yellow warning that the next signal would be yellow giving a driver a better knowledge of the state of the line while the extra warning phase allowed more sections and thus greater line capacity. Some signals had the aspects arranged vertically, while others were in clusters, the latter placed where vertical aspects were unsuitable for drivers' viewing. Two new signal boxes replaced seven of the manual pattern.

Not all SR employees went on strike on 4 May 1926 in support of the miners, with 12,000 of the total of a workforce of 73,000 continuing work, and the railway did not come to a halt as employees and volunteers kept the trains running. This demonstrated to trade union leaders that the public was against them and that they were inflicting injury on their fellow workers. This resulted in the general strike ending on 12 May 1926, but it was not until 14 May 1926 that the railway companies agreed to their employees returning to work.

One result of the strike was that it was found that road transport was a viable alternative to rail; some firms who used road transport during the strike never returned to rail.

On 19 July 1926 electrified lines were opened from North Kent East Junction to Dartford, Lewisham to Charlton, Blackheath to Slades Green, and Hither Green to Dartford Junction. Carriage sheds for the electric stock were erected at Orpington and Addiscombe while the former engine shed at Slades Green was converted to an electric depot and a new building erected as a repair shop. It consisted of steel frames covered with corrugated asbestos sheets.

2 July 1926 marked a change to railways in the Margate and Ramsgate area. Competition between the SER and the LCDR had given rise to duplication, which could now be avoided. The two termini at Ramsgate were closed and a new line laid from a point south of Broadstairs to St Lawrence, thus permitting through running between Chatham and Ashford via these resorts. A station was built on this new line at Ramsgate and another at Dumpton Park.

The property of the Newhaven Harbour Commissioners was purchased in 1926, and in view of the development of the Kent coalfield the unissued capital of the East Kent Light Railway serving it was purchased. As an cost-saving measure the Folkestone to Flushing service was discontinued in 1926.

On 9 August 1926 it was announced that the next electrifications would be London Bridge to Norwood Junction, Sydenham to Crystal Palace (Low Level), Crystal Palace (Low Level) to Beckenham Junction, Putney to Caterham and Tattenham Corner, Herne Hill to Wimbledon, Streatham North Junction to Epsom, and Sutton to Epsom Downs.

About forty goods trains ran from the LNER and LMS to Hither Green sidings for exchange purposes. As they passed through Ludgate Hill, they could only run outside of the rush hours. It was obvious that if use could be made of the line through Elephant & Castle and Nunhead this would improve the situation and to facilitate this, a curve was installed from the Greenwich Park line to the St John's to Blackheath line, and another from Lewisham Junction to the Hither Green line. These connections also offered direct access between the West London Extension line and Hither Green and permitted the roughly twenty-five trains daily from the GWR and the LMS that formerly exchanged elsewhere to use Hither Green.

Although in 1876 the LBSCR had obtained powers to purchase Newhaven Harbour Board's property, these were not exercised. In 1926 the SR obtained powers to do so and replaced the timber east pier with a concrete structure.

In 1927 work started on quadrupling the line between Kent House and Beckenham Junction, this abolishing a bottleneck for Up boat trains that had hindered the development of electric services.

On 25 March 1928 electric trains commenced between London Bridge and Norwood Junction and Caterham, and Purley and Tattenham Corner, while Sutton–Epsom Downs opened 17 June 1928. Also on 17 June the Elevated Electric DC services were inaugurated between London Bridge and Coulsdon North and Norwood Junction, Sutton and Epsom Downs via Wallington. The AC Victoria–Crystal Palace line was converted to DC on 3 March 1929 and Victoria–Coulsdon North on 22 September 1929.

At the AGM on 6 March 1929 the chairman, Brigadier-General the Hon. Everard Baring, said that in 1928 306,673,000 passengers had been carried and in the electrified area passenger journeys had increased by 6 million. Depression in trade and competition from road transport had caused goods receipts to suffer, but reduced rates and better methods, including the use of containers, were improving matters. Meat traffic from Southampton to London, which had been lost to road, had been regained by the use of containers.

The Act of 3 August 1928 enabled the Big Four to own and operate road transport. The SR owned Southern National and Southern Vectis buses and had shares in Aldershot & District, Devon General Omnibus & Touring Company, East Kent Road Car, Hants & Dorset Motor Services, Maidstone & District Motor Services, Southdown Motor Services, Thames Valley Traction and Wilts & Dorset Motor Services. With the GWR, LMS and LNER, the SR had acquired Carter Paterson & Co. and Hays Wharf Cartage Co., including Pickfords Ltd. On 31 December 1930 Messrs Spiers & Pond's contract for catering on the Western and Eastern sections of the SR was terminated, Frederick Hotels Ltd, refreshment contractors for the steamers, securing the tender.

Between 1929 and 1939 the number of motor vans and lorries rose from 278 to 757, while in addition the SR owned 360 mechanical horses.

In 1929 the SR obtained power to run air services, but only in the Metropolitan Police District or areas served by SR lines. It could also work in co-operation with other railway companies. The Railway Air Services set up by the Big Four from 21 March 1934, on 30 July 1934, inaugurated a Birmingham–Bristol–Southampton–Cowes service and a London–Isle of Wight service from 20 August 1934, while in 1937 a joint service was worked with the GWR to the Channel Islands. The SR could claim the first railway airport station when one was opened at Shoreham on 1 July 1935, and Tinsley Green opened 30 September 1935, renamed Gatwick Airport on 1 June 1936.

In his 1929 budget the Chancellor of the Exchequer announced that the Railway Passenger duty levied on first- and second-class fares would be abolished on condition that the railway companies spent the capitalised value of the duty on improvement and development schemes to relieve unemployment. The SR decided to use the offer to electrify lines to Brighton and Worthing. The new signalling on the line was to be colour light. Electrification opened to Brighton 30 December 1932.

In November 1929 the SR and LMS decided to end running the Somerset & Dorset as a separate railway. Track maintenance became the responsibility of the SR, while the LMS took over motive power; coaching vehicles were divided between the two companies, while the wagon stock had been split already in 1914. The Somerset & Dorset Joint Committee continued with three directors from each company. The SR took responsibility for S&D ships, but not for long as this department was closed in 1934.

An important land reclamation scheme was started in June 1931, recovering 407 acres of mudland at Southampton and creating a new quay 7,400 ft in length. The new docks were opened by King George V on 26 July 1933.

On 30 April 1932 the SR made its last slip coach workings, the slip at Horley running through to Forest Row, and that at Hayward's Heath continuing as a slow train to Brighton. With the suburban electrification virtually complete, the first section of that to Brighton opened as far as Three Bridges on 17 July 1932 and the extension to Brighton and Worthing on 30 December 1932. Twenty-three six-coach multiple units were provided comprising five corridor coaches and one Pullman. Colour-light signalling was installed from Coulsdon to Brighton.

The south side of the Thames estuary failed to develop the popular resorts that had grown up on the north bank. When a development was proposed at All Hallows, the owners of the estate offered to give the land required for the 1¾-mile-long branch and contribute £20,000 towards its construction. It opened from Stoke Junction Halt on the Port Victoria branch on 16 May 1932. Unfortunately it did not prove popular and failed to become a second Westcliff-on-Sea.

Summer holiday traffic was heavy and as most people travelled on a Saturday this meant large crowds that day and not spread evenly through the week. As many passengers did not book tickets in advance, providing the correct number of coaches for various destinations required a certain amount of guesswork. On 4 August 1934, the

Saturday preceding the bank holiday, the SR conveyed from Waterloo about 70,000 passengers of whom only 23,000 had reserved their seats in advance. From Victoria 33,263 travelled to Brighton, 44,929 to the Kent coast and 10,538 to the continent. In all, 971,400 passengers left SR London termini in 2,538 trains. 41,929 used the Portsmouth-Ryde service, which also carried 553 cars.

Downsizing in the 1930s included either closure to passenger traffic, or complete closure, of several branch lines, including the narrow-gauge Lynton & Barnstaple. On the Chichester to Midhurst branch, the extensive station at Singleton, built to serve Goodwood race course, closed to passenger traffic 8 July 1936, the line remaining open for goods. Singleton had approximately three-quarters of a mile of sidings, which could hold fourteen trains of normal length, while the station buildings complete with refreshment rooms and the two island platforms, were a surprise to the casual visitor on days when races were not taking place.

On 29 June 1934 the Southern Belle all-Pullman train was renamed the Brighton Belle. Its riding left something to be desired as C. F. Klapper in *Sir Herbert Walker's Southern Railway* saw a lurch by a motor coach throw a cup of tea over a passenger's shoulder. That summer cheap evening return tickets were available from Victoria to Brighton at a fare of 4s 0d, with lower fares to the resort from East Croydon and Redhill.

The formal opening of the electrified Hastings line via Eastbourne took place on 4 July 1935. An important flyover, opened on 17 May 1936, enabled electric trains to approach any Wimbledon platform without conflicting with any other movement.

Keen on publicity, the SR was the first of the Big Four to set up a publicity department, and in addition to encouraging tourism they advertised housing developments with such posters as 'Live in Kent and be Content', or 'Live in Surrey free from Worry'. Booklets were printed such as 'Southern Homes in the Kentish Hills' and 'Southern Homes on the Conqueror's Coast', thus endeavouring to augment sales of season tickets. In the summer of 1929 the SR introduced weekly season tickets for holiday areas. The idea proved popular and in 1930 the issue was extended to cover twelve more areas.

On 25 and 26 January 1936, the SR, using seven steamers, ten special trains and thirteen special coaches attached to normal workings, conveyed four kings, a president, five princes and thirteen delegations to Victoria for the funeral of King George V. Due to the development of air transport, any similar travel by European crowned heads in the future is unlikely.

In 1932 news that the LNER was contemplating a Harwich–Calais train ferry meant that the SR had to take steps to combat this competition. On 13 October 1936 the Dover–Dunkirk train ferry began working *Wagons-Lits* sleeping cars between Victoria and Paris. Although in theory you could go to bed in London and wake in Paris, in reality the shunting of the cars on to the various roads on the ferry and then chaining them to the deck was likely to wake all but the most deep sleepers.

When the Waterloo–Portsmouth electrification opened 4 July 1937, Sir Herbert Walker considered electrifying the Hundred of Manhood & Selsey Tramway and also the Hayling Island branch.

In 1937, authorisation for upgrading the Waterloo & City tube was given. It included replacing rolling stock, cables, switchgear and signalling, welding rail joints, renewing and replacing the third rail in the standard position and introducing noise shields and pinch-wire communication between driver and substation.

On 3 July 1938 electrification reached Bognor Regis, while the formal opening to Reading was on 30 December 1938. The final pre-war electrification reached Gillingham and Maidstone, officially opened on 30 June 1939, giving the SR the world's largest suburban electric network.

Landowners and farmers were concerned about safety in rural areas. It was explained that fatalities due to electrification were few and only occurred to trespassers. Ten-wire fencing was used on electrified lines and wire mesh added where children or animals might get through. The conductor rail stopped where a footpath or occupation crossing passed over the line and wooden cattle grids were provided to prevent cattle straying from the crossing.

In 1938 the SR ran 46.7 million miles by steam at a cost of £3,079,000, while 37.47 million miles had been worked by electricity at £1,642,000. Wages for steam mileage was £1,668,000, but for electric only £327,000. The electricity cost £1,190,000 against £1,295,000 for coal and water.

The railways were well prepared for the Second World War. When hostilities seemed inevitable the Railway Executive Committee was formed on 24 September 1938, with Gilbert Szlumper representing the SR. Plans were prepared for mobilising troops, evacuating cities, taking air-raid precautions, working under blackout conditions, bringing privately owned wagons into common usage and providing ambulance trains. A wartime headquarters was set up at Deepdene, Dorking.

The order to begin the evacuation was given on 31 August 1939. To ease pressure on the SR termini, Richmond, Wimbledon and New Cross Gate were also used, seventy-five trains daily carrying children from London. In addition, twenty-seven trains daily moved children from the Medway towns, while 127 trains took 30,000 evacuees from Portsmouth, Gosport and Southampton.

From 1 September 1939 the Ministry of Transport took over; armed guards were placed at vital river crossings such as Charing Cross Bridge, while the Port of Dover was closed to civilians and Pullman and restaurant cars withdrawn. Some services were cancelled to allow stock to be used for evacuation trains.

To avoid being seen from the air, during the black-out no lights were to be shown externally, so windows had to be screened. Platform lighting was limited to blue electric lights, or enclosed gas lamps below verandas. Colour-light signals were fitted with long hoods and anti-glare sheets fixed between cab and tender to obscure firebox glow.

On 28 September 1939 a landslip occurred between Abbot's Cliff and Shakespeare tunnels. Reopened on 7 January 1940, a further fall occurred on 24 February 1940.

With the invasion of Holland, Belgium and France in May 1940 another evacuation was organised. Then the evacuation of 319,000 troops from Dunkirk between 27 May and 4 June 1940 required 327 trains from Dover, eighty-two from Ramsgate, seventy-five from Margate plus seventy-five ambulance trains; sixty-four trains left Folkestone and seventeen from Sheerness. The SR lost five vessels at Dunkirk and Dieppe.

For the first nine months of war, the Channel Islands were almost unaffected, railway ships carrying potatoes to England as usual. With the fall of France, it was obvious that the Channel Islands would be almost impossible to defend so evacuation was offered to women, children and men willing to join the armed forces. From 17 to 28 June, five SR cargo ships carried 8,000 from Jersey, 17,00 from Guernsey and 1,500 from Alderney. Despite the partial evacuation of the islands, the SR continued to operate a service. On 27 June 1940 the *Isle of Sark* was attacked at Guernsey. The ship was undamaged, but it was an indicator that the service should be withdrawn.

The SR, like the other main railway companies, set up Local Defence Volunteer Corps, later to become the Home Guard, to protect vulnerable railway facilities such as goods yards, tunnels, bridges and viaducts. Initially making do with makeshift weapons, they were later supplied with guns and ammunition; other railwaymen manned anti-aircraft batteries near marshalling yards and major stations.

Following the evacuation of Dunkirk it was believed that the beaches in North Devon near the mouth of the Taw offered potential sites for a German invasion. To assist the defence of this area it was decided to move Armoured Train F from Ashford, where it had been patrolling the Ashford–Hastings–Lewes line, to Barnstaple. Motive power was provided by ex-LNER F4 class 2-4-2T No. 7077. No spare engine was provided, but boiler washout and repair did not interfere with patrols. No. 7077 was maintained by SR staff at Barnstaple Junction shed, and the Royal Engineers provided a driver and fireman. By the spring of 1942, fears of the south-west peninsula being invaded had receded to such an extent that the armoured train was moved to Tilbury and left Barnstaple on 20 April 1942.

In the event of an air raid, on receipt of a Red warning, passenger trains were required to stop at the first station, allow any passengers who wished to step out to do so, and then proceed at not more than 15 mph. Goods trains were required to stop at the first signal box to receive instructions and then continue not in excess of 10 mph. As so many warnings were given in the summer and autumn of 1940, rail transport was chaotic, In July an extra warning, Purple, was added to indicate that enemy aircraft were in the vicinity and that all lights should be extinguished. Speed restrictions were eased in November 1940 and only at night were trains stopped and drivers instructed to proceed at not over 30 mph.

On 15 October 1940 a high-explosive bomb struck the west chimney of the Durnsford Road power house and damaged the boiler house so badly that its capacity was reduced by half, but 127 days later it was back on full power. On 1 January 1941 an electric train was bombed while at No. 4 platform, Portsmouth Harbour, and a gap blown in the viaduct on the landward side of the damaged coaches. They were left as they were until craned out in September 1946.

As in the poor visibility of the blackout it was impossible to ensure that first-class passengers obtained the accommodation for which they had paid, trains in the London area became third class only from 6 October 1941. This move also had the advantage of making the maximum use of the available accommodation. Indications on the doors were painted out and rugs removed from the compartments. Knowledgeable travellers then sought out ex-first-class compartments where they could avail themselves of more luxurious accommodation and greater legroom.

At Dunkirk, seventy-nine British locomotives fell into German hands. As these needed to be replaced and more engines were required to help with the war effort, the Railway Executive Committee ordered 400 LMS class 8F 2-8-0s from the Big Four, the SR building no less than 130. In 1940, Brighton works, which had been threatened with closure was re-equipped in order to repair locomotives in the event of damage to other works, while in 1942 it commenced building 93 LMS Class 8F 2-8-0s for use by all the Big Four.

To avoid damage to rolling stock, some was dispersed overnight to safe places – Brighton stock was removed to Kemp Town Tunnel and likewise at Dover to a nearby tunnel. Deliberate bombing by the enemy did not cause very serious damage, but some of the worst effects were just unlucky chance. On 19 April 1941, a parachute mine destroyed the Southward Street Bridge, severing eight roads, while in May 1943 a bouncing bomb wrecked a pier and two arches of the viaduct at Brighton. A German bomber crashed on the roof of Victoria station. The official report read, 'Many important missions have arrived at Victoria, but never before in this fashion.'

Railwaymen could work surprisingly quickly. At 12.10 p.m. on 2 October 1943 the SR Exeter Divisional superintendent received a phone call from the United States Army asking for a temporary siding on the Exmouth branch in order to unload 150 wagons arriving from the north. By 7 October the sidings, reached by a new embankment, had been laid and signalling installed. Another wartime installation was at Lockerly on the Salisbury to Romsey line, where the United States Army Supply Depot required 15 miles of sidings and 134 large sheds.

An advantage of the SR's density of lines came in setting up diversionary routes when lines were damaged or overcrowded; for example, there were no less than 136 routes from the London area to Folkestone.

In less densely populated areas, to cope with the event of a major route being severed by bombing, new connections were made between the SR and GWR at St Budeaux, Lydford, Launceston and Yeovil to enable trains to use an alternative route. These new connections were built at government expense and were government not railway property, although they were managed by the SR and GWR.

As many SR passenger trains were cancelled, it had a superfluity of locomotives which were loaned to companies desperately in need: ten King Arthur 4-6-0s were sent for use in north-east England and Scotland; three Z class 0-8-0Ts went to Scotland; five D1 0-4-2Ts and three H class 0-4-4Ts to the LMS in Scotland; one T9 4-4-0, all the S11 class 4-4-0s, eight F1 4-4-0s, two B1 4-4-0s, four K10 4-4-0s and six T1 class 0-4-4Ts to the LMS; all the Remembrance class and four S15 class 4-6-0s to the GWR; seven I2 4-4-2Ts to the Longmoor Military Railway.

On 25 October 1941 the Waterloo & City Line closed for a week to enable the old stock to be removed and new stock lowered. This was done by lift, one car at a time. The five four-car sets were replaced by five five-car sets in silver livery, each capable of carrying 600 passengers. Before being placed in regular operation, one new set made a trip to Brighton and back. The old single cars remained in use for off-peak trains.

On 26 November 1942, near Lydd on the New Romney branch, D3 class 0-4-4T No. 2365 had its boiler punctured by enemy fire, but retaliated when the escaping jet of steam caused the attacking aircraft to crash. Its pilot was flung out and drowned in a ditch. The aircraft was destroyed but No. 2365 was repaired.

Two D1 class 0-4-2Ts, No. 2220 and No. 2252, were fitted with firefighting equipment with pumps fitted behind the bunker.

Dover was shelled by long-range guns and five railwaymen were killed. Long-range rail-mounted guns on the SR fired back a few rounds before moving on to a new firing point before enemy plotters could get the range.

In preparation for the 1944 invasion of Europe, fourteen 0-6-0Ts built in the USA assisted the B4 0-4-0Ts with the shunting at Southampton Docks. Post-war they were purchased by the SR and continued work there.

In 1944, German flying bombs caused a certain amount of havoc, especially at Cow Lane Viaduct, Peckham, where the LCDR viaduct collapsed on the LBSCR track. A V2 rocket fell in front of a Kent coast express killing several passengers. A particular morale-booster was the display at Waterloo of a Nazi flag hauled down from the St Malo offices of the SR by a company employee serving in the Navy.

By the end of 1944 a million US troops had sailed from Southampton and between D-Day and VE-Day no less than 2,840,346 personnel had been embarked or disembarked. With the advent of peace it was announced that during the war a Pullman train left Victoria every night at 7.08 p.m. adjacent to the British Airways Corporation building to carry service personnel, many being VIPs, to Hurn Airport and the Poole flying boat base. Between 1941 and 1945 this train carried 30,000 passengers.

During the Second World War the SR works built tank landing craft, tail pieces for aerial-launched torpedoes, Horsa glider tail pieces, pontoon bridges, gun barrels, rocket guns to protect merchant ships, 1,000 pre-fabricated railway wagons sent to Russia in pieces ready for assembly, bridge-carrying tanks, fast motor boats, LCPs (landing craft personnel), ALCs (assault landing craft) and old howitzers were reconditioned.

283 rail blockades were prepared for setting up on SR territory in the event of invasion. An ambulance train ferry worked from Cherbourg to Southampton and later Calais to Dover.

During the war the SR had one engine destroyed and 189 damaged, while 153 carriages were damaged beyond repair and over 4,000 damaged. Although about 1,000 wagons were destroyed, Ashford built 11,935 new wagons, over 7,000 of which were for SR use, the others being for the other main-line companies and the government. 170 railwaymen were killed on duty.

Between 3 September 1939 and 8 May 1945 the SR carried 9,367,886 troops in 30,890 trains; 582,005 prisoners-of-war in 1,127 trains; 408,051 (including medical staff) in 1,797 ambulance trains.

In March 1942 post-war plans were considered for electrifying all the Central and Eastern sections. In November 1946 this was realised as too costly and the plan was modified to 284 miles of principal routes. Some SR officers visited the USA early in 1946 to study the possibility of diesel traction on non-electrified lines.

With the end of the Second World War the Channel Islands and Folkestone–Ostend services were restored on 9 October 1945; Jersey–Granville on 15 January 1946; the Golden Arrow express on 15 April 1946 and on 16 April 1946 the *Autocarrier* resumed the Jersey–St Malo service.

From August 1946 cheap day returns were issued to south coast resorts and from September 1946 cheap day returns to London were issued from suburban stations after 9.30 a.m.

Post-war plans were that 70 per cent of the mileage on the Eastern section would be worked by electric multiple-unit trains, electric locomotives handling continental boat trains and goods trains. Diesel-electric multiple-unit trains would cover the non-electrified routes, with diesel-electric locomotives handling freight.

Severe snow in January 1947 caused problems and the SR used de-icing trains spreading warm oil on the third rail. Bad weather kept miners from work, while coal in trucks was frozen by melted snow re-freezing and almost impossible to unload. By early February 1947 the SR only had enough coal for one week. Cuts were made in services to eke out the available fuel. Early in March a blizzard brought more snow and the 4.25 p.m. from Brighton to Victoria took over 8 hours for the journey. When the thaw began on 8 March, landslips and flooding occurred.

At the company's AGM in March 1947 the chairman reported that sixty-five stations had been renovated and 30 acres of glass in the roofs of main stations had been replaced.

The Transport Act nationalising all major British railways was passed on 6 August 1947, becoming operative on 1 January 1948. Management of the British Transport Commission would be delegated to five executives: railways, docks and inland waterways, hotels, road transport and London Transport. The Railway Executive to administer the nationalised lines was chaired by the former SR general manager Sir Eustace Missenden.

On 15 December 1947 the Dover–Dunkirk train ferry service was restored, the three ships working the route having been reinstated following their wartime workings.

On 16 January 1948 the new West Country class 21C158 *Sir Frederick Pile* appeared with its number prefixed by the letter 'S', though much of the SR flavour was retained in the Southern Region of British Railways for many years.

The SR identified the longest signal box pull was from Worgret Junction to the distant signal sited 1,678 yards away – nearly a mile.

In its lifespan of twenty-five years, the SR had erected forty-seven new stations, rebuilt thirty-five and opened thirty-one new halts. Its target-style name boards were virtually a copy of the underground emblem, but in green.

The SR was publicity conscious, anxious to make the most of its resources: continental traffic and coastal resorts from Kent to Cornwall. Some of its posters were famous, particularly the one published in 1925 showing a boy talking to a driver of a Urie 4-6-0 and saying, 'For Holidays I always go Southern 'cos it's the Sunshine Line.' Then there was Sunny South Sam. 'Why do they call me Sunny South Sam? Because the sun shines most on the SOUTHERN coast.'

Unlike its constituent companies, the publicity-minded SR had quite a number of named trains, they were:

The Atlantic Coast Express

In July 1925 *The Southern Railway Magazine* held a competition for naming the principal West of England express. It was won by Guard Rowland who suggested the Atlantic Coast Express. It started running on 19 July 1926 and was notable for the number of parts run to various destinations. The train was commonly referred to as the ACE.

At busy times the Atlantic Coast Express could run in about six parts, and even when just a single train it carried through coaches to various destinations that were detached, or coupled en route. It was the most multi-portioned train in the country, having no less than nine sections: for Lyme Regis, Seaton, Sidmouth, Ilfracombe, Torrington, Padstow, Bude, Plymouth and Exeter.

West of Salisbury the locomotive running was particularly exciting, and as there was practically no speed limit drivers made the utmost use of falling gradients to gain impetus for the succeeding ascents, 80 mph being frequently attained.

Due to no water troughs being provided, engines were changed at Salisbury. At the height of the holiday season the ACE ran in several parts.

Bournemouth Belle

Starting on 5 July 1931 it ran to Bournemouth Central where five coaches were sent to Weymouth, while the other five terminated at Bournemouth West. In pre-Second World War days it was handled by a Lord Nelson 4-6-0. Withdrawn during the war, when restored on 7 October 1946 it was headed by a Merchant Navy 4-6-2.

Bournemouth Limited

This train with a two-hour timing was limited to ten carriages and began on 8 July 1929. The non-stop run of 107.9 miles was one of the longest in Britain without the aid of water troughs. Initially worked by 4-6-0s, in the years immediately preceding the Second World War the eleven bogie coaches were headed by a Schools class 4-4-0 and one was recorded as covering the distance in a net time of 108 minutes.

Brighton Belle

This was a renaming of the Southern Belle when worked by multiple electric units from 29 June 1934. It had the only motor-driven Pullman cars in the world. Every day the set made three return journeys, a total of 306 miles.

The coaches rode rather roughly so menus carried the disclaimer: 'Our staff take every care and precaution in the service of refreshments, and the company cannot be held responsible for accidents or spillage etc., which may occur on account of excessive movement of the train.' Its ventilation system was controlled by photo-electric cells which prevented smoke from steam engines penetrating the interior. Between 1934 and 1972 the Brighton Belle was unusual in that it was an electric all-Pullman train.

City Limited

This train was started by the LBSCR 7 February 1921 and in the morning ran non-stop from Brighton to London Bridge, returning in the evening. When the line was electrified special six-car sets were built, the entire twelve-coach train seating 276 first- and 240 third-class passengers. During the Second World War, unlike most of the other expresses, it still retained its sixty-minute schedule.

City Expresses

Originally introduced by the LCDR, these were morning trains from Ramsgate Harbour and Margate to Cannon Street. The titles were dropped in 1927.

Cliftonville Express

Originally introduced by the SECR, running from Victoria to Ramsgate Harbour, the title was dropped by the SR in 1927.

Devon Belle

On 20 June 1947, the all-Pullman Devon Belle was inaugurated to run from Waterloo with up to ten cars for Ilfracombe and four for Plymouth. Its special feature was a Pullman observation car at the rear. In order for Up passengers to have a good view rearwards, this car was placed on the turntable at Ilfracombe before being placed on the rear of the train. The Devon Belle was ostensibly run non-stop from Waterloo to Exeter but in fact required a locomotive exchange at Salisbury, the actual exchange being made at Wilton, just west of the city.

Eastbourne Sunday Limited

An LBSCR train non-stop from Victoria to Eastbourne. In October 1923 the SR reduced the time to 85 minutes and 80 minutes on 1 January 1933.

Golden Arrow

A Victoria–Dover Marine Pullman service was inaugurated 15 May 1929 and allowed Paris to be reached in 6 hours 35 minutes, this faster time being achieved by improving customs examinations. The Golden Arrow was originally first class only, but as the Depression caused reduced traffic Pullmans were supplemented by first- and second-class coaches. Lord Nelsons generally monopolised the workings, though King Arthurs appeared. Withdrawn at the start of the Second World War, it was reinstated 15 April 1946.

Granville Express
A Ramsgate Harbour to Victoria train reintroduced by the SECR on 11 July 1921. The SR dropped the title in the summer of 1927.

Night Ferry
Inaugurated 14 October 1936, it was a through sleeping car train for London to Paris, vehicles crossing the Channel by ferry. Pre-war the heavy train was hauled by two 4-4-0s, but after the war a Bulleid light Pacific was used.

Southern Belle
Started by the LBSCR on 1 November 1908, it was the first daily all-Pullman train in Britain. An unusual feature was that it ran twice daily in each direction. It last ran on 28 June 1934 when it was superseded by the Brighton Belle.

Thanet Express
Initiated by the SECR, it ran between Victoria and Ramsgate Harbour twice daily. The SR dropped the title in 1927.

The Tourist
Beginning in the summer of 1933, three trains with this name ran daily from Ventnor to Freshwater, each carriage carrying a board with the title in gold letters on a red ground.

In addition to the SR's own trains, several cross-country services were run in conjunction with other railways. The LMS ran the Pines Express from Liverpool and Manchester via the Somerset & Dorset Railway to Bournemouth, while the Sunny South Special ran through from Liverpool and other northern cities on the LMS to Brighton and Eastbourne, the GWR providing a similar train from Birkenhead to Deal, Brighton and Hastings; the GWR also provided through trains between Cardiff, Bristol and Portsmouth. The LNER ran through carriages from Glasgow and Edinburgh to Southampton Docks.

Accidents

The first serious accident on the SR occurred on 24 August 1927. K class 2-6-4T No. 800 *River Cray* was hauling the 5.00 p.m. Cannon Street to Folkestone, which was booked to run the 56 miles to Ashford in 65 minutes. Driver W. H. Buss was very experienced and aware of the tendency of this class to roll. About midway between Dunton Green and Sevenoaks he heard a knocking from the front of the engine; the sound continued, and he closed the regulator.

The pony truck had derailed and after about 500 yd burst open a pair of trailing catch points, derailing the whole train. Unfortunately this happened near the overbridge carrying Shoreham Lane, and this bridge had separate arches for Up and Down roads. The engine and first two coaches passed through, but the fourth coach became jammed across under the bridge. The fifth vehicle was the Pullman car *Carmen*, which stood up to the impact well, its strong construction saving passengers. Thirteen passengers were killed, twenty-one seriously injured and a further forty less seriously hurt. An odd feature was that several uninjured passengers had their shoes torn off; they recovered them from the wreckage with the laces still tied, although their feet were unhurt.

It transpired that there had been three previous derailments of this class of engine all on former SECR lines, yet when the River class appeared on ex-Brighton lines no complaints of poor riding were made.

Pending the Ministry of Transport enquiry led by Col Sir John Pringle, Sir Herbert Walker withdrew all River class engines. Col Sir John Pringle chose to test certain SR locomotives, including the River class, on a stretch of the LNER between St Neots and Huntingdon which had reverse curves. Tested with both full and half-empty tanks and bunkers, the engines ran smoothly. These tests exonerated Maunsell, the derailment being caused by poor track drainage.

Sir Herbert Walker sought similar trials on the SR between Woking and Walton-on-Thames. Despite special track maintenance being given, both tender and tank locomotives rolled at high speed, even when running on straight track. Nigel Gresley commented, 'If the location of the irregular depressions in the road should coincide with the rolling periods of engines, a dangerous and unstable condition would arise. As it is not so likely that such irregularities would occur as close to each other as to coincide with the shorter rolling periods of Tender engines, there is less probability of this dangerous condition arising with Tender engines than with Tank engines.'

These investigations resulted in the upgrading the SR permanent way by using Meldon stone rather than shingle, which offered a less stable track, and rebuilding the 2-6-4Ts into U and U1 class 2-6-0s, two-cylinder and three-cylinder respectively.

On 9 July 1928 B2X class 4-4-0 No. B210 was placed on a siding at London Bridge preparatory to shunting. The driver misunderstood his instructions and, believing he should run to New Cross Gates, when the colour light signal for the Down local line changed to green he moved off, ignoring the ground signal controlling the exit from his siding. Actually this signal had been cleared for the 7.22 p.m. to Epsom Downs, and as it emerged from behind the signal box it was struck by No. B210, killing one passenger instantly and injuring six others seriously, one fatally.

A serious accident occurred on 24 October 1947 towards the end of the SR. Thick fog was causing delays as drivers had to proceed slowly in order to see the position of the semaphore signals. The signalman at Purley Oaks accepted the 7.33 a.m. Haywards Heath to London Bridge. It comprised a four-coach electric set with steel body panels fixed to timber framing set on steel underframes. Although not booked to call at Purley Oaks, because the previous train had not cleared the section ahead the 7.33 had to stop – unfortunately out of the signalman's sight.

As the signalman at the previous box had not received 'Out of section', he phoned Purley Oaks to discover the situation. The Purley Oaks signalman then realised from his block instruments that the Haywards Heath train had not been cleared by the automatic treadle – which was quite correct because it should not have been cleared because the train had not passed it.

Sadly the signalman jumped to the conclusion that the lock-and-block had failed, freed it with the release key, gave 'Out of section' to Purley North and accepted the 8.04 a.m. Tattenham Corner to London Bridge composed of ex-LBSCR timber-bodied coaches. On clearing the starting signal the Haywards Heath train, still hidden in the fog, moved forward, but approaching South Croydon it slowed for an adverse distant signal. Unfortunately this deceleration occurred just as the Tattenham Corner train caught up. The leading vehicle was smashed to matchwood, while all but three compartments of the last coach of the steel-panelled Haywards Heath train were destroyed. With approximately 800 passengers on the Haywards Heath and about 1,000 on that from Tattenham Corner, it was surprising that fatalities were only thirty-one passengers and the driver of the Tattenham Corner train. Despite Col Sir Alan Mount's recommendation that track circuits and colour-light signals be installed, this did not happen until May 1955.

On 6 November 1947, in thick fog, the 4.45 p.m. from Holmwood to Waterloo ran into the 5.16 Waterloo–Chessington South as it crossed to the Chessington branch, killing four passengers. The accident was caused through a fogman showing a green handlamp to the driver of the Holmwood–Waterloo train. He had not climbed the signal to check its actual position, but merely relied on the sound of it rising and falling.

20

SR LOCOMOTIVES, ROLLING STOCK & STEAMER SERVICES

On Amalgamation, as numbers were duplicated on engines from the LBSCR, LSWR and the SECR, initially Brighton numbers were given the prefix 'B', LSWR 'E' (for Eastleigh) and those from the SECR 'A' (for Ashford). In 1931 Ashford engines had 1000 added to their number and Brighton engines 2000. An exception to the rule were some elderly LSWR engines which had 3000 added.

In 1925, ten N15 class 4-6-0s appeared and were named after personalities featured in the tales of King Arthur. These engines appeared at the head of all the important expresses, including the Atlantic Coast Express, the Continental Express and the Southern Belle. On the Central and Eastern sections, except on the Continental Express, they ran with six-wheeled Maunsell tenders, whereas on the Western section they drew the large Urie bogie tenders with great water capacity.

Maunsell's L1 class 4-4-0, a development of Wainwright's L class, appeared in 1926, but the SR had a need for a locomotive that could haul a 500-ton train at an average speed of 55 mph. The answer to this was the four-cylinder 4-6-0 Lord Nelson, which appeared in 1926. Its tractive effort of 33,500 lbs enabled the company's publicity department to produce a poster proclaiming the 'Most powerful passenger engine in Great Britain'. To aid publicity, drivers were asked to blow the whistle for longer when passing through a major station to attract attention. One driver rather over-egged the pudding when he kept it open for a mile when running through Ashford. Although fast, the Nelsons were not so good at climbing as King Arthurs.

On 23 January 1930, while hauling the Up Golden Arrow, when approaching Kent House the leading and centre driving wheels of Lord Nelson No. E853 *Sir Richard Grenville* became derailed at 50–55 mph. The middle wheels soon rerailed themselves at a crossing, but the leading set ran 880 yd before getting back on the track. Its crew was quite unaware of this event.

One interesting feature of a Nelson was that the angles of the cranks was such that there were eight small blasts for each revolution of the driving wheels, rather than four stronger ones. This led to less unconsumed smoke and coal drawn through the tubes.

Because suburban electrification had rendered the E1 0-6-0Ts superfluous, from 1927 they were economically rebuilt as Class E1R 0-6-2Ts with spare pony trucks bought from Woolwich Arsenal, given a larger bunker and were thus ideal for lightly laid lines such as the North Devon and Cornwall Junction.

Nelsons were followed in 1930 by the V class 4-4-0 and were the most powerful 4-4-0s in Europe. They were fitted with three Lord Nelson cylinders fed by a King Arthur firebox married to a shorter boiler barrel. Named after public schools, those locomotives named after schools in the SR area made a courtesy visit to the station nearest the school.

In the post-war period, to assist the gradual running-down of the ordnance factory at Woolwich, N class 2-6-0s of Maunsell's SECR design were constructed there and sent to some SR lines in the West of England. In 1930 Maunsell equipped N class No. A816 with the Anderson steam heat conservation equipment. Semi-condensing, draught was supplied by a fan driven by a rotary steam engine in the smokebox door. It ran successfully for three years before the makers ran out of cash. The locomotive was notable for its almost total silence.

Complaints from drivers of vision being obstructed by drifting steam led to the adoption of smoke deflector plates beside the smokebox. An additional advantage was that the carcases of any pheasants struck were safely secured.

As the LBSCR I1 class 4-4-2Ts proved underpowered they were rebuilt with larger boilers, while additionally SECR R class 0-4-4Ts were moved to the Central section. The rebuilding of the C2 0-6-0s with larger, higher-pitched boilers ceased, but the useful C2X engines could be seen on empty coaching stock trains in the London area until 1962.

Five W class 2-6-4Ts with three cylinders and 5 ft 6 in. wheels were constructed at Eastleigh in 1932, principally for working goods trains between the SR and marshalling yards in north London. The eight Z class 0-8-0Ts built at Brighton in 1929 for shunting were considered by many to be the best British engine for this purpose.

The final Sentinel steam railcar to enter service on a British railway was a rail bus specially designed for the steeply graded Brighton to Dyke branch. Extraordinarily light, it only weighed 17 tons 4 cwt. It had a compound engine driving through a cardan shaft and reduction gearing. Each bogie side frame was in two halves, slightly unequal in length. The wheels were fitted with external brake drums with road-pattern brake shoes inside. Supplies of coal and feed water were automatic so the car could be manned by just a driver. Forty-four seats were provided in the bus-type body. Both ends were streamlined and the roof had domed ends. It entered service on 1 May 1933.

It was quick, economical and comfortable, and on test its acceleration was phenomenal and it achieved a maximum of 61 mph. Over the 109 miles from Birmingham to Willesden it consumed an average of 4.88 lbs of coal per mile.

It entered service on 1 May 1933 but when overloaded in 1935 its frame broke. Following repairs at Brighton works, it was transferred to the Westerham branch on 2 March 1936, before being withdrawn in 1936.

In the 1930s U class 2-6-0 No. 1629 was fitted experimentally to burn powdered fuel, the necessary plant being erected at Eastbourne locomotive depot, where No. 1629 was shedded. The experiment was abandoned when spontaneous combustion of the pulverised coal caused the container to explode and a black cloud of fuel descended on the town.

In 1937 three 0-6-0 diesel shunters were built at Ashford, while the last steam locomotive erected there was the London, Midland & Scottish Railway Class 8F 2-8-0 No. 8674.

The 4-6-4T Remembrance class were converted to tender engines in 1934, the vacuum replacing the Westinghouse brake. Subsequent to Maunsell's retirement in 1937 his last class appeared, the Q class 0-6-0, useful on both goods and passenger workings.

His replacement was O. V. Bulleid, who came from the LNER and had startling new ideas. His aim was a locomotive capable of hauling 600-ton trains at 70 mph. The 4-6-2 Merchant Navy class engines which appeared in 1941 had many innovations. The exterior was air-smoothed, and they had patent disc wheels, chain-driven valve gear, a steel firebox rather than copper, and electric lighting. Other innovations were a multiple-jet blast giving a comparatively soft exhaust; a pressure of 280 lb per sq. in., the highest to date on a British railway using a normal boiler and firebox; the firebox being welded steel with two Nicholson thermic syphons; the fire-hole door being steam-operated from a floor treadle; and the cab and tender being built to the same external contour used on the coaches. The numbering system was different: 21C1 indicated two leading axles, a trailing axle, while the C showed three driving axles, the last numeral being the engine's number in the class. To overcome the wartime restriction on building express locomotives, it was classified 'mixed traffic'.

Being revolutionary, it was not without faults: the oil bath tended to leak and the lubricant ran on to the rails and caused slipping and occasionally fire; the steam reverser suffered steam leakage and could move from 25 per cent cut-off to 75 per cent accidentally.

To create paths for military trains some services to the West Country were combined, the 10.05 a.m. from Waterloo having sixteen coaches. On 2 December 1941 No. 21C10 *Blue Star* hauled twenty carriages from Waterloo – a tremendous feat considering the additional friction caused by reverse curves.

On 17 January 1941 a Co-Co electric locomotive designed by A. Raworth, chief electrical engineer, appeared from Ashford works numbered CC1, and made its first demonstration run. In 1945 Ashford produced a second, CC2.

Each of the six axles was driven by a 245 hp force-ventilated motor with current supplied by means of a booster set consisting of a 600V motor direct-coupled to a 600V generator. Each booster-set had a heavy flywheel mounted between the motor and generator which stored sufficient energy to keep the set running over the longest gap in the live rails. A pantograph was fitted for use if sidings were equipped with overhead wires.

In 1937 English Electric and Bulleid produced three 350 hp diesel-electric 0-6-0s.

Bulleid's Q1 class 0-6-0s appeared in 1942. Although about the same length and weight as Maunsell's Q class engines, the Q1 had a much larger firebox based on a modified Lord Nelson design and a boiler pressure of 230 lbs rather than 200. Weight was kept down by using welding with the result that the engine was able to travel over 93 per cent of the company's system. The spacious cab was well arranged and the tender had a modified cab at its front end.

In 1945 a lightweight Merchant Navy appeared with slightly smaller cylinders and weighing 86 rather than 92½ tons. It had two groups of names: those for use in the West Country being allocated suitable titles, while the Battle of Britain section of the class were named after fighters and persons associated with the defence of Britain in 1940.

In 1946, the SR purchased fourteen ex-US Army Transportation Corps 0-6-0Ts built in 1942 and after being fitted with a modified cab and bunker were used for shunting in Southampton Docks.

Although designed during the SR era, Bulleid's final class did not appear until 1949. This was what proved to be a step too far, the 0-6-6-0 Leader class. With a driving cab at both ends, and looking similar to a diesel-electric, the fireman occupied the central cab which was completely closed and became far too hot. Another important failure was that the boiler failed to produce adequate steam. Only one engine was actually completed.

Another SR design which did not appear until the BR era was an order placed in August 1947 for three 1,600 hp diesel-electric locomotives. No. 10203 uprated to 2,000 hp and became the prototype for the BR Class 40.

By 1958 the R1 class 0-6-0Ts used for banking trains up the severe incline from Folkestone harbour were life-expired. BR had to hunt for suitable replacements and on 15 October 1958 Western Region 57XX class 0-6-0PT No. 9770 arrived for trials. It proved successful and this class took over all the workings.

A Drewry four-wheeled petrol-engine railcar was purchased by the SR in 1928 and worked between Andover and Romsey; Reading and Blackwater; and Appledore, New Romney and Dungeness, ending on the Fareham–Gosport service Works No. 1650 it had a 50 hp engine,

20 ft wheelbase, weighed 10 tons 17 cwt. It seated twenty-six until around 1930 when a luggage compartment was added, reducing seating to twenty-two. It was numbered 5, Nos 1–4 being two railcars and two overhead inspection vehicles ex-LBSCR. It was sold in 1934 to the Weston, Clevedon & Portishead Light Railway for £272.

At the formation of the SR in 1923, only the LSWR had supplied an appreciable number of corridor coaches, the SECR coaches for longer-distance trains having only internal corridors and lavatories serving first- and second-class passengers, while the LBSCR never built any corridor coaches. Therefore the first coaches built by the SR were a modified LSWR design, with bogies based on those of the SECR. In 1929 some new coaches appeared for use on the best expresses of the Eastern and Western sections, Central receiving only a few due to the forthcoming electrification, which would bring new stock to the area. Some of these vehicles were first and third composites for use on the Atlantic Coast Express, where only one coach might be required for a destination.

Due to a variety of loading gauge limitations the SR had inherited, a standard 59 ft long body required three different body widths: 9 ft for Portsmouth, Bournemouth, West of England and Brighton services; 8 ft 6 in. for Eastbourne and the Kent Coast; and 8 ft for the Hastings/Bexhill via Battle trains, coaches in the latter two categories being straight-sided.

A feature which the SR continued from all its constituents was the practice of marshalling coaches in permanent sets with the set number painted on the solebars and on the outer ends of the brake coaches. Large numbers of non-set coaches – called 'swingers' – were kept for strengthening trains.

The first SR electric stock were twenty-one bogie motor cars with four 250 hp motors for the Balham–Coulsdon North and Sutton via Selhurst overhead electric scheme, opened 1 April 1925. After withdrawal when the line was converted to third rail DC, in 1934 these motors were converted to 27-ton bogie goods brake vans.

Just as in 1915 the LSWR had electric trains using converted steam stock, so did the Eastern section in 1925, built with the difference that for stock less than 64 ft in length the difference was made up either by extending the original coach or by mounting two non-bogie vehicles on a single frame. Each motor coach in a three-car set had two 275 hp motors. Some new steel-panelled three-car sets were built for both the Western and Eastern sections. The Eastern section followed the LSWR practice of running at busy times, a two-car trailer set between two three-car motor sets.

The SR developed a code for describing sets, one figure indicating the number of coaches and three letters its make-up or duty. Hence 3SUB was a three-coach suburban unit and 5BEL the five-coach Brighton Belle.

In 1934, seventy-seven two-car sets were converted from LSWR steam stock for use on the more rural electrified lines. As they had no toilet accommodation, they were classified 2-NOL. For trains to Three Bridges and Reigate new four-car sets were built (4-LAV) with one of the trailers being a first/third with a lavatory. For Brighton expresses six-car sets were used with corridors between coaches, but not at the ends of the set. Each end coach had two motor bogies each with two 225 hp motors. Each set had one Pullman car, so the sets were designated 6-PUL. Three sets, also with a Pullman, were 6-CITY and had a greater number of first-class seats. Three five-car entire Pullman sets (5-BEL) were built for the Brighton Belle. For the electrification to Eastbourne and Hastings, six-car units like the 6-CITY were used except with a pantry car replacing the Pullman. These sets were 6-PAN. For Brighton–Hastings service and Horstead Keynes–Seaford, two-car corridor sets with lavatories, 2-BIL, supplemented the 2-NOL sets.

In 1934 the SR stock consisted of:

For steam working
3,431 carriages either first, second (for use on boat trains) or third class
1,416 first/third composites
69 restaurant cars

For electric working
1,031 motor coaches
964 trailers

Goods stock
24,469 open wagons
5,054 covered wagons
851 mineral wagons
2,770 wagons for special traffic, e.g. cattle, rails, timber
928 goods brake vans

In 1935 some corridor thirds were constructed for the Waterloo–Bournemouth expresses, some at peak times still using non-corridor stock. For carrying passengers' luggage, a four- or six-wheeled van formed part of each coach set, but new carriage stock incorporated enough luggage space to obviate the need for vans except on continental expresses where a greater amount of luggage was carried. Maunsell designed some long-wheelbase utility vans, some of which also contained guards' compartments and periscope, enabling him to observe signals and the line ahead.

The LNER introduced camp coaches in 1933 as an economical scheme for using old rolling stock, the SR copying this idea in 1935, placing vehicles at picturesque locations on its system.

For the electrification to Portsmouth in 1937, two types were used: 4-RES, with a restaurant car, and 4-COR, without; as one of each type was normally coupled together, to enable passengers in the 4-COR to use the eating facilities a through corridor was at each end of a set, an end view showing driver's window, corridor connection and route indicator panel. As there was but one window at the front, they were nicknamed 'Nelsons'. Power for the kitchen equipment was 660V DC.

In 1938, Eastleigh turned out thirteen 4-BUF sets with buffet facilities. In 1938–9, seventy-six two-car 2-HAL units were built, each unit having just one lavatory, which explains the 'half'. 2-HALS were built for the North Kent electrification in 1939, and unlike previous 2-HAL sets these did not have a side corridor or lavatory in the motor coach.

In 1938 the Waterloo & City Railway was reconditioned, running rails welded into 315 ft lengths, automatic signalling installed and five new five-car trains provided, arranged motor, three trailers and motor. The motor cars had two 190 hp motors and could be used singly in the slack hours.

Late in 1941 Bulleid's new coach appeared, with passengers seated in compartments six a side and the coach classified 4-SUB. Its flush steel-panelled sides curved inwards from waist to eaves. In 1946 a 4-SUB was constructed at Eastleigh with two eight-compartment motors and a nine- and ten-compartment trailer, The nine-compartment trailer was provided in case first-class accommodation was reintroduced in the post-war period. Also in 1946 a similar series was built, having two groups of four compartments with central gangway in each motor coach while the ten-compartment coach had groups of three, four and three.

As a result of passenger research, in 1948–9 it was decided to generally adopt the centre gangway, thus each eight-compartment motor coach had a centre gangway throughout, with a centre gangway trailer and another trailer with ten compartments.

Post-war rolling stock shortage was alleviated by the construction of thirty-five new four-car electric sets and 116 trailers, seating six a side, making 420 seats per set. The odd trailer coaches were used to bring as many as possible of the three-car suburban sets up to four-car.

In the post-war period, to obtain foreign currency the best steam coal was exported, leaving poor-quality coal for home use. To alleviate the shortage of good steam coal, encouraged by the Ministry of Transport, early in 1947 the SR converted 100 locomotives at Eastleigh and Ashford for oil-burning, the shed at Fratton being almost entirely oil-burning. Then, after many locomotives had been converted and money invested in oil fuelling plants, the Treasury announced that there was insufficient foreign exchange available to purchase the oil! The left hand was ignorant of what the right hand was doing.

On 2 November 1949, Bulleid's two double-deck four-coach trains were placed in service. Weighing the same as a normal set, they seated 508 passengers rather than the 386 capacity of the normal design. They were really half-decks, as the feet of the upper passengers were between the backs of those sitting lower. Due to the loading gauge, windows in the upper deck could not be opened, but pressure ventilation was provided. An entrance to each upper-deck compartment was provided from a lower-deck compartment. Due to the fact that access to the upper compartment meant pushing through a lower compartment, the coaches were unpopular with passengers; the railway staff also did not like them, as they needed a longer time at stations for passengers to get out and in.

Surrey Warner from the LSWR was appointed the SR's assistant mechanical engineer for carriages, wagons and road vehicles. His chief draughtsman was Lionel Lynes, and when Warner retired in 1929, Lynes was his replacement.

The livery of dark green was changed to malachite in 1937. It came about because in 1936 Sir Herbert Walker, with three fellow officers, was travelling to the Isle of Wight and discussed colour schemes. After lunch Walker went into an optician's where reels of spectacle cord were displayed. He emerged with a length of malachite green cord, cut off a length for each officer and proclaimed, 'Now, argument shall cease; that will be the colour Southern engines and coaches shall be painted in future This reel shall remain in my office safe as the standard to which reference shall be made.' Thus when Bulleid was appointed CME in 1937, the livery had been made inevitable by a manager who had retired a fortnight before he was appointed.

The SR concentrated the construction of new steam and electric coaching stock at Eastleigh, space being made by transferring carriage repairs to Lancing. These works assisted in converting steam stock to electrical operation, the actual conversion carried out at Ashford, coaches being sent to Lancing for the fitting of the electrical equipment in the motor coaches and for the motors and trailers to be painted. All SR electric trains were fitted with the Westinghouse brake, whereas steam-worked rolling stock on the Central section had their Westinghouse equipment replaced with vacuum so as to be standard with the Western and Eastern sections. Steam trains on the Isle of Wight retained their Westinghouse brakes. By the mid-thirties 1,400 men at Lancing repaired 2,200 carriages annually, and during the Second World War the works constructed tail units for Horsa gliders.

When General Montgomery was informed that the Germans planned to land on nearby beaches and use the Lancing works for maintaining their road vehicles, either the works manager or his assistant slept at the works so that in the event of invasion, vital machinery could be removed at short notice and taken inland in a special train which was always kept standing by.

The SR never built any locomotive-hauled non-corridor stock as electrification enabled pre-1923 stock to be sufficient to cater for non-electrified areas. Very few new suburban electric trains were built due to this policy of converting old stock.

The SR concentrated new wagon building at Ashford, and the works was also the site of the chemical laboratory opened by the SECR in 1915.

Feltham locomotive depot was rebuilt, with four roads each accommodating seven engines, and running the length of the shed was a 50-ton electrically driven engine hoist. Adjacent was an electrically worked turntable and coaling plant, offering an average time of 2½ minutes for coaling an engine.

The new shed at Exmouth Junction contained twelve storage roads and one lifting road. Exmouth Junction also possessed an electric turntable and mechanical coaling plant. Coaling plants were also found at Nine Elms, Ramsgate and Stewarts Lane.

As much of the SR was located in areas of chalk, water-softening plants were installed at various locations.

SR Steamers

In 1923, the SR inherited twenty-seven steamers of over 250 tons, ten being jointly owned with the French State Railways. Five SR vessels were exclusively for cargo. Additionally, there were fourteen smaller vessels.

On 15 May 1929, the first-class-only *Canterbury* came into service in connection with the Golden Arrow. The *Autocarrier* appeared in 1931 to carry about thirty-five cars and was licensed for 120 passengers. *Tonbridge* and *Minster* were cargo vessels which came on the Dover–Folkestone route in 1924, followed by *Hythe* and *Whitstable* in 1925, and *Maidstone* in 1926.

Worthing was placed in service between Newhaven and Dieppe on 5 September 1928 and *Brighton* in April 1933. These had a speed of 25 knots, necessary for a passage of 64 nautical miles compared with the 21 between Dover and Calais and 28 from Folkestone to Boulogne. The high speed of the crossing and the shorter rail journey placed the Newhaven route favourably in the competition of routes between London and Paris; the through fares were cheaper too. The cargo steamer *Rennes* arrived in 1925.

New vessels to the Southampton route were *Dinard* and *St Briac* in 1924, running to St Malo. The cargo ships *Fratton*, *Ringwood* and *Haslemere* were brought into use in 1925–6. *Isle of Jersey* and *Isle of Guernsey* came into service in the spring of 1930, while *Isle of Sark* followed in March 1932; this latter vessel was the first in the world to be fitted with an activated fin stabiliser. In June 1932 a service was launched between Jersey, Granville and St Malo, this being taken over by a new ship, *Brittany*, in June 1933. On 1 May 1932 the night service to Paris, which had been operated by the LMS between Tilbury and Dunkirk, was transferred to Folkestone.

The Dover–Ostend and Gravesend–Rotterdam services were not owned by the SR.

The SR introduced *Shanklin* to the Portsmouth–Ryde service in 1924 and *Merstone* and *Portsdown* in 1928, *Southsea* and *Whippingham* following in 1930 and *Ryde* in 1937.

The PS *Freshwater* came on the Lymington–Yarmouth crossing in June 1927, while in 1938 came *Lymington*. July 1927 saw the inauguration between Portsmouth and Fishbourne of a ferry boat service principally intended for cars. The *Fishbourne* was double-ended, which allowed cars to board at one end and leave at the other. In July 1928 she was joined by *Wootton* and *Hilsea* in 1930.

In 1936 three steamers were provided for the Dover–Dunkirk train ferry: *Twickenham Ferry*, *Hampton Ferry* and *Shepperton Ferry*. Each could carry twelve sleeping cars or forty goods wagons spread over four roads. On board, passengers were locked in – which could have proved dangerous had the ship been struck by a rock or other vessel.

During the Second World War, the train ferries were equipped with 84-ton derricks at the stern for transferring rolling stock on open beaches. Twelve SR vessels were lost in the Second World War.

BIBLIOGRAPHY

Allen, C. J., *Titled Trains of Great Britain* (London: Ian Allan, 1953)

Allen, P. C. & MacLeod, A. B., *Rails on the Isle of Wight* (London: George Allen & Unwin, 1967)

Bradley, D. L., *The Locomotives of the South Eastern Railway* (Railway Correspondence & Travel Society, 1963)

Bradley, D. L., *Locomotives of the LSWR Part 1 and Part 2* (Railway Correspondence & Travel Society, 1965/1967)

Bradley, D. L., *A Locomotive History of Railways on the Isle of Wight* (Railway Correspondence & Travel Society, 1982)

Bulleid, H. A. V., *Bulleid of the Southern* (Shepperton: Ian Allan, 1977)

Casserley, H. C., *London & South Western Locomotives* (Shepperton: Ian Allan, 1971)

Christopher, J. (editor), *Locomotives of the London, Brighton & South Coast Railway 1839-1903* (Stroud: Amberley, 2014)

Chivers, C., *Feltham Concentration Yard* (South Western Circle, 2016)

Course, E., *The Railways of Southern England: The Main Lines* (London: Batsford, 1973)

Course, E., *The Railways of Southern England: Secondary and Branch Lines* (London: Batsford, 1974)

Course, E., *The Railways of Southern England: Independent and Light Railways* (London: Batsford, 1976)

Ellis, H., *British Railway History 1830-1876* (London: Allen & Unwin, 1954)

Ellis, H., *British Railway History 1877-1947* (London: Allen & Unwin, 1959)

Ellis, H., *The South Western Railway* (London: Allen & Unwin, 1956)

Faulkner, J. N. & Williams, R A., *The LSWR in the Twentieth Century* (Newton Abbot: David & Charles, 1988)

Klapper, C. F., *Sir Herbert Walker's Southern Railway* (London: Ian Allan 1973)

Marshall, C. F. D., *A History of the Southern Railway,* revised by R. W. Kidner (London: Ian Allan, 1963)

Moody, G. T., *Southern Electric 1909-1979* (London: Ian Allan, 1979)

Pattenden, N., *Salisbury 1906. An Answer to the Enigma?* (South Western Circle 2015)

Robertson, K., *Leader, Steam's Last Chance* (Gloucester: Alan Sutton, 1988)

Rolt, L. T. C., *Red For Danger* (London: Pan, 1960)

Ruegg, L. H., *The History of a Railway* (Sherborne: Journal Offices, 1878)

Rush, R. W., *British Steam Railcars* (Lingfield: Oakwood Press, 1971)

Sekon, G. A., *The London & South Western Railway: Half a Century of Railway Progress to 1896* (London: Temple, 1896)

Staines, D., *Kent Railways* (Newbury: Countryside Books, 2010)

Thomas, D. St J. & Whitehouse, P., *A Century and a Half of the Southern Railway* (Newton Abbot: David & Charles, 1988)

Turner, J. H., *The London Brighton and South Coast Railway* (London: Batsford, 1977)

Weddell, G. R., *LSWR Carriages Vol 1 1838-1900* (Didcot: Wild Swan, 1992

White, H. P., *A Regional History of the Railways of Great Britain, Volume 2 Southern England* (Newton Abbot: David & Charles, 1969)

White, H. P., *A Regional History of the Railways of Great Britain, Volume 3 Greater London* (Newton Abbot: David & Charles, 1971)

Williams, R. A., *The London & South Western Railway Volume 1 The Formative Years* (Newton Abbot: David & Charles 1968)

Williams, R. A., *The London & South Western Railway Volume 2: Growth and Consolidation* (Newton Abbot: David & Charles 1973)

Wragg, D., *Southern Railway Handbook* (Sparkford: Haynes, 2011)

APPENDIX I

DATES LINES OPENED

London & South Western Railway Main Lines (geographical order)

Waterloo–Nine Elms	11 July 1848
Nine Elms–Woking Common	19 May 1838
Public opening	21 May 1838
Woking Common–Shapley Heath (Winchfield)	24 Sept 1838
Shapley Heath–Basingstoke	10 June 1839
Basingstoke–Andover	3 July 1854
Andover–Salisbury	1 May 1857
Salisbury–Gillingham (passengers)	2 May 1859
(goods)	1 Sept 1860
Gillingham–Sherborne (passengers)	7 May 1860
(goods)	1 Sept 1860
Sherborne–Yeovil (passengers)	June 1860
(goods)	1 Sept 1860
Yeovil–Exeter (Queen Street) (passengers)	18 July 1860
(goods)	1 Sept 1860
Exeter (Queen Street)–Exeter (St David's)	1 Feb 1862
Exeter–Crediton	12 May 1851
Crediton–Fremington	1 Aug 1854
Freminlington–Bideford	2 Nov 1855
Barnstaple–llfracombe	20 July 1874
Barnstaple Junction–Barnstaple (Victoria Road)	31 July 1885
Bideford–Torrington	18 July 1872
Coleford Junction–North Tawton	1 Nov 1865
North Tawton–Okehampton Road	8 Jan 1867
Okehampton Road–Okehampton	3 Oct 1871
Okehampton–Lydford	12 Oct 1874
Lydford–Devonport	1 June 1890
Plymouth (North Road)–Devonport	17 May 1876
Meldon Junction–Holsworthy	20 Jan 1879

Holsworthy–Bude	10 Aug 1898
Halwill–Launceston	21 July 1886
Launceston–Tresmeer	28 July 1892
Tresmeer–Camelford	14 Aug 1893
Camelford–Delabole	8 Oct 1893
Delabole–Wadebridge	1 June 1895
Wadebridge–Padstow	27 Mar 1899
Basingstoke–Winchester	11 May 1840
Winchester–Southampton	10 June 1839
Northam curve	1858
Southampton Junction–Blechynden	29 July 1847
Blechynden–Brockenhurst	1 June 1847
Brockenhurst–Christchurch	5 Mar 1888
Bournemouth (New) –Bournemouth West (ceremonial)	6 Mar 1888
Christchurch–Bournemouth East	14 Mar 1870
Bournemouth–Poole	15 June 1874
Branksome curve	1 June 1893
Hamworthy Junction–Poole (Holes Bay curve)	1 June 1893
Alderbury Junction–West Moors	20 Dec 1866
Hamworthy Junction–Dorchester	1 June 1847
Dorchester–Weymouth	20 Jan 1857
Woking–Guildford	5 May 1845
Guildford–Godalming (old station)	15 Oct 1849
Godalming–Havant	1 Jan 1859
Havant–Portsmouth	14 June 1847
Portsmouth Town–Portsmouth Harbour	2 Oct 1876
(Joint with LBSCR)	

LSWR Suburban Lines, branches, spurs, etc.

Bodmin–Wadebridge	4 July 1834
Boscarne–Wenford Bridge	30 Sept 1834
Grogley Halt–Ruthern Bridge	30 Sept 1834
Bishopstoke–Gosport	29 Nov 1841
Gospsort–Clarence Victualling Yard	21 Sept 1845
Battersea (Clapham Junction) –Richmond	27 July 1846
Bishopstoke–Salisbury (goods)	27 Jan 1847
(passenger)	1 Mar 1847
Brockenhurst–Dorchester (via Wimborne)	1 June 1847
Weybridge–Chertsey	14 Feb 1848
Farlington Jc & Portscreek Jc–Cosham (goods)	26 July 1848
Richmond–Datchet	22 Aug 1848
Fareham–Cosham	1 Sept 1848
Cosham–Portsmouth (goods)	1 Sept 1848
(passenger)	1 Oct 1848
Southcote Junction–Basingstoke	1 Nov 1848

Hampton Court Junction–Hampton Court	1 Feb 1849
Guildford–Ash Junction	20 Aug 1849
Barnes–Smallbury Green	22 Aug 1849
Ash Junction–Farnham	8 Aug 1849
Shaford Junction with SER	15 Oct 1849
Datchet–Windsor	1 Dec 1849
Loop Line Feltham Junction	1 Feb 1850
Smallberry Green–Hounslow	1 Feb 1850
Farnham–Alton	28 July 1852
Brookwood Cemetery Branch	Dec 1854
Staines–Ascot	4 June 1856
Ascot–Wokingham	9 July 1856
Lymington Junction–Lymington	12 July 1858
Epsom–Leatherhead	1 Feb 1859
Raynes Park–Epsom	4 Apr 1859
Havant–Cosham (via Farlington Junction)	2 Jan 1860
Exeter–Exmouth	1 May 1861
Kew curve; Barnes curve	1 Feb 1862
Ringwood–Christchurch	13 Nov 1862
West London Extension	2 Mar 1863
Gosport–Stokes Bay	6 Apr 1863
Chard Junction–Chard	8 May 1853
Botley–Bishop's Waltham	1 June 1863
Twickenham–Kingston	1 July 1863
Petersfield–Midhurst	1 Sept 1864
Strawberry Hill–Shepperton	1 Nov 1864
Andover–Redbridge	6 Mar 1865
Alton–Winchester	2 Oct 1865
Weymouth–Portland (goods)	16 Oct 1865
(passenger)	1 Sept 1889
Weymouth Harbour Tramway (goods)	16 Oct 1865
(passenger)	1 Sept 1889
Longhedge Junction–Ludgate Junction	1866
Portwood–Netley	5 Mar 1866
Chertsey–Virginia Water	1 Oct 1866
Midhurst extension	17 Dec 1866
Colyton Junction–Beer (Seaton)	16 Mar 1868
Tulse Hill spur	1 Oct 1868
Tooting, Merton, Wimbledon	1 Oct 1868
Malden–Kingston	1 Jan 1869
Kensington (Addison Road) –Richmond	1 Jan 1869
Pirbright Junction–Farnham	2 May 1870
Callington–Calstock Quay	7 May 1872
New Poole Junction–Poole	2 Dec 1872
Sidmouth Junction–Sidmouth	6 July 1874
Studland Road Junction	1 June 1877

Friary. Junction–Friary Road Goods Depot	1 Feb 1878
Ascot–Sturt Lane Junction	18 Mar 1878
Ash–Aldershot spur	1879
Frimley Junction–North Camp	2 June 1879
Friary–North Quay	22 Oct 1879
Twickenham flyover	1882
Twickenham and Hounslow connecting curve	1 Jan 1883
Raynes Park dive-under	16 Mar 1884
Leatherhead–Effingham Junction	2 Feb 1885
Hampton Court Junction–Guildford	2 Feb 1885
Wareham–Swanage	20 May 1885
Hurstbourne–Fullerton	1 June 1885
Fratton–Southsea	1 July 1885
Staines curve	4 July 1887
East Putney–Wimbledon	June 1889
Spur to Point Pleasant	1 July 1889
Netley–Fareham	2 Sept 1889
Brookwood–Bisley	4 July 1889
Winchester–Shawford	1 Oct 1891
Plymstock branch	5 Sept 1892
Ascot–Frimley Junction	11 June 1893
Fort Brockhurst–Lee-on-the-Solent	12 May 1894
Wadebridge–Bodmin joined to main line	1 Nov 1895
Tipton St John's–Budleigh Salterton	15 May 1897
Yealmpton branch	17 Jan 1898
Lynton–Barnstaple Town	16 May 1898
Waterloo & City Railway	8 Aug 1898
Easton–Church Hope (goods)	1 Oct 1900
(passenger)	1 Sept 1902
Basingstoke–Alton	1 June 1901
Newton Tony Junction–Amesbury	1 Oct 1901
Byfleet Junction dive-under	1903
Alton–Fareham	1 June 1903
Budleigh Salterton–Exmouth	1 June 1903
Axminster–Lyme Regis	24 Aug 1903
Amesbury Junction–Newton Tony Junction	7 Aug 1904
Fareham Tunnel avoiding line Up	2 Oct 1904
Down	Sept 1906
Bentley–Bordon	11 Dec 1905
Amesbury–Bulford	1 June 1906
Calstock–Bere Alston	2 Mar 1908
Hampton Court Junction dive-under	21 Oct 1908
Hampton Court branch flyover	July 1915
Dinton–Fovant	15 Oct 1915
Bisley–Deepcut	25 July 1917
Deepcut–Blackdown	Dec 1917

Bovington Camp branch   9 Aug 1919

Southern Railway (Western Section)

Totton–Fawley	20 July 1925
Halwill Junction–Torrington	27 July 1925
Wimbledon–South Merton	7 July 1929
South Merton–Sutton	5 Jan 1930
Motspur Park–Tolworth	29 May 1938
Tolworth–Chessington South	28 May 1939
Winchester Junction spur	5 May 1943

Isle of Wight (Date order)

Cowes–Newport	16 June 1862
Ryde (St John's Road)–Shanklin	23 Aug 1864
Brading–Brading Quay	23 Aug 1864
Ryde Pier Tramway	28 Aug 1864
(Extension Esplanade–St John's Road)	1 Aug 1871
Shanklin–Ventnor	10 Sept 1866
Sandown–Shide	1 Feb 1875
Shide–Pan Lane	6 Oct 1875
Smallbrook Junction–Newport	20 Dec 1875
Pan Lane–Newport	1 June 1879
Ryde Pier Head–Esplanade (railway replacing tramway)	5 Apr 1880
Ryde Pier Head–Esplande (railway in addition to tramway)	12 July 1880
Brading–Bembridge	27 May 1882
Newport–Freshwater (goods)	10 Sept 1888
(passenger)	20 July 1889
Merstone–St Lawrence	20 July 1897
St Lawrence–Ventnor	1 June 1900

Somerset & Dorset Joint Railway (Date order)

Somerset Central Railway	28 Aug 1854
Highbridge–Burnham-on-Sea	3 May 1858
Glastonbury–Wells	15 Mar 1859
Wimborne–Blandford	1 Nov 1860
Cole–Templecombe	3 Feb 1862
Evercreech–Glastonbury	3 Feb 1862
Templecombe–Blandford	31 Aug 1863
Broadstone Junction–Poole	2 Dec 1872
Evercreech–Bath	20 July 1874
Corfe Mullen Junction–Broadstone Junction	14 Dec 1875
Edington Junction–Bridgwater	21 July 1890

London, Brighton & South Coast Railway Main Lines (Geographical order)

London Bridge Junction–Corbetts Lane Junction	14 Dec 1836
Corbetts Lane Junction–West Croydon	5 June 1839

Norwood–Haywards Heath	12 July 1841
South Croydon–Stoats Nest	5 Nov 1899
Stoats Nest–Earlswood (goods)	5 Nov 1899
(passengers)	1 April 1900
Haywards Heath–Brighton	21 Sept 1841
Brighton–Shoreham	12 May 1840
Preston Park–Hove (spur)	1 July 1879
Shoreham–Worthing	24 Nov 1845
Worthing–Arundel and Littlehampton	16 Mar 1846
Arundel and Littlehampton–Chichester	8 June 1846
Ford–Littlehampton	17 Aug 1863
Littlehampton direct	1 Jan 1887
Barnham–Bognor	1 Jun 1864
Chichester–Havant	15 Mar 1847
Havant–Langston	19 Jan 1865
Langston–South Hayling	17 July 1867
Havant–Portsmouth	14 June 1847
Fratton–Southsea	1 July 1885
Portsmouth Town–Harbour	2 Oct 1876
Watering Island Jetty Line	15 Jan 1878
Brighton–Lewes	8 June 1846
Kemp Town Branch	2 Aug 1869
Keymer Junction–Lewes	1 Oct 1847
Southerham Junction–Newhaven Wharf	8 Dec 1847
Newhaven Harbour–Seaford	1 June 1864
Extension along Newhaven Quay	17 May 1886
Lewes–St Leonards	27 June 1846
Polegate–Eastbourne	14 May 1849
Stone Cross spur	1 Aug 1871

London, Brighton & South Coast Railway Suburban lines, branches etc. (Date order)

West Croydon–Epsom Town	10 May 1847
Three Bridges–Horsham	14 Feb 1848
Polegate–Hailsham	14 May 1849
Deptford Wharf Branch	2 July 1849
Sydenham–Crystal Palace Low Level (goods)	27 Mar 1854
(passengers)	10 June 1854
Three Bridges–East Grinstead	9 July 1855
Commercial Dock Branch	July 1855
New Cross–Lift Bridge Junction	Aug 1855
West Croydon–Wimbledon	22 Oct 1855
Crystal Palace Low Level–Wandsworth	1 Dec 1856
Crystal Palace Low Level–Norwood Junction	1 Oct 1857
New Wandsworth–Battersea Pier	29 Mar 1858

Lewes–Uckfield	18 Oct 1858
Epsom–Leatherhead	1 Feb 1859
Epsom Town–Epsom	8 Aug 1859
Horsham–Petworth	10 Oct 1859
Battersea Pier Junction–Victoria	1 Oct 1860
Shoreham–Partridge Green	1 July 1861
Partridge Green–Itchingfield Junction	16 Sept 1861
Battersea Wharf Branch	30 Apr 1862
Norwood Fork South–Windmill Bridge Junction	1 May 1862
Birkbeck–Norwood Junction spur	18 June 1862
Windmill Bridge Junction–Balham	1 Dec 1862
Norwood Fork–Selhurst	1 Dec 1862
Clapham Junction–Kensington	2 Mar 1863
Hardham Junction–Ford	3 Aug 1863
Ford–Littlehampton	17 Aug 1863
Barnham Junction–Bognor	1 June 1864
Sutton–Epsom Downs	22 May 1865
West Croydon–Selhurst Fork	22 May 1865
Cow Lane–Barrington Road	1 Aug 1865
South Fork–Itchingfield Junction	2 Oct 1865
West Horsham–Peasmarch	2 Oct 1865
Lavender Hill Junction–Factory Junction	1 Mar 1866
London Bridge–East Brixton	13 Aug 1866
East Grinstead–Groombridge	1 Oct 1866
Groombridge–Tunbridge Wells	1 Oct 1866
Petworth–Midhurst	15 Oct 1866
Midhurst (LBSCR)–Midhurst (LSWR)	17 Dec 1866
Leatherhead (Old Joint Station)–new LBSCR station	4 Mar 1867
Leatherhead–Dorking	11 Mar 1867
Barrington Road Junction–Battersea Park	1 May 1867
Dorking–Horsham	1 May 1867
Dorking spur to SER	1 May 1867
Battersea (High Level line)	1 Dec 1867
Central Croydon Branch	1 Jan 1868
Groombridge–Uckfield	3 Aug 1868
Peckham Rye–Sutton	1 Oct 1868
Balham spur–Sutton	1 Oct 1868
Tooting–Merton Park	1 Oct 1868
Streatham–Wimbledon	1 Oct 1868
Hamsey–Lewes (East)	1 Oct 1868
Deptford Wharf–Old Kent Road	15 May 1869
New Cross–Wapping	7 Dec 1869
Lower Norwood–Tulse Hill	1 Nov 1870
South Bermondsey spur	1 Jan 1871
Old Kent Road–Deptford Road Junction	13 Mar 1871
Tulse Hill–Streatham Hill spur	1 Aug 1871

Eastbourne spur	1 Aug 1871
Cambria Road–LCDR spur	1 July 1872
Tunbridge Wells–Grove Junction (goods)	1867
(passenger)	1 Feb 1876
Hailsham–Heathfield	5 Apr 1880
Heathfield–Redgate Mill Junction	1 Sept 1880
Midhurst–Chichester	11 July 1881
Polegate–Hailsham	3 Oct 1881
East Grinstead–Culver Junction	1 Aug 1882
Horsted Keynes–Haywards Heath	3 Sept 1883
South Croydon–East Grinstead (Low Level)	10 Mar 1884
East Grinstead (High Level)–East Grinstead (Low Level)	10 Mar 1884
Crowhurst Junction SER spur	10 Mar 1884
New Cross (Up side)–Deptford Road Junction	1 Oct 1884
Woodside–Selsdon Road Junction	10 Aug 1885
Streatham Common–Streatham	1 Jan 1886
Dyke branch	1 Sept 1887
Hurst Green Junction–Edenbridge	2 Jan 1888
Edenbridge–Groombridge	1 Oct 1888
Eridge spur	1 Oct 1888

SER Main Lines (Geographical order)

Charing Cross–London Bridge	11 Jan 1864
Cannon Street extension	1 Sept 1866
London Bridge–Corbett's Lane	14 Dec 1836
Corbett's Lane–Norwood Junction	5 June 1839
Norwood Junction–Redhill	12 July 1841
Redhill–Tonbridge	26 May 1842
Tonbridge–Headcorn	31 Aug 1842
Headcorn–Ashford	1 Dec 1842
Ashford–Folkestone (west of viaduct)	28 June 1843
Folkestone (west of viaduct)–Folkestone Junction	18 Dec 1843
Folkestone–Dover	7 Feb 1844
Ashford–Canterbury	6 Feb 1846
Canterbury–Ramsgate	13 Apr 1846
Ramsgate Town–Margate Sands	1 Dec 1846
Minster–Deal	1 July 1847
North Kent East Junction–New Cross (St John's)	30 July 1849
New Cross (St John's)–Chislehurst	1 July 1865
Chislehurst–Tonbridge Junction	3 Feb 1868
Chislehurst–Sevenoaks	3 Mar 1868
Sevenoaks–Tonbridge	1 May 1868
Tonbridge–Tunbridge Wells	20 Sept 1845
Tunbridge Wells–Robertsbridge	1 Sept 1851

Robertsbridge–Battle	1 Jan 1852
Battle–Bopeep Junction	1 Feb 1852
Bopeep Junction–Hastings	13 Feb 1851

SER Suburban Lines, Branches etc. (Date order)

Canterbury–Whitstable	3 May 1830
Whitstable Harbour branch	19 Mar 1832
London Bridge–Spa Road	14 Dec 1836
Spa Road–Deptford	8 Feb 1836
Deptford–Greenwich	24 Dec 1838
Bricklayers' Arms branch	1 May 1844
Paddock Wood–Maidstone	25 Sept 1844
Gravesend–Strood	10 Feb 1845
Folkestone Harbour branch (goods)	1843
(passengers)	1 Jan 1849
Dorking–Redhill	4 July 1849
Reading–Farnborough	4 July 1849
North Kent East Junction–Gravesend	30 July 1849
Farnborough–Ash Junction	Aug 1849
Dorking–Shalford	20 Aug 1849
Guildford–Ash Junction	20 Aug 1849
Shalford–Guildford	15 Oct 1849
North Kent West Junction–Surrey Canal Junction	1 Sept 1849
Bopeep Junction–Ashford	13 Feb 1851
Angerstein Wharf branch	Oct 1852
Rye–Rye Harbour	Mar 1854
Strood–Maidstone	18 June 1856
Purley–Caterham	5 Aug 1856
Lewisham Junction–Beckenham Junction	1 Jan 1857
Reading– junction with GWR	1 Dec 1858
St Lawrence Loop	July 1863
New Beckenham–Addiscombe Road	1 Apr 1864
Dartford Loop	1 Sept 1866
Parks Bridge Junction–Ladywell	Sept 1866
Dorking spur	1 May 1867
Maze Hill–Charlton	1 Jan 1873
Sandling Junction–Sandgate	10 Oct 1874
Grove Park Junction–Bromley	1 Jan 1878
Greenwich–Maze Hill	1 Feb 1878
Blackfriars spur	1 June 1878
Aldershot Junction–Aldershot Town	May 1879
Dunton Green–Westerham	7 July 1881
Buckland Junction–Deal	15 June 1881
Appledore–Lydd	7 Dec 1881
Lydd–Dungeness (goods)	7 Dec 1881
(passengers)	1 Apr 1883

Hoo Junction–Sharnal Street	1 Apr 1882
Elmers End–Hayes	29 May 1882
Kearsney Curve	1 July 1882
Sharnal Street–Port Victoria	11 Sept 1882
Lydd–New Romney	19 June 1884
Selsdon–Woodside	10 Aug 1885
Cheriton Junction–Barham	4 July 1887
Barham–Harbledown Junction	1 July 1889
Strood Junction–Rochester Common	20 July 1891
Rochester Common–Chatham	1 Mar 1892
Paddock Wood–Goudhurst	1 Oct 1892
Goudhurst–Hawkhurst	4 Sept 1893
Blackheath (near)–Slades Green (near)	1 May 1895
Purley–Kingswood	2 Nov 1897

SECR (South Eastern section)

Kingswood–Tadworth	1 July 1900
Tadworth–Tattenham Corner	4 June 1901
Crowhurst–Bexhill West	1 June 1902
Bickley–Orpington (Down loop)	8 Sept 1902
(Up loop)	14 Sept 1902
Chislehurst–St Mary Cray Junction	19 June 1904

SR (South Eastern section)

Ramsgate loop	2 July 1926
Minster loop	7 July 1929
Lewisham loops (Nunhead–Lewisham (goods)	7 July 1929
(Lewisham–Hither Green)	7 July 1929
(Nunhead–Lewisham) (passengers)	30 Sept 1935
Stoke Junction–Allhallows-on-Sea	14 May 1932
Greatstone Deviation, New Romney Branch	4 July 1937
Crayford Curve	11 Oct. 1942

LCDR Main Lines (Geographical order)

Victoria–Battersea	3 Dec 1860
Stewarts Lane Junction–south end Victoria Bridge	20 Dec 1866
Stewarts Lane–Herne Hill	25 Aug 1862
Herne Hill–Penge Junction	1 July 1863
Bromley Junction–Shortlands	3 May 1858
Shortlands–Bickley	5 July 1858
Bickley–Strood	3 Dec 1860
Strood–Chatham	29 Mar 1858
Chatham–Faversham	25 Jan 1858
Faversham–Canterbury	July 1860
Canterbury–Dover Town	22 July 1861
Dover Town–Harbour	1 Nov 1861

Admiralty Pier Branch	30 Aug 1864
Faversham–Whitstable	1 Aug 1860
Whitstable–Herne Bay	13 July 1861
Herne Bay–Margate and Ramsgate Harbour	5 Oct 1863

LCDR Suburban lines, branches etc (Date order)

Chatham–Strood	29 Mar 1858
Faversham Creek branch	12 Apr 1860
Sittingbourne–Sheerness	19 July 1860
Swanley–Bat & Ball	2 June 1862
Herne Hill–Elephant & Castle	6 Oct 1862
Brixton–Loughborough Junction	1 May 1863
Elephant & Castle–Blackfriars	1 June 1864
Blackfriars–Ludgate Hill (temporary station)	21 Dec 1864
Longhedge Junction–Factory Junction	1 July 1865
Canterbury Road–Barrington Road	1 Aug 1865
Peckham Rye–Crystal Palace (High Level)	1 Aug 1865
Stewarts Lane–Longhedge works	7 Oct 1865
Ludgate Hill–Farringdon Street	1 Jan 1866
Victoria Bridge–Prince of Wales Road	20 Dec 1866
Factory Junction–Shepperds Lane Brixton	1867
Tulse Hill–Herne Hill spur	1 Jan 1869
Bat & Ball–Tubs Hill	1 Aug 1869
Nunhead–Blackheath Hill	18 Sept 1871
Ludgate Hill–Holborn Viaduct	2 Mar 1874
Otford Junction–Maidstone	1 June 1874
Queenborough Pier branch	15 May 1876
Chatham Dockyard branch	16 Feb 1877
Toomer loop re-opening	2 Apr 1877
Buckland Junction–Deal	15 June 1881
Kearsney loop	1 July 1882
Sheerness Town branch	1 June 1883
Maidstone–Ashford	1 July 1884
Fawkham–Gravesend	10 May 1886
Blackheath Hill–Greenwich Park	1 Oct 1888
Ashford LCDR–SER	1 Nov 1891
Nunhead–Shortlands	1 July 1892

SECR (LCDR section)

Queenborough–Leysdown	1 Aug 1901
Sheerness-on-Sea spur	2 Jan 1922

APPENDIX II

DATES LINES CLOSED

Nine Elms Junction–Nine Elms (passengers)	11 July 1848
Surrey Canal Junction–Bricklayers' Arms (passengers)	Jan. 1852
Stewarts Lane Junction–Pimlico	1 Oct 1860
Itchingfield Junction South Fork	1 Aug 1867
Pouparts Junction–Battersea Pier Junction (passengers)	1 Dec 1867
Hamsey–Uckfield Junction	1 Oct 1868
Havant–Hayling Island (re–opened Aug 1869)	Jan 1869
Central Croydon branch (re-opened 1 June 1886)	1 Dec 1871
Hailsham (old junction)	3 Oct 1881
Eastbourne (old junction)	3 Oct 1881
Angmering–Ford Junction	1 Jan 1887
Lewes–Southerham Junction	3 Oct 1889
Central Croydon branch	1 Sept 1890
Hamworthy Junction–Hamworthy (passengers)	1 July 1896
Waterloo (SECR)–Waterloo (LSWR)	1911
Strood–Chatham Central	1 Oct 1911
Fratton–Southsea	Aug 1914
Southampton Town–Royal Pier	Sept 1914
Queenborough Pier Branch (passengers)	Nov 1914
Gunnersbury–Chiswick Junction (passengers)	22 Feb 1915
(goods)	24 July 1932
Forton Junction–Stokes Bay	1 Nov 1915
Snow Hill Junction–Holborn Viaduct Low Level	2 Apr 1916
Holborn Viaduct L.L.–Ludgate Hill	1 June 1916
Woodside–Selsdon Road	1 Jan 1917
Kensington (Addison Road)–Studland Road Junction	5 June 1916
Basingstoke–Butts Junction (re-opened 18 Aug 1924)	1 Jan 1917
Nunhead–Greenwich Park	1 Jan 1917
Norwood Junction–Spur Junction	1 Jan 1917

Nunhead–Crystal Palace (High Level)	
First closure	1 Jan 1917
Re-opened	1 Mar 1919
Re-closure	22 May 1944
Re-opened	4 Mar 1946
Closure	20 Sept 1954
Ramsgate Harbour Branch	2 July 1926
Ramsgate Town–Margate Sands	2 July 1926
Tooting Junction–Merton Park	4 Mar 1929
Fort Brockhurst–Lee-on-Solent (passengers)	1 Jan 1931
(goods)	30 Sept 1935
Canterbury–Whitstable (passengers)	1 Jan 1931
(goods)	1 Dec 1952
Hythe–Sandgate	1 Apr 1931
Hurstbourne Junction–Fullerton Junction	6 July 1931
Fort Bockenhurst–Lee-on-Solent	30 Sept 1935
Basingstoke–Alton (passengers)	12 Sept 1932
(goods)	1 June 1936
Botley–Bishop's Waltham (passengers)	2 Jan 1933
Dyke Branch (goods)	2 Jan 1933
(passengers)	1 Jan 1939
Kemp Town Branch (passengers)	2 Jan 1933
Ruthern Bridge Branch	30 Dec 1933
Chichester–Midhurst (passengers)	8 July 1935
Lynton–Barnstaple Town	30 Sept 1935
Ringwood–Christchurch	30 Sept 1935
New Romney Branch (Greatstone Deviation)–Dungeness	4 July 1937
Ash Junction–Farnham	4 July 1937
Canterbury–Lyminge (passengers)	2 Dec 1940
Lyminge–Folkestone	3 May 1943
(restored)	7 Oct 1946
(suspended)	16 June 1947

APPENDIX III

DATE SERVICES ELECTRIFIED

* Overhead system

Victoria–London Bridge	*1 Dec 1909
Battersea Park–Crystal Palace L.L.	*12 May 1911
Crystal Palace–Norwood Junction–Selhurst	*1 June 1912
Peckham Rye–West Norwood	*1 June 1912
Waterloo–East Putney	25 Oct 1915
Point Pleasant Junction–Shepperton	30 Jan 1916
Clapham Junction–Wimbledon–Strawberry Hill	30 Jan 1916
Hounslow Loop	12 Mar 1916
Malden–Hampton Court	18 June 1916
Hampton Court Junction–Claygate	20 Nov 1916
Balham–Coulsdon North	* 1 Apr 1925
Sutton	* 1 Apr 1925
Victoria–Orpington	12 July 1925
Raynes Park–Dorking North	12 July 1925
Nunhead–Crystal Palace H.L.	12 July 1925
Leatherhead–Effingham Junction	12 July 1925
Holborn Viaduct–Orpington	12 July 1925
Claygate–Guildford	12 July 1925
Hayes–Elmers End	21 Sept 1925
Charing Cross & Cannon Street–Orpington/Bromley North/Addiscombe/Hayes	28 Feb 1926
Charing Cross & Cannon Street–Dartford via Blackheath	19 July 1926
London Bridge–Crystal Palace L.L.	25 Mar 1928
Charing Cross–Caterham/Tadworth	25 Mar 1928
London Bridge–Victoria (replacing overhead system)	17 June 1928
Streatham Hill–London Bridge	17 June 1928
London Bridge–Coulsdon North	17 June 1928

London Bridge–London Bridge via Norwood Junction and Selhurst	17 June 1928
London Bridge–Epsom Downs	17 June 1928
London Bridge–Crystal Palace L.L.	17 June 1928
London Bridge–Dorking North and Effingham Junction	3 Mar 1929
Victoria–Epsom	3 Mar 1929
Victoria–Beckenham Junction	3 Mar 1929
Victoria/Holborn Viaduct–Wimbledon	3 Mar 1929
Wimbledon–South Merton	7 July 1929
Victoria–Coulsdon North and Sutton	22 Sept 1929
South Merton–Sutton	5 Jan 1930
Whitton Junction/Hounslow Junction–Windsor	6 July 1930
Dartford–Gravesend Central	6 July 1930
Wimbledon–West Croydon	6 July 1930
Purley–Three Bridges/Reigate	17 July 1932
Three Bridges–Brighton/Hove/Worthing	1 Jan 1933
Lewisham–Hither Green	16 July 1933
Bickley/Chislehurst–Sevenoaks (Tub's Hill)	6 Jan 1935
Orpington–Sevenoaks (Tub's Hill)	6 Jan 1935
Brighton/Haywards Heath–Eastbourne	7 July 1935
Brighton–Hastings and Ore	7 July 1935
Haywards Heath–Horsted Keynes	7 July 1935
Brighton–Seaford	7 July 1935
Nunhead–Lewisham	30 Sep 1935
Woodside–Sanderstead	30 Sep 1935
Hampton Court Junction–Chertsey/Staines	3 Jan 1937
Hampton Court Junction–Guildford	3 Jan 1937
Woking–Farnham	3 Jan 1937
Waterloo–Portsmouth (via Woking/Haslemere)	4 July 1937
Woking–Alton	4 July 1937
Motspur Park–Tolworth	29 May 1938
Dorking North–Havant (via Horsham and Arundel)	3 July 1938
Littlehampton Branch	3 July 1938
Barnham–Bognor Regis	3 July 1938
Virginia Water–Ash Vale (via Ascot)	1 Jan 1939
Ascot–Reading South	1 Jan 1939
Frimley Junction–Sturt Lane Junction	1 Jan 1939
Aldershot–Guildford	1 Jan 1939
Tolworth–Chessington South	28 May 1939
Otford–Maidstone East	2 July 1939
Swanley–Gillingham	2 July 1939
Gravesend–Maidstone West and Rochester (via Strood)	2 July 1939

APPENDIX IV

CHIEF ADMINISTRATORS AND OFFICERS

LSWR (London & Southampton Railway until 1839)
CHAIRMEN

Sir Thomas Baring, Bart, MP	1832–1833
John Wright	1834–1836
John Easthope	1837–1840
Robert Garnett MP	1841–1842
W. J. Chaplin	1843–1852
Hon. Francis Scott MP	1853
Sir William Heathcote, Bart	1854
W. J. Chaplin	1854–1858
Capt Charles Mangles	1859–1872
Charles Castleman	1873–1874
The Hon Ralph H. Dutton	1875–1892
Wyndham S. Portal	1892–1899
Lt-Col the Hon H. W. Campbell	1899–1904
Sir Charles Scotter Bart	1904–1910
Sir Hugh Drummond Bart	1911–1922

GENERAL MANAGERS

C. Stovin (Traffic Manager)	1839
A. Scott (Traffic Manager)	1852
(General Manager)	1870
Sir Charles Scotter	1885
Sir Charles Owens	1898
Sir Herbert Walker	1912

SECRETARIES

E. L. Stephens	1832
W. Reed	1835

A. Morgan	1841
P. L. Campbell	1846
W. Harding	1849
C. J. Brydges	1852
A. Bulkley	1853
L. Crombie	1853
F. Clarke	1862
F. J. Macaulay	1880
G. Knight	1898

ENGINEERS

Francis Giles	1834
Joseph Locke	1837
Albino Martin	1840
John Bass	1849
John Strapp	1853
W. Jacomb	1870
E. Andrews	1887
J. W. Jacomb-Hood	1901
A. W. Szlumper	1914

LOCOMOTIVE SUPERINTENDENTS

Joseph Woods	1835
John Gooch	1841
Joseph Beattie	1850
William Beattie	1871
William Adams	1878
Dugald Drummond	1895
Robert Urie	1912

LBSCR (London & Brighton Railway until 1846)
CHAIRMEN

John Harman	1837–1843
J. M. Parsons	1843
Rowland Hill	1843–1846
C. P. Grenfell	1846–1848
Samuel Laing	1848–1855
Leo Schuster	1856–1866
P. N. Laurie	1866–1867
Col W. B. Barttelot MP	1867
Samuel Laing	1867–1896
Lord Cottesloe	1896–1908
Earl of Bessborough	1908–1920
C. C. Macrae	1920–1922
G. W. E. Loder	1922

GENERAL MANAGERS

Peter Clarke (Manager)	1846
G. Hawkins (Manager)	1850
J. P. Knight (Traffic Manager)	1869
(General Manager)	1870
Sir Allen Sarle (Secretary and General Manager)	1886
J. F. S. Gooday	1897
Sir William Forbes	1899

SECRETARIES

T. J. Buckton	1846
F. Slight	1849
Sir Allen Sarle	1867
J. J. Brewer	1898

ENGINEERS

R. Jacomb-Hood	1846
F. D. Banister	1860
Sir Charles Morgan	1895
Sir James Ball	1917
O. G. C. Drury	1920

LOCOMOTIVE SUPERINTENDENTS

-, Statham	?
John Gray	1845
S. Kirtley	Feb 1847
John Craven	Dec 1847
William Stroudley	1870
Robert Billinton	1890
D. Earle Marsh	1905
Lawson Billinton	1911

SER

CHAIRMEN

P. St Leger Grenfell	1836–1838
T. W. Tyndale	1838–1841
J. Baxendale	1841–1845
Sir John Kirkland	1845
J. MacGregor	1845–1854
Sir John Campbell	1854
Hon James Byng	1855–1866
Sir Edward Watkins	1866–1894
Hon James Byng	1894
Sir George Russell, Bart	1895–1898
H. Cosmo O. Bonsor	1898–1922

GENERAL MANAGERS
Capt R. H. Barlow	1854
C. W. Eborall	1855–1873
Sir Myles Fenton	1880
W. R. Stevens (Chief Officer)	1895
A. Wills	1898

SECRETARIES
J. S. Yeats	1836
John Whitehead	1841
Capt O'Brien	1845
G. S. Herbert	1845
Samuel Smiles	1854
T. A. Chubb	1866
John Shaw	1868
W. R. Stevens	1887
C. Sheath (Deputy Secretary)	1895
(Secretary)	!898
C. Davis (Acting Secretary)	1922

ENGINEERS
William Cubitt	1836
Peter Barlow	1844
Thomas Drane	1851
Peter Ashcroft	1854
Francis Brady	1870
P. C. Tempest (Resident Engineer)	1897

LOCOMOTIVE SUPERINTENDENTS
Benjamin Cubitt	1842
James Cudworth	1845
Alfred Watkin	1876
Richard Mansell	1877
James Stirling	1878

LCDR (East Kent Railway 1852–1859)
CHAIRMEN
Lord Sondes	1852–1866
Lord Harris	1866–1867
G. Hodgkinson	1867–1873
J. Staats Forbes	1873–1904
Sir E. L. Pemberton	1904–1908
Sir William Hart Dyke Bart	1908–1922

GENERAL MANAGER
J. Staats Forbes	1862–1904
William Forbes (Traffic Manager)	1890–1899

SECRETARIES

G. F. Holroyd	1852
W. E. Johnson	1863
G. W. Brooke	1867
John Morgan	1876
E. W. Livesey	1900
J. R. Dowdall	1916

ENGINEERS

John S. Valentine & William Mills	(?)1852
Sir William & Joseph Cubitt	1853
William Mills	1858
G. B. Roche	1891

LOCOMOTIVE SUPERINTENDENTS

Sir William Cubitt	(?) 1853
William Martley	1860
William Kirtley	1874

SECR
CHAIRMAN

H. Cosmo O. Bonsor	1898–1922

GENERAL MANAGERS

A. Willis	1898
Vincent W. Hill	1900
F. H. Dent	1911
P. C. Tempest	1920

SECRETARIES

John Morgan & C. Sheath (Joint)	1898
C. Davis (Acting)	1922

ENGINEER

P. C. Tempest	1898

LOCOMOTIVE SUPERINTENDENTS

Harry S. Wainwright	1898
Richard E. Maunsell (CME)	1913

SR
CHAIRMEN

Brig-Gen Sir Hugh Drummond, Bart CMG	1923
Brig-Gen The Hon. Everard Baring, CVO, CBE	1924
The Rt Hon Lord Wakehurst	1932
Robert M. Holland-Martin CB	1935
Col Eric Gore-Brown DSO	1944

GENERAL MANAGERS
Sir Herbert Ashcombe Walker KCB 1923
G. S. Szlumper CBE 1937
Sir Eustace Missenden 1939
John Elliot 1947

SECRETARIES
John Jennings Brewer 1923
Geoffrey Knight 1923
Francis Henry Willis 1930
Brig L. F. S. Dawes MBE 1936
T. E. Brain (Acting) 1939
S. E. Clarke (Acting) 1944
Brig L. F. S. Dawes MBE 1946

CHIEF ENGINEERS
A. W. Szlumper 1923
G. Ellson 1927
V. A. M. Robertson 1944

CHIEF ELECTRICAL ENGINEERS
H. Jones 1923
A. Raworth 1938
C. M. Cock 1945

CHIEF MECHANICAL ENGINEERS
Richard E. Maunsell CBE 1923
Oliver V. S. Bulleid CBE 1937

LONDON & SOUTH WESTERN RAILWAY.
GENERAL MAP.

Lines owned or leased, thus: ▬▬▬

Lines jointly owned or leased, thus: ▬▬▬

Lines projected or in course of construction, thus: ══

Lines not used for passenger traffic, thus: ───

LONDON
WATERLOO
ADDISON ROAD
HAMMERSMITH

HAMMERSMITH
GUNNERSBURY
BRENTFORD
HOUNSLOW
FELTHAM
STAINES

CLAPHAM JUNC.

WINDSOR
VIRGINIA WATER
ASCOT
CHERTSEY

WOKINGHAM
Reading
FARNBOROUGH
BISLEY

BROOKWOOD
GUILDFORD
GODALMING
HASLEMERE
MIDHURST
PETERSFIELD

LEATHERHEAD
EFFINGHAM JK.
WOKING

ALDERSHOT
FARNHAM
BENTLEY
ALTON

BASINGSTOKE
ALRESFORD

WHITCHURCH
HURSTBOURNE
ANDOVER
GRATELEY
STOCKBRIDGE
FULLERTON

WINCHESTER
EASTLEIGH
ROMSEY
REDBRIDGE
ST. DENYS
BOTLEY

FAREHAM
GOSPORT
PORTSMOUTH
EAST SOUTHSEA
STOKES BAY
SOLENT

SOUTHAMPTON
NETLEY
BROCKENHURST
LYMINGTON PIER
ISLE OF WIGHT

AMESBURY
BULFORD CAMP

SALISBURY
WILTON
RINGWOOD
WIMBORNE
WEST MOORS

CHRISTCHURCH
BOURNEMOUTH
POOLE
SWANAGE
CORFE CASTLE
WAREHAM

BATH
RADSTOCK
SHEPTON MALLET
EVERCREECH JUNC.
WELLS
GLASTONBURY
EDINGTON
HIGHBRIDGE
BURNHAM
BRIDGWATER

SOMERSET C. & S.W.JT.

TEMPLECOMBE JUNC.
YEOVIL JUNC.
YEOVIL
CREWKERNE
CHARD JNC.
CHARD
AXMINSTER
LYME REGIS
SEATON JNC.
SEATON
SIDMOUTH

BLANDFORD
BAILEY GATE
BROADSTONE
DORCHESTER JNC.
WEYMOUTH
PORTLAND
EASTON

HONITON
SIDMOUTH JUNC.
TIPTON ST. JOHNS
BUDLEIGH SALTERTON
EXMOUTH
TOPSHAM

EXETER
CREDITON
YEOFORD JNC.
OKEHAMPTON
LYDFORD
TAVISTOCK

PLYMOUTH
DEVONPORT
TURNCHAPEL
YELAMPTON

ILFRACOMBE
BARNSTAPLE
BIDEFORD
TORRINGTON
HALWILL JNC.
HOLSWORTHY
LAUNCESTON
BUDE
CAMELFORD
WADEBRIDGE
PADSTOW
BODMIN

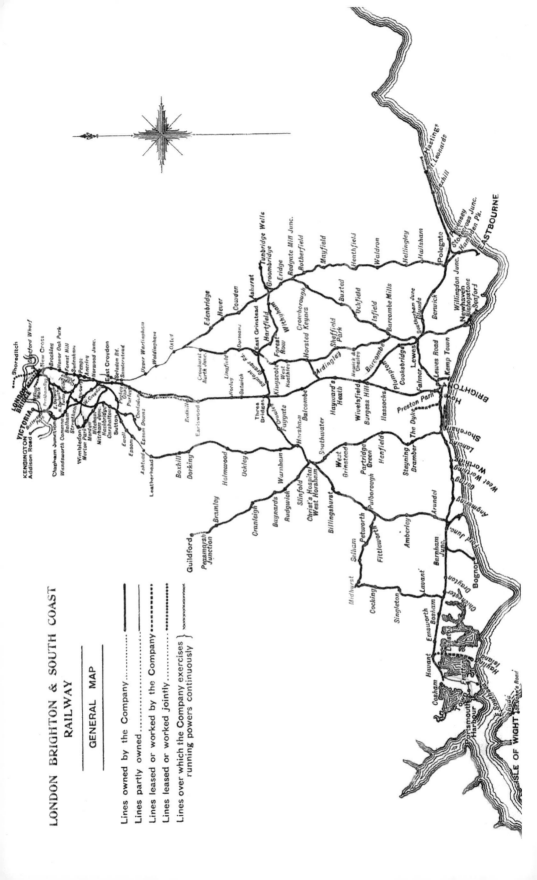

LONDON BRIGHTON & SOUTH COAST
RAILWAY

GENERAL MAP

Lines owned by the Company............
Lines partly owned............
Lines leased or worked by the Company............
Lines leased or worked jointly............
Lines over which the Company exercises }
running powers continuously }

SOUTH EASTERN & CHATHAM RAILWAY. GENERAL MAP.

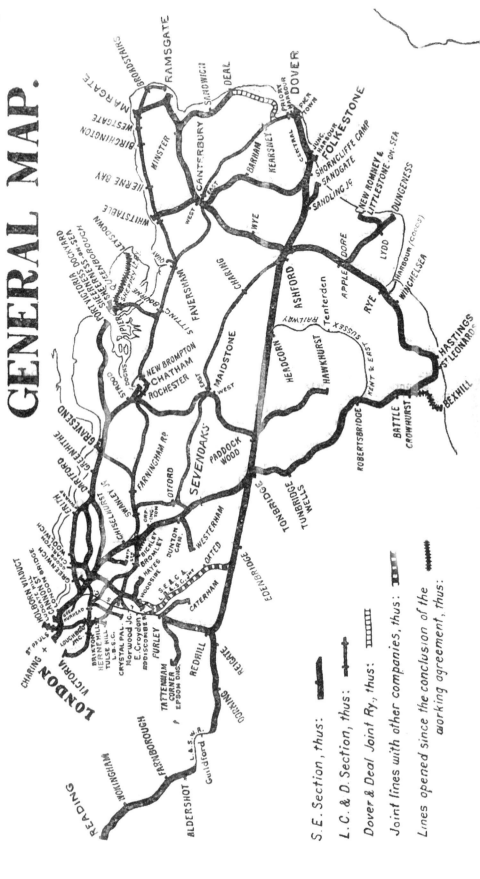

S. E. Section, thus:

L. C. & D. Section, thus:

Dover & Deal Joint Ry., thus:

Joint lines with other companies, thus:

Lines opened since the conclusion of the working agreement, thus:

INDEX

Index

Also available from Amberley Publishing

'Comprehensive and full of charming anecdotes'
CHRISTIAN WOLMAR

A HISTORY OF THE

GREAT
WESTERN
RAILWAY

COLIN MAGGS

Available from all good bookshops or to order direct
Please call **01453-847-800**
www.amberley-books.com

Also available from Amberley Publishing

TRAIN
DRIVER'S
MANUAL

Available from all good bookshops or to order direct
Please call **01453-847-800**
www.amberley-books.com